PeaceTech: Digital Transformation to End Wars

Christine Bell

PeaceTech: Digital Transformation to End Wars

palgrave
macmillan

Christine Bell
School of Law, Old College, University of Edinburgh
PeaceRep, Peace and Conflict Resolution Evidence Platform
Edinburgh, UK

ISBN 978-3-031-38896-5 ISBN 978-3-031-38894-1 (eBook)
https://doi.org/10.1007/978-3-031-38894-1

This Palgrave Macmillan imprint is published by the registered company Springer Nature Switzerland AG.
The registered company address is: Gewerbestrasse 11, 6330 Cham, Switzerland

Disclaimer and Conflict of Interest

None of the funders or those thanked bear any responsibility or liabilities for the contents of the book.

April 2023 Christine Bell

Acknowledgements

This book has grown out of practice and learning in PeaceTech undertaken as part of a dynamic research team. I am very grateful to the many people who have given their time to the interdisciplinary PeaceTech initiatives that are described in this book and underpin it. I would in particular like to pay tribute to the work of Sanja Badanjak (PeaceRep Director of Data), on the PA-X Peace Agreement Database, and her work on 'all things data' as she puts it. I also owe profound thanks to the whole of the Edinburgh PeaceRep team, who can be seen here: https://peacerep.org/about/people/.

I would also like to give personal thanks to Harriet Cornell, Programme Manager PeaceRep (and earlier related programmes); Tim Epple, Managing Director (Research), PeaceRep; Sanja Badanjak, Director of Data, PeaceRep; Stephanie Lewis, Programme Finance Director, PeaceRep; and Shauna Thomson, Head of Research, Knowledge Exchange and Impact, School of Law, University of Edinburgh. All in a variety of ways stepped up to a range of new tasks to support me in the writing of the book.

I am indebted to Adam Farquhar, Sanja Badanjak, Harriet Cornell, Deval Desai, Niamh Henry, Roy Gardiner, Robert Wilson and Laura Wise for research review of the manuscript and assistance with diagrams and proof-reading.

Funding

I would also like to thank the funders of PeaceRep, the Foreign, Commonwealth and Development Office (FCDO), UK, that enabled the research described in the book, the time to write the book, and its open access format. This funding is for the benefit of overseas development. I also thank UN Women for supporting the work on the PeaceFem App; the Covid Collective for support to the Ceasefire Tracker; and Edinburgh Law School for providing additional support for the research leave to write this book.

Contents

About the Author

Christine Bell grew up in Belfast, Northern Ireland, studied at Selwyn College Cambridge, Harvard Law School, and Queen's University Belfast. She is Executive Director and Principal Investigator for the Peace and Conflict Resolution Evidence Platform—PeaceRep, and part of the team responsible for the PA-X Peace Agreement Database. She has a long-standing mediation practice and academic engagement in peace and transition processes that aim to end violent conflict. Her work on peace processes has won the Francis Deak Prize of the American Association of International Law, and the Hart Socio-Legal Book Prize, and in 2023 the PeaceRep team won the Royal Society of Edinburgh Mary Somerville Prize for excellence in team research, in recognition for its PeaceTech work relating to digital support for peace processes.

She is also Professor of Constitutional Law, University of Edinburgh, and Assistant Principal (Global Justice), University of Edinburgh, and Honorary Professor, The Senator George J. Mitchell Institute for Global Peace, Security and Justice, Queen's University of Belfast.

PeaceRep is a programme that provides comparative research and PeaceTech innovation to support peacebuilding efforts in violent conflicts. In particular, the programme provides evidence-based support to the mediation, design and implementation of peace and transition processes globally with a focus on inclusion. PeaceRep focuses on some of the most complex contemporary conflicts, working with local researchers both within country and among displaced diaspora communities from: Afghanistan, Ethiopia, Iraq, Myanmar, Somalia, South Sudan, Sudan, Syria, Yemen and Ukraine.

Christine Bell's full research profile can be seen here.

Christine Bell, ORCID ID https://orcid.org/0000-0003-0233-4410

List of Figures

CHAPTER 1

PeaceTech World

Abstract The PeaceTech World described in this book is a racy, developing and exciting one. It harnesses peacebuilders, digital technology entrepreneurs and often local communities of activists, in pursuit of peace process innovation and influence. Their aim? To promote more peaceful relationships, more just structures and fairer outcomes, so as to prevent, de-escalate or resolve conflict. This chapter introduces PeaceTech World.

Keywords PeaceTech • United Nations

1.1 PeaceTech in Action

1.1.1 Seán

Seán sits in his air-conditioned office in the capital city of a very hot country with a 'peace process'. He works for the United Nations (UN). His job involves deciding how to spend funds pooled by countries who cooperate to support the peace process. The money is used to support local peacebuilding projects in-country. There is one problem. There is not much of a peace process in evidence. There was a peace agreement many years ago. Then a revised one when the first did not work. Then more revisions. Each

C. Bell, *PeaceTech: Digital Transformation to End Wars*,
https://doi.org/10.1007/978-3-031-38894-1_1

agreement tried to make the preceding ones work—amending them, adding new 'implementation matrixes' and new timelines. Despite these efforts, the 'peace process' barely exists.

Seán works and lives in the country. Except for the one week in six that he gets off which he uses to go home or recuperate in tourist spots in neighbouring countries. As an 'international' he works in a building in a 'compound'—a gated community where lots of the diplomatic embassies and international offices are behind the same perimeter fence. Seán's credentials as an international mean he cannot leave the compound easily: it is considered too unsafe. He does not just work in the compound but lives there too—in a different building in a more residential section. His world exists between these two buildings, and in the cafes and coffee shops around them. Except for a few days every two months, when the team visits projects 'out there' in the countryside. His home life is through his screen. He does not like that things are the way they are.

Seán's job involves monitoring and reporting on how all the funded projects are going, so he has to put together a lot of project reports, and data relating to the country. He spends huge amounts of time gathering data, and cutting and pasting it into his reports. It is much more boring than what his family thinks he does. He tries to use this information to present to the donors how their money is spent, and what it is achieving. It takes forever, so he and his colleagues are working on an automated system to try to capture the data, and decrease the manual work.

1.1.2 Paul

Sitting in Geneva, Paul works on this same country, and sort of for the UN. He works to deliver food aid to places where people are going hungry. Many of those places are in countries experiencing armed conflict. Today he gathers international experts online. The organization he works for has just won a major award for peace. In fact, this organization does not 'do peace': it does food aid. Now his boss has questioned, if people think that food and peace are connected and have given us a prize for peace, should the organization try to measure the 'peace impacts' of its food aid? Sometimes they have been aware that programmes such as enabling people to get cattle are co-opted by armed groups for income, or trigger cattle rustling between warring communities.

When does food aid build peace and when might it have a negative peace impact? His boss has asked Paul to help to design a dashboard to help measure peace impacts, or warn of war impacts. This dashboard could then help the organization to think more systematically about how their proposed delivery of food aid might affect the conflict or help encourage peace.

When we say that Paul 'sort of' works for the UN, what does that mean? He works for an agency within the United Nations that operates almost as an independent organization within the UN's broad umbrella (see Foley, 2023, p. 4). While in some deep sense Seán and Paul work for the same organization, in another sense they do not. Their different sub-organizations will not ask them to work together, and in a sense do not trust each other. Trust cannot exist within departments, even less so across them, as much of the data is sensitive to the particular job each agency does. Sometimes the information is sensitive because it could be helpful to 'war tech'. Information on networks of civic groups, for example, can be used to target activists. Sometimes, however, there is no trust between agencies for much duller bureaucratic reasons. It is sensitive that the organization views things a certain way. Views of particular armed groups, or state armies, for example, need to be discussed within organizations, but can cause a diplomatic incident if they are seen as the formal or even informal position of the organization.

Seán and Paul may never learn of each other, and their projects will be locked down to those 'who need to know' within their own agency or department. If they do meet in 'shows and tells', they will never be asked to collaborate, and will not be allowed access the other's finished data system. Could it not be a different way, they wonder?

1.1.3 Atem

Out beyond the capital city, Atem who is from the country works as part of a Churches project trying to support local agreements to end conflict arising from cattle theft and kidnapping. He gets money from Seán's fund. The conflict Atem is engaged with is between local communities and armed groups. But it has curious links to the 'national conflict'. For example, there is overlap between local organizations and the main armed groups that operate country-wide. Conflict in his area can trigger conflict in other places, and vice versa. Atem's childhood friend Samuel—also with activist commitments—is doing a PhD on local agreements and peacebuilding initiatives 'from the bottom up' at a University in Norway. Samuel is studying there on a scholarship targeted at people from his country. But he spends most of the time 'in the field', or in other words 'back at home'. Atem and Samuel figure that—if they created a simple

App, they could support information sharing between social activists and create a crowd-sourced way to monitor the implementation of agreements and perhaps even help support new ones being reached.

Everyone 'knows' when kidnappings or killing of cattle that signifies an agreement's breakdown is going to happen. If they had a safe and secure and fast way to communicate with each other, perhaps attacks could be prevented, by simply moving people and animals out of harm's way. Could Atem and Samuel provide this? A 'data-driven initiative' in Samuel's Norwegian university offers funding, and the Informatics Department offers to help. Samuel and eager young computing academics design and deliver a prototype App for communication. Atem works with Samuel to develop the App and trial it in the field. It proves quite simple and effective, where there is connectivity, or at least for some reason agreement violations subside. The difficulty is that when the App does not work quite right or needs improved, the Norwegian Informatics Department staff cannot always spare the time and resources to develop it.

1.1.4 Aker

Aker is Atem's sister. She listens to her brother talk, and wonders if a similar App could help with her work. She works in an organization supporting victims of sexual violence. Sexual violence existed before the conflict, during it as part of armed violence, and has continued even in moments when peace has been celebrated. Could they have a similar App to assist in prevention and reporting of sexual violence? She wonders about whether this would really work for the issues and people she serves. Have Atem and Samuel thought about whether women will be able to participate in their initiatives? Most of the people with information about imminent attacks will be women: they hear and swap information from across communities as they go to collect fire wood to cook, or to get water. This is also often when attacks against women occur as they stray farther from safe areas when climate change makes both water and wood scarce. But women often don't own phones, and when technically they do, they often don't control when they are used, or get to take them outside the home.

Is sexual violence not also something that should be reported on and taken seriously as violence 'to do' with the conflict? What is peace, she wonders, if resolving conflict is does not resolve this violence? Peace processes and wars come and go, and the reasons given for violence against women change, but their experience of violence does not.

1.1.5 Nick

Nick is sitting in an office in an Ivy League University in North America. He and his team are looking down on the same country from above. They have developed a capacity to use open-source satellite technology and images to monitor agricultural development. They have worked collaboratively across social science and geospatial technology and can now use the many publicly available satellite images to try to understand drought and where crops are doing well and where they are failing. This work sheds light on how the lives of people are affected by climate change and helps inform development organizations to support local communities to be 'resilient'. Nick's team also monitors what happens when crop failure becomes a driver of displacement as people move in search of food. Until recently Nick's research would not have existed, but has been made possible because publicly accessible geospatial imagery is now free or very cheap.

Today, as they monitor crops they notice something strange. In the area they are zoning in on, all the roofs have disappeared from the houses. This triggers alarm: people take the roofs off houses when they are moving. The houses contain metal that has a value. But the crops are still in the ground, so why are people on the move? Nick and his colleagues get other satellite imagery, and look more closely down the road. They see villages burning just a short distance away. The villagers seem to know that an armed group is moving through with violence, and are fleeing. Nick and his team triangulate their satellite data with local evidence by WhatsApping some contacts in the area—yes, this is what is happening. There are other villages further down the road who do not seem to know they are in the pathway of a marauding armed group. Nick and his team agonise—there is a prospect of huge violence and civilian death, if villagers down the road do not move. The team faces a dilemma. Will they go public with what they know and warn villages down the road? Or is this something they should not interfere in? After all, they were only trying to look at crops. Nick makes a decision and goes public, warning people locally of what is coming.

Something he did not expect happens. Another armed group further down the road mounts an ambush, and kills many of the first armed group. In the North American University, Nick and his team feel uneasy. This is not what they meant to happen. But was it their fault? What do they think should have happened? Are they playing God?

1.2 Introducing PeaceTech

These PeaceTech stories are all drawn from real life, amended a little: the country and their coincidence in it are mostly fictional, as are some of the details. The key elements, however, are drawn from practices I have encountered across a number of violent conflicts going on in the world, and often do all co-exist in some form within a single country. The stories illustrate real-world efforts concerning the business of peace, the business of development, and the business of war, all of which rely on digital technology to achieve their goals. As you go through this book, you may recognise some real-life examples that resemble those above, and we will see yet other examples of digital innovation and peace-focused applications.

These are stories of what we are calling 'PeaceTech'—that is—innovation in the use of digital technologies to support peacebuilding. This book maps out 'PeaceTech' as an emerging set of peacebuilding activities that connect to a wider digital revolution that affects all aspects of all our lives. The book assesses how PeaceTech aims to end violent conflict in deeply divided societies.

PeaceTech World, however, operates alongside 'WarTech World', where the same technologies also carry significant risk for escalating conflict, targeting civilians, or undermining the political institutions that offer an alternative to violence. Can tech really be used for good and to end conflict? Or do the risks outweigh the benefits? Or are PeaceTech and WarTech inevitably part of the same picture—each attempting to outwit the other, in a mutually building dynamic?

1.3 About This Book

This book aims to set out PeaceTech as used to support peace and transition processes, and introduce some of its potential and some of its challenges. I hope the book will support those who aspire to 'do PeaceTech' in some form or other. I draw on my own experience in incubating PeaceTech projects as part of a dynamic research group in PeaceRep, www.peacerep.org which has innovated to produce what I term in Chap. 11—'Peace Analytics'. Through this work I have been part of what is being termed the 'PeaceTech Ecosystem' that I talk about in Chap. 6—that is, a set of practitioners, researchers, funders, tech entrepreneurs, and people living in conflict, that are seeking to support use of technology in peacebuilding, and who have a sense of being in a network with each other.

them, and point to new emerging frameworks. In conclusion, I assess the future directions of PeaceTech and contribute a short 'manifesto' to shape it if it is to do good rather than harm.

Throughout I draw on the PeaceTech work that I and the team I am part of have engaged in and learnt from.

Questions

1. What is your reaction to the stories?
2. What examples of PeaceTech can you think of?
3. Is PeaceTech a good term, or can you think of other terms to use for digital technology and peacebuilding?

References[1]

Foley, C. (2023). *The protection paradox: How the UN can get better at saving civilian lives.* Palgrave Macmillan.

Hirblinger, A. T., Hansen, J. M., Hoelscher, K., Kolås, Å., Lidén, K., & Martins, B. O. (2022). Digital peacebuilding: A framework for critical–reflexive engagement. *International Studies Perspectives, 24*(3), 265–284. https://doi.org/10.1093/isp/ekac015

[1] All last accessed 1 May 2023.

PART I

What Is PeaceTech?

CHAPTER 2

PeaceTech: What Is It?

Abstract This chapter examines definitions of PeaceTech and associated terms such as digital innovation and peacebuilding. It explains that the book is focused on digital innovation to end wars through mediated processes, and illustrates how this focus connects to wider understandings of peacebuilding and PeaceTech.

Keywords Civicness; Digital innovation; Peacebuilding; Peace processes; Technology

2.1 Legacies

In the year after the Belfast/Good Friday Peace Agreement of 1998 was signed in Northern Ireland, a brilliant two-minute radio programme called 'Legacy' was broadcast as the Agreement was implemented, including its provisions releasing those convicted and imprisoned. Each Legacy programme provided a short audio testimony of an anonymous person whose relative had been killed in the conflict, talking about how the killing. If you wish, you can listen to these heartbreaking testimonies at Legacy Series.

Over 1999, daily stories came from people such as: the policeman's widow; the 'totally innocent' child killed because they were in the 'wrong place at the wrong time'; the pro-state armed actor killed by his own side for informing; or the IRA member shot dead by security forces.

C. Bell, *PeaceTech: Digital Transformation to End Wars*,
https://doi.org/10.1007/978-3-031-38894-1_2

The series played an innovative peacebuilding role. It exposed people to the common loss and grief of relatives of those killed, across divisions, and regardless of perceptions of the person's 'victim status' in terms of perceived complicity in the conflict. The stories focusing on the experience of those left behind, created a powerful public conversation regarding the bottom common denominator of grief and loss. It was a daily reminder of the costs of the conflict that quietly bore witness to what was at stake in maintaining the peace.

The Legacy Series contributed to peacebuilding, it used technology, and it was innovative. So was it PeaceTech? PeaceTech sounds new, but the technology—radio—was very old. In an interesting aside, some of the first attempted cross-Atlantic wireless signals by Guglielmo Marconi were transmitted from Rathlin Island and Ballycastle, Northern Ireland, across the Atlantic in 1898. You can still see the 'Marconi cottage' where he worked from—now a fancy coastal house. Marconi was to return to Italy during the Second World War where he was a Mussolini supporter—not what we would think of as pro-peace, or associated with the Nobel Physics prize that he had won. Marconi PLC, the company which emerged from his work, still exists as a major player in communications including mobile technology, with a central role in digital innovation (see its history here).

2.2 Defining PeaceTech

The 'Legacy' radio programme poses the question—what *exactly* is PeaceTech? As we will see PeaceTech is experimental in nature and there are many diverse examples that we could label as PeaceTech. This experimentalism makes it difficult to define or to draw good boundaries as to what is PeaceTech and what is something else.

The following definition is a useful starting point:

PeaceTech is the use of digital innovation to support peacebuilding practices to improve and extend.

There are other possible definitions that have overlaps and are set out in the Box below. Our definition, however, needs more definitions to make better sense.

PeaceTech Definitions

PeaceTech is….

… an umbrella term for technologies (software and hardware) that are being developed and used in efforts to prevent or end cycles of violence in society, building and sustaining peace. (Carl, 2023).

…the movement to use technology to end violent conflict and extremism. (Heidebrecht, 2022, p. 101).

…

– Products and services that help foster relationships between groups, protect people from the effects of violent conflict, disrupt the tactics of violence, or respond to the root causes of conflict.

– Tools that foster positive outcomes like enhanced social well-being, sustainable economies, stable governance, rule of law, and safe and secure environments.

– And so much more. (Peacetechlab)

…. The field of technology for peacebuilding. (Peace Direct, 2020)

2.3 What Is Digital Innovation?

PeaceTech involves digital innovation, what then is 'digital innovation'? Is it the use of a new technology, such as the use of satellite imagery such as Nick was using in Chap. 1? Or is it the innovative application of an existing technology to a new peacebuilding application—say the use of SMS text messaging to survey a population with little internet connectivity, on their desires for particular outcomes for the peace process (see e.g., Firchow & Mac Ginty, 2020)? Is use of SMS texting really 'digital innovation'? People have been texting for decades. It is not a terribly innovative technology. But then come to think about it, the first satellite was Sputnik 1, launched in 1957, so satellite technology is in fact older than SMS texting (which seems to have arrived only in 1992).

Yet, both the examples above involve forms of innovation. If you read Firchow and Mac Ginty's work, you will find out about an interesting project called 'Everyday Peace Indicators', involving a creative attempt to measure the success or failure of peace processes 'from the bottom up' (see also Everyday Peace Indicators). They used SMS texting to generate bottom up peace indicators and measure perceptions of peace in hard-to-access populations. No-one engaged in implementing the peace process had ever really bothered to ask people what they thought peace should look like, or what they wanted from it—what would have to change for them to experience peace? Yet, why should international supporters of peace processes define what 'peace' looks like from a perspective of 'when can we leave'? Is it not important that peace is felt in people's everyday lives, far from the capital cities that international actors reside in? Everyday Peace Indicators are now taken seriously by international organization as a way of benchmarking positive change, these include organizations like the World Bank that we think of as disconnected from local communities.

What was new in Mac Ginty and Firchow's use of SMS was the design of a localized participative process of defining peace by ordinary people in hard-to-reach communities. Using SMS contributed to a transformation of how we define and monitor peace, and whose experience 'counts', although it raised its own challenges in terms of who has access to mobile phones in terms of inclusion (for discussion of these challenges and how to navigate them, see Firchow et al., 2017; Demombynes et al., 2013). *Legacy* and radio broadcasting are even more 'analogue' than SMS. But in societies with low connectivity, radio may be a very effective way to reach large sections of the population. Is new always good when it comes to technology?

Similarly, what is new about use of satellites for peacebuilding is not satellite imagery per se, but the new capacities for producing images, and producing them cheaply enough and open source enough that researchers, citizens, and non-governmental organizations can now sometimes gain capacity to use them for new purposes such as peace monitoring. We will look at satellite technology more in Chap. 10.

2.4 What Is Peacebuilding?

The second definition that our starting PeaceTech definition would need to clarify is: what is peacebuilding?

Civicness is a useful word to capture the focus and spirit of 'peacebuilding'. It was coined by Mary Kaldor and colleagues who work as members of our PeaceRep team, and the term is at the heart of our PeaceRep programme as a way of working that seeks to counter-act logics of war. They describe civicness as:

> (i) as a logic of public authority, that speaks to ideas of rights-based, inclusive rather than exclusive political orders; (ii) as a form of behaviour, acting 'as if' such a logic existed; and (iii) as a political position, articulated against un-civic politics, in particular the combination of endemic corruption, ethnic or religious sectarianism and economic and social injustice. (Kaldor & Radice, 2022, p. 125)

Is peacebuilding everything that has some sort of 'peace impact' or that attempts to create civicness? Well my goodness, this could be literally everything. PayPal and Airbnb for example, work in interesting ways to generate 'trust between strangers'. Is 'creating trust between strangers' a form of peacebuilding? To use PayPal as an example, complete strangers enter into transactions with each other at a distance without even knowing if their identity is real. In 2022, PayPal had 392 million active users who conducted 15.4 billion transactions that generated $21.4 billion revenue (Galov 2023). Four hundred and twenty six million users transacted at least once in that year. Fraud rates were only 0.12%—less they claim than most competitors. So PayPal generates and depends on a lot of trust and its success in getting people to use it, depends on this trust.

PayPal see their system as rooted in four core commitments, three of which appear to be more connected to a morality of 'civicness' than what we might think of as money-making commitments. These are:

- transparency—that we might think of as a public good
- data protection—that we might view as rooted in individual rights
- a commitment to fighting fraud—that we might view as a commitment to civicness by tackling uncivic behaviour of corruption.

Their fourth core commitment is 'using payment methods that are popular with customers' which appears more business-oriented. But in fact we could also see this commitment as having something to do with civicness if we put it a different way, for example: being 'responsive to people', or delivering maximum 'digital financial inclusion'. By using technologies that people already use, PayPal aims to include more people by meeting them where they are at, rather than assuming they will become more 'tech-savvy'.

While I have suggested that PayPal's values encapsulate a form of civicness, PayPal likely committed to these values because they generate the trust that is central to their business model. They need people to trust the service to use it.

So is PayPal 'peacebuilding'? Let us review: it creates peaceful interactions between people, and promotes trust based on commitments which have a moral dimension rooted in civicness—something I have suggested is at the heart of peacebuilding. PayPal also improves the world in a lot of peaceful ways by enabling commerce, charity payments and gifts to friends and family. But we would probably hesitate to call it an exercise in 'peacebuilding' as the 'peace' element is indirect, unintentional and really an accidental side-product of trying to enable on-line commerce.

But perhaps we should not be so hesitant. One of the greatest threats to peace of our times, is currently disinformation. People fighting against social media circulation of disinformation as a threat to peace, are doing all sorts of innovative thinking on how to address this threat. These people find themselves thinking a lot about the ways in which systems themselves work to generate trust or distrust.

Some of those concerned with peace and human rights, lobby social media companies to engage in 'content moderation', that would remove illegal content, or disinformation (see Barrett & Hendrix, 2022; Barrett 2022). While the stated intent for Twitter/X was that it should merely be a platform for views, there is now greater awareness that its real-world power to shape views, and its use for vile purposes, have brought pressure to moderate what is put on the platform.

A second focus of people concerned with peace, however, has concerned the more invisible ways that social media constructs interchanges between even civically minded people to be 'uncivic'. These people seek to understand the algorithms (essentially maths formula that try to predict what you will most click on), that control what pops up on your social media feeds on Twitter/X, or Facebook (see Fournier, 2021).

Peacebuilders have noted that social media uses algorithms to promote 'engagement' to keep people scrolling and expose them to more advertising (also chosen by algorithms). These algorithms promote emotionally provocative feed more than factually correct feed, because the former has been found to better promote 'engagement' (see Lanier, 2018). Social media platforms defend the neutrality of algorithms on the grounds that they merely reflect user preferences and interactions that increase engagement. For those concerned about peace, accentuating dispute is a choice that leads to social polarization and is particularly invidious, because it happens without users fully realising how they are being drawn in. If you are pro-peace, this is not neutral.

The ways in which social media controls what you see happens invisibly under a cloak of 'neutral algorithms'. However, there are now peace counter-responses, that look to the trust-creating mechanisms of online commerce such as Airbnb or PayPal to understand how a platform creates trust rather than polarization. For example, a new Global Partnership on Artificial Intelligence (GPAI) was set up in 2020, as 'a multi-stakeholder initiative bringing together leading experts from science, industry, civil society, international organizations and government that share values to foster international cooperation'. It subscribes to Organization for Economic Cooperation and Development (OECD) Principles for Artificial Intelligence (AI) focused on 'how governments and other actors can shape a human-centric approach to trustworthy AI'. Experts involved in groups like this consider how trust is built or destroyed using AI, such as social media algorithms, to drive platforms, based on issues such as the 'transparency' of how the AI does its job. Broadly speaking this move to responsible AI, is in some deep sense 'about peacebuilding'.

2.5 The Problem With Definitions

Returning to our definitions: discussion illustrates the difficulties of deciding how 'new' and how 'innovative' digital innovation, and how peace-focused an activity has to be to be PeaceTech. There is no exact way to draw a circle around PeaceTech. It depends what we want to give the label to.

The good news is that we do not need to get too agitated about the exact boundaries of PeaceTech: labels are merely useful ways to create a bounded conversation to help us talk to each other about the same thing. If we understand peacebuilding to be broad and 'everything that is to do with peaceful co-existence', then we will have a broad definition and conversation about PeaceTech involving all the ways in which technology is being used by those who have an agenda of peace, and even those who work on values such as 'trust' that we associate with peace. This approach can see PeaceTech applications in countries such as the US or UK where there is no violent conflict with armed actors (even though some forms of organised crime and state violence come close to creating similar conditions in some areas).

However, the term peacebuilding sometimes has a narrower meaning amongst communities of practice and scholars as:

Activities taken in response to violent conflict within societies, that aim to address the conflict around them directly or indirectly, to produce more peaceful outcomes.

Again there are different definitions of peacebuilding or similar concepts, some of which are set out in the box below and are useful to read to see how peacebuilding is talked about. But the definition above captures things well enough for our purposes.

Peacebuilding Definitions

Sustaining peace 'should be broadly understood as both a goal and a process ... which encompasses activities aimed at preventing the outbreak, escalation, continuation and recurrence of conflict, addressing root causes, assisting parties to conflict to end hostilities, ensuring national reconciliation, and moving towards recovery, reconstruction and development...'. (UN GA Resolution 70/262 (2016) and UN SC Resolution 2282 (2016))

Peacebuilding is the development of constructive personal, group, and political relationships across ethnic, religious, class, national, and racial boundaries. It aims to resolve injustice in nonviolent ways and to transform the structural conditions that generate deadly conflict. (Kroc Institute for International Peace Studies, University of Notre Dame)

Peacebuilding refers to efforts to assist countries and regions in their transitions from war to peace and to reduce a country's risk of lapsing or relapsing into conflict by strengthening national capacities for conflict management, and laying the foundations for sustainable peace and development. (United Nations)

Conflict prevention 'is about creating incentives for actors to choose actions that resolve conflict without violence. Effective prevention requires acting before grievances harden and the threat of violence narrows the choices available for leaders and elites, understood as groups who hold power or influence in a society'. (World Bank, 2018, p. xxi)

2.6 Peacebuilding Ripples

To understand the examination of PeaceTech in this book, and the possible scope of the PeaceTech field in general, it can be useful to think about types of peacebuilding activities as nested within each other from and connecting in and out like ripples. Fig. 2.1 illustrates.

In the inner circle are peace and transition processes to end conflict as an active practice of trying to stop people from fighting by creating a process to mediate its end.

In the second circle, a broader range of activities take place in war zones with or without a clear conflict resolution process, whereby individuals and organisations address aspects of violent behaviour or things like distrust that create violence; or try to counter violence by creating spaces of dialogue or civicness as an alternative; or work to support those who are affected by violence. These activities could be things like women's groups,

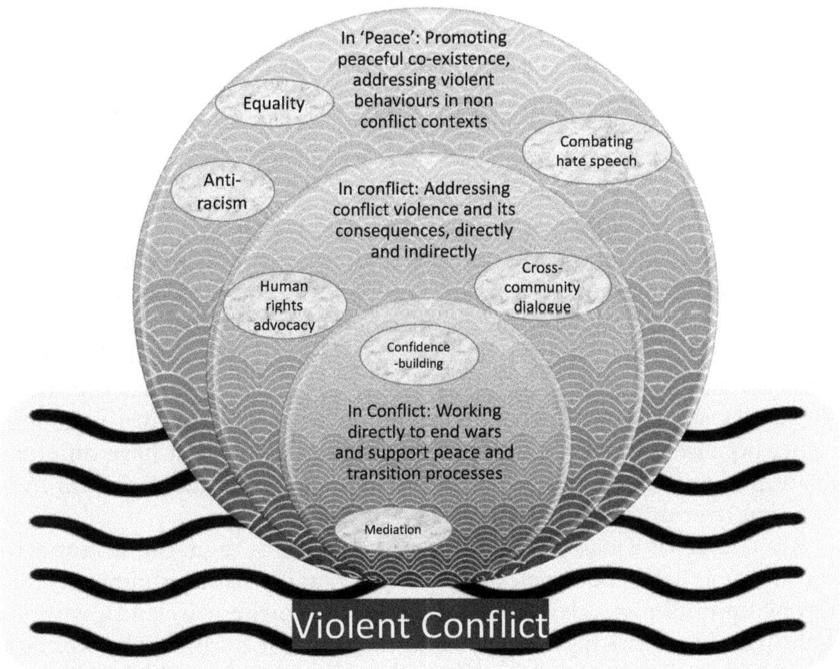

Fig. 2.1 Peacebuilding Ripples

meeting across divides to try to address common problems of poverty. They could be victims groups supporting those hurt by the conflict regardless of where they come from. They could be an inter-schools reconciliation group that attempts to create understanding across social divisions. All of these activities try to build civicness in the face of uncivic violent behaviour that seeks to destroy people and their relationships and communities.

In the widest circle are all peace-focused activities that operate even in societies that we do not think of as having violent conflicts (albeit that most societies have violent practices and spaces). These could be an anti-racist group seeking to combat racial polarization, injustice and violence against minorities; they could be people seeking to address inter-gang rivalries and knife crime; or groups trying to address 'polarization'. The International Catalan Institute for Peace, located in Barcelona, for example, has recently been committed to conducting surveys on polarization in an attempt to understand the nature of polarization and what it means for 'a culture of peace' in Catalonia and more widely (International Catalan Institute of Peace, 2020). The survey produces interesting results on what types of polarised views people can hold without it affecting their emotional relationship to people different to them, and what types of polarized views translate into treating others badly.

2.7 PeaceTech and Ending Wars

What will this book discuss as PeaceTech? Which circle is it focusing on? The book will focus on the innermost circle of peace processes to end conflict, and the use of technology to support attempts to create and sustain ceasefires and agreements to that end. The book therefore mainly focuses on the narrowest circle, but throughout I will give a flavour of PeaceTech as an activity that inhabits all of the circles. The activities in all the circles are important to understanding what goes on in the central circle, because different circles pull in different actors that have different relationships to peacebuilding, and different capacities for digital innovation that over time connect.

My choice of a narrow circle of PeaceTech—as digital innovation to end wars—is partly personal. Quite simply, that is what most interests me. I grew up until my early 20s in a conflict (in Northern Ireland), without realising what was happening around me was not normal. The weirdest part of life, as I look back, was the curious way that normal life and completely abnormal life were all mixed together until you couldn't really tell what normal was. As a young child, I never really understood that the conflict was not normal, what it was about, or how I and my family were positioned as regards its various 'sides'. Over time, I learnt of course, and experienced directly the violence.

Jumping forward to when I was an adult and the peace process arrived I realised that without some sort of agreement with those involved in the fighting, the fighting would not stop. Since that time, I have been interested and involved in how conflicts are brought to an end, not by victory or defeat, but by agreement. I am therefore interested in how and when PeaceTech supports attempts to end conflict through mediation and the peace processes that unfold.

Questions

1. Do you agree with the definitions of PeaceTech?
2. Is it new? Does that matter?
3. Is the PeaceTech label a helpful one, or does it lump too many things together?
4. What do you view as peacebuilding? Which of the three circles are you most interested in?

References[1]

Barrett, P. M. (2022, September). *Spreading the Big Lie: How social media sites have amplified false claims of U.S. election fraud*. Stern Center for Business and Human Rights report, New York University. https://bhr.stern.nyu.edu/tech-big-lie

Barrett, P. M., & Hendrix. J. (2022, June). *A Platform 'Weaponised': How youtube spreads harmful contents—And what can be done about it*. Stern Center for Business and Human Rights, New York University. https://static1.squarespace.com/static/5b6df958f8370af3217d4178/t/62a38fc022745a7274601da0/1654886337000/NYU+CBHR+YouTube_Final_June10.pdf

Carl, A. (2023). Understanding PeaceTech [Peace Analytics Series]. PeaceRep: The Peace and Conflict Resolution Evidence Platform, University of Edinburgh. https://peacerep.org/publication/understanding-peacetech

Demombynes, G., Gubbins, P., & Romeo, A. (2013). *Challenges and opportunities of mobile phone-based data collection: Evidence from South Sudan*". The World Bank Africa Region Poverty Reduction and Economic Management Unit Policy Research Working Paper. https://papers.ssrn.com/sol3/papers.cfm?abstract_id=2202683

Firchow, P., Martin-Shields, C., Omer, A., & Mac Ginty, R. (2017). Peacetech: The liminal spaces of digital technology in Peacebuilding. *International Studies*

[1] All last accessed 1 May 2023.

Perspectives, 18, 4–42. https://cpb-us-e1.wpmucdn.com/blogs.gwu.edu/dist/8/846/files/2017/11/ekw007-1y3cfw7.pdf

Firchow, P., & Mac Ginty, R. (2020). Including hard-to-access populations using mobile phone surveys and participatory indicators. *Sociological Methods and Research, 49*(1), 133–160. https://doi.org/10.1177/0049124117729702

Fournier, J. (2021, November 10). *How algorithms are amplifying misinformation and driving a wedge between people.* Changing America, The Hill blog. https://thehill.com/changing-america/opinion/581002-how-algorithms-are-amplifying-misinformation-and-driving-a-wedge/

Galov, N. (2023, March 30). *17+ Impressive PayPal statistics to pay attention to in 2023.* Webtribunal blog. https://webtribunal.net/blog/paypal-statistics/#gref

Heidebrecht, P. (2022, September 16). *Peacetech commentary.* IEEE Technology and Society Magazine: 101–2. https://ieeexplore.ieee.org/stamp/stamp.jsp?tp=andarnumber=9893514; https://technologyandsociety.org/peacetech

International Catalan Institute of Peace. (2020, October). *Co-existence and polarization in Catalonia.* ICIP Survey. https://www.icip.cat/wp-content/uploads/2021/01/Enquesta_ICIP2020_Eng.pdf

Kaldor, M., & Radice, H. (2022). Introduction: Civicness in conflict. *Journal of Civil Society, 18*(2), 125–141. https://www.tandfonline.com/doi/full/10.1080/17448689.2022.2121295

Lanier, J. (2018). *Ten arguments for deleting your social media accounts right now.* Vintage Penguin Random House.

Peace Direct. 2020. *Digital Pathways to Peace: Lessons and Insights from a Global Online Conversation.* Peace Direct. https://www.peacedirect.org/digital-pathways-for-peace/

World Bank. (2018). *Pathways for peace: Inclusive approaches to preventing violent conflict.* World Bank and UN Report. http://hdl.handle.net/10986/28337.

CHAPTER 3

PeaceTech Technologies

Abstract This chapter sets out the key PeaceTech technologies and considers the drivers of PeaceTech as an area of activity.

Keywords Cloud computing • Internet of things • Artificial intelligence • Remote-sensing • Geographic information systems

3.1 Running Hard to Stand Still

The fastest runners in the world are Ethiopian and Kenyan (Douglas, 2022). Theories of their speed have included: analysis of genetics; expanded lung capacity from training at the high altitudes in each country; cultural and historic attitudes to running; team training methods; and nature of training schedules.

Both these countries have had complex conflicts and peace processes that have continued many years. These are seldom discussed in running magazines, although, for example, in 2023 unexpected London marathon winner Sifan Hassan, had fled Ethiopia aged 15 as a refugee from war.

Ethiopia reached a peace and transition agreement in 1991 as a result of a victory by a range of groups from different areas and ethnicities, against a vicious dictatorship known as 'the Derg' (Transitional Period Charter of Ethiopia, 1991). In 1994, a creative Constitution built a federal country, but conflicts have remained in different areas, as have peace processes.

C. Bell, *PeaceTech: Digital Transformation to End Wars*,
https://doi.org/10.1007/978-3-031-38894-1_3

I worked on and off for several years with people of Somali identity in the Ogaden region of Ethiopia, who built over time what is presently a successful peace process reaching a peace agreement, which interestingly was mediated by a Kenyan government facilitation team (Joint Declaration, 2018). Other conflicts continue and emerge—this last year a conflict in the Tigray region of Ethiopia has been brutal and involved allegations of war crimes, with an estimated 600,000 killed. In Kenya, post electoral violence in 2007–2008 saw over 1000 people killed, and led to transition agreements and a transition that in a sense remains perpetually ongoing (see further, Paffenholz, 2021).

Back to running. For those of us who are not so swift, in countries that are predominantly located in the western or developed world, the search for improvement in running has involved Fitbits, Garmins, Apple i-watches, and a range of wrist 'fitness trackers', which track steps, speed, route, and when and how you did the activity.

3.2 What Are the Key New PeaceTech Technologies?

We often talk about PeaceTech without really talking about the Tech. It is important to understand the key technologies, their distinctive terminologies, and how they interact to create new ways of working, if one is seeking to understand their use in peacebuilding. Fitness watches are a good, if trivial, example of how a range of technologies work. If you came to hear about peacebuilding, bear with me here.

Fitness watches are fitness trackers that look like watches. However, they are really little computers that log data from your wrist. They work as part of a system of interrelated computing devices that include phones and computers and satellites. Each wrist tracker has a unique identifier—like a name that only they have, that mark them out as a distinct 'thing'. When you sign up to their systems, they will give you a unique identifier—you too will be a 'thing'. These computers have ability to transfer information over a network without any human being involved. They are part of what we call **'the internet of things'** or **IoT** for short (see Box 3.2).

> **Internet of things**: the network of physical objects—'things'—that are embedded with sensors, software, and other technologies for the purpose of ongoing connecting and exchanging data over the internet in automated ways, with other devices and systems. Oracle, India.

To illustrate: for you to analyse your performance and compare it with others, your watch will count the steps, and measure your elevation with reference to already coded data on maps and sensors within the watch, and satellites in the sky. This will be recorded on the watch's mini-computer which will then transmit this data to **the Cloud**. 'The cloud, as its metaphorical name suggests, is like a big computer and storage system in the sky (see Box). Cloud computing is available on-demand and offers both computing power and ways of storing data without your active management.

The Cloud: a network of global servers, with software that enables remote storage and computing accessible widely through the internet. Cloud computing is computing happening on those servers, rather than the user's own computer.

Sometimes you get access to the cloud for free (like your free email such as Gmail, or file storage, such as Dropbox or SharePoint, both of which are on 'the cloud'). Except that free is not really free—you 'pay' for it, by permitting your personal data to be connected to a range of other products and services. Sometimes you get access as part of your deal with the watchmakers. Sometimes you get access by paying for it with money—like when Gmail or Dropbox charge because you have 'run out of free storage'.

Use of the cloud storage is not bought permanently as if it were a warehouse, but in-effect rented for a periodic fee. There is a word for this: **Servitization** that connotes the shift from buying to in a sense renting—by subscribing to a 'service' (sometimes referred to 'software as a service' or SaaS).

We will come more to servitization in Chap. 12, but let's explain it a little here. Sell a thing and the person pays for it once. Change it to a 'service' and it is paid for on an ongoing and even indefinite basis. Servitization goes hand-in-hand with digital innovation as it is a way for businesses to create revenue streams to support ongoing development of their product and continue to make profit.

Servitization is not just a cunning new capitalist tool to keep charging you (although it's that too): it makes some sort of sense in the field of digital provision because digital innovation is fast-paced. Email systems such as Gmail, for example, are constantly being improved and integrated into other products. The storage service fee enables system maintenance and improvement, including ever-improved security.

The Cloud of course is not a magical storage container in the sky, but is a complex set of machines and software that has a physical existence 'on-the-ground' somewhere. Amazon, for example, which started as a book-seller, expanded to selling more and more things until it has become the world's biggest marketplace. Part of its success lies in how Amazon can provide data about its customers and their purchases to create sophisticated user data models that inform predictions about item sales that can enable targeted advertising, and predictive storage and shipping. Over time this led to collection of more and more data, so that Amazon dominates online selling because it can quite simply do more of it more efficiently than others. Amazon has had to build the **data facilities** needed to sustain all this data-crunching. These data facilities, are now themselves a major thing that Amazon markets. One can buy storage on amazon and use its 'data facilities' (see details here).

This short digression shows us that behind digital innovation and 'the cloud', is a computing power and software housed very much on-the-ground in a hardware of data facilities that require architected physical actual warehouses, and architecture in computer engineering terms.

Back to your fitness watch. As you run, your watch can calculate and produce **real time analytics**, such as: how fast you are running, what your average pace is, and your 'cadence' is (how many steps a second you are running). Sometime real time analytics will also tell you how fast your heart is beating and what 'zone' of exertion it is in—for which it will compare your heart-rate to statistical norms for people your age and size, at different levels of exertion, something that itself requires a lot of data and algorithms. Real time analytics are therefore 'right now' analytics, and they can be useful in helping you adjust things in the moment—in my case, run a bit slower to bring my heart down from the heart attack zone.

Once you have completed your run, your watch may transmit your data to the cloud. Computer programmes in the cloud can then put it together with other fitness watch user data to tell you how your run compared with other previous runs you did, how high you ran elevation wise on that run, and have run over the year, how you compare with others in your age group, etc. This is part of what we might call **data analytics**. In fact, this is often data analytics that uses **big data** capacity, as it lets you compare your data with hundreds, thousands and even millions of others. These 'others' might be others with your same watch and App, but if you have linked to some broader fitness App, such as Strava, this may have connections to users of lots of different types of watch. Strava might link to Instagram and Facebook, and have data-sharing agreements that enable it to pool information from even more people to create big data. This data then needs to be analysed using **machine learning**, which for example can 'cluster' groups of similar users, that would simply be beyond human computation given the number of data points.

> **Big data**: data of a very large size, typically to the extent that its manipulation and management present significant logistical challenges. Oxford English Dictionary. It is characterized by 'the three 'vs': high **variety**, high **volume**, and requirements for high computing power to process at **velocity**.

Your data together with this **big data**, will be fed into data analytic systems that use algorithms to tell you things about yourself and others around you: who you might want to connect with, who ran past you, who took the same route, who has run that route most frequently, etc. These systems will often try to sell you things as well.

You may see all this on your watch face, but you may find it easier to look at on your computer or your phone. In fact, your watch will automatically synchronise with your phone. It does not do this by linking into the cloud: it does so by Bluetooth that is a way your phone has of connecting with other devices. This means of connection means that the data goes straight from the computer on your watch to your phone without being beamed up to the cloud and back down again. In essence a quick form of mini network connects the two devices (IOT again). So, your phone and watch will be set up to automatically synchronise without any action from you, as soon as they are in close enough proximity for their wireless (Bluetooth) connectivity to reach.

While data going to a central computer or cloud takes some time, your watch and phone connect at what is called **the edge**. The transfer from watch to phone is known as **edge computing**. Typically, this sort of transfer of data offers more speed, because it reduces the distance between devices, and that can be useful. More speed equals less 'latency', which all sounds very complicated, but latency is just 'delay'. The faster something moves, and the closer the distance, the less time it takes to get there. Edge computing therefore brings efficiencies.

Machine learning (ML): a branch of artificial intelligence (AI) and computer science that works to build models and use them to classify data and predict outcomes, typically using statistical methods.

Your fitness watch can do other things. It can show you maps, and your route as you run, and after. It can jiggle on your wrist when you go past a turn-off you should have taken. It does this by being linked to a **Geographic Information System** or **GIS**, which enables it to plot runs on an online maps. The watch uses a range of sensors to 'locate' you, and geocodes the information into location data that can be put on a map. Typically, your watch will try to place you by linking you to a satellite thousands of feet above the sky. It will tell you 'GPS' on. The **GPS** is the **'Global Positioning System'** involving a satellite navigation system that can tell within around 20 meters where you are. It will triangulate this data (data analytics again), with where you are in relation to wireless networks around you (the cloud again), and sometimes in relation to other devices near you (internet of things again) to improve the location detail. Sometimes you will connect to the GPS through wireless technology or mobile data technology. Sometimes you will do it without either because your watch or phone contains a 'remote sensor' that can be picked up by the GPS. **Remote-Sensing** is something that we will see feature as part of Early Warning Systems in the PeaceTech World (Chap. 9).

Remote-sensing/sensors. Remote-sensing is the process of detecting and monitoring the physical characteristics of an area by measuring its reflected and emitted radiation at a distance (typically from satellite or aircraft). Special cameras collect remotely sensed images, which help researchers 'sense' things about the Earth. United States Geological Survey.

Finally, your watch may track other things than running. Here **AI** or **Artificial Intelligence** may come in (see, e.g., Bosch account of AI in fitness watches). Artificial intelligence using algorithms might give you new statistics such as your 'fitness' score over time (see for example Strava on how they calculate a fitness score,). Your watch may have artificial intelligence software that enables it even to 'learn' activities that were not programmed in in the place. The software, for example may calculate the lengths in a swimming pool, by using previous swims and matching length with strokes counted. Artificial intelligence perhaps now conjures to mind Open AI's 'GPT-4', an online tool that produces 'human like' responsive answers to any question you write. However, AI is any system of computing that produces responsive and changing predictive outputs based on the data it holds and computes, and it is involved throughout our lives already.

Artificial Intelligence: The simulation of human intelligence by machines, often using machine learning, neuronal networks and sophisticated models and algorithms.

3.3 The Fourth Industrial Revolution

Who knew fitness watches were so complex and used so many multiple innovative technologies? They are one small part of a wider digital revolution that touches every aspect of life, characterised by the 'blurring of boundaries between the physical, the digital, and biological worlds' (McGinnis, 2023). This revolution, emerging in the last decade or so, has been called 'the fourth industrial revolution'. There is a little debate as to what the first three were (see further Schwab, 2015).

Most noticeably, the current digital revolution has revolutionised business, whether of watch-makers or in other areas, by reshaping connectivity, production, consumption, and the speed and efficiency at which things can be done. In fact, regular watchmakers are not the makers of fitness watches. The makers of fitness watches are the makers of phones such as Samsung and Apple. We will come back to this.

Interestingly, while I said the digital revolution has 'noticably' revolutionised business, many underlying technologies are designed to remain unnoticed. Digital innovation now permeates most of the online tools we use, and many of the 'things' around our house. It includes the cookies that stalk us invisibly as we search through the internet, gathering information about us from our google searches until they know us better than our best friend and perhaps more even than we know ourselves. It includes Apps we sign up to for much daily business (that also gather data on us), and the things around us such as the sensors that switch on lights or heating automatically.

Here the main purpose of digital transformation is to build competitive advantage and increased sales and profit. We probably also think of it as a 'developed country' thing, gone a bit mad. I am not sure my fitness watch has in fact improved my fitness. But I do now at least know how unfit I am.

What, then, are the incentives for PeaceTech as digital transformation of peacebuilding?

3.4 Key PeaceTech Technologies

I spent so long talking about fitness watches in the middle of a PeaceTech book because I have found it is important to think in fairly simple ways about how these technologies actually work in real life. Understanding what they do and do not do, where they do it, and what types of capacities and infrastructure are needed to use them, is necessary to using digital technology wisely in a live conflict. Conflict creates challenging infrastructure, security and capacity issues, and using technology to challenge conflict is more complicated than using it to measure running.

Also, trying to use digital innovation for peacebuilding, involves knowing at least a little bit about the difference between 'the cloud', and 'the edge', or between artificial intelligence and machine learning, or GPS and GIS. Technicians will use these terms lightly and quickly. You will have to trust them to do their work. However, if you are going to have a sense of how to hire or contract the right skills, write specifications for the work, or be able to interrogate the adequacy of security of the digital products that emerge with reference to particular conflict contexts, then you will need some technical knowledge. Just as, technical experts will ideally have some commitment to understanding what it is you do, and the particular constraints relating to your work.

PeaceTech and the use of technology to resolve conflict also has to be pursued understanding the wider moment of digital transformation that is happening at speed. Digital transformation is driven by both business interests and ongoing technological innovation. Business courses on digital transformation often map the key technologies driving change within businesses, to consider how they drive change. These courses are designed to help people work with digital transformation within their business as people who understand the business rather than the 'tech', but also see that they need tech to remain competitive. I have found these courses very helpful to seeking to 'do PeaceTech' better. They tend to cover a list of 'digital transformation technologies' that is made from many of the things which the fitness watch mechanisms illustrated.

In Part II of this book we will look further at how the above technologies have been used for a range of peacebuilding activities, and in particular those focused on creating and sustaining peace mediation, agreement and implementation. I focused on fitness watches because if we focus in on how digital innovation can assist in ending wars, the new bundles of technologies that fitness watches illustrate, are the technologies that have had a real traction in the PeaceTech field. We will explore how through the chapters as follows.

Peacebuilding as Hack: Mobile and cloud technology to produce a range of practical peacebuilding tools often for local communities, to support any peace process. PeaceTech has often worked to support 'app-ization' of peacebuilding support tools (that is, turning ways of doing things into usable phone Apps); gaming, used as a mechanism of trust-building, communication and even data-collection; and other forms of digital consultation, that are crucial to peace processes. Distinctions between edge computing, and cloud computing, become important for low band-width communities because they enable some things to be done without being on line, and uploaded in moments of connectivity. Edge-cloud decisions also have implications for personal security—for example if sensitive information is on personal devices and needs transmitted off them. We will consider the ways that PeaceTech offers new 'hacks' to analogue peacebuilding modalities.

Conflict Early Warning Systems: Geocoded Information Systems (GIS). Geocoded, spatial knowledge technologies, for example, geolocation of data, satellite imaging, remote-sensing, and drones, are key to trying to develop Early Warning Systems to alert people to conflict. Interestingly, the use of satellites and drones often does not get dedicated attention on business courses because they are not germane to marketing. They may seem a strange technology to think of with regard to peacebuilding, because we often understand things like satellite and drones to be more associated with conflict, or at least securitization, than with peace.

However, GIS often provide important ways of mapping conflict, that can be used to support its prevention, for example through 'Conflict Early Warning Systems' (CEWS) that attempt to combine observed phenomenon such as troop movements, that can be correlated with other data, such as rise in conflict events such as killings. We will consider how this type of innovation is used with other data, and machine learning to try to create CEWS, in Chap. 9. Once only available to militaries, are increasingly becoming part of the tool-kit of political and peacekeeping missions put in place to implement peace and transition agreements.

Peace Analytics: Data analytics, involving real time analytics, and big data. Data relating to conflict events, to other indicators of peace, such as political stability or democracy, and on peace processes themselves (including our own PA-X peace agreement data), is now all part of PeaceTech. Monitoring conflict, creating dashboards on conflict drivers (such as poverty), and trying to map change over time, or provide easy access to ways of measuring 'peace impacts', are all key to peace process implementation activities. Also often used in the PeaceTech field, are techniques of using population-wide analysis of social media feed—Twitter/X and Facebook—to understand perceptions of a conflict or peace process. This data can be used for purposes such as, understanding perceptions on peace agreement proposals; engaging in more effective or 'strategic communications' around a peace agreement initiative such as a referendum; or for understanding and combat the types of disinformation and hate speech that are at play in undermining peace efforts. We will consider Peace Analytics in Chap. 11.

Underpinning connective tissue: Artificial Intelligence (AI), and Machine Learning (ML). Forms of natural language processing, machine learning and Artificial Intelligence, underlie CEWS, GIS, and Peace Analytics in different ways, drawing on the now extensive—and ever growing—data relating to peace and conflict.

3.5 Conclusion

We now turn to examine the drivers of PeaceTech and how to locate it in terms of other types of innovation in connected fields.

Questions

1. In what ways do you notice you are in the middle of a 'digital revolution'?
2. What advantages does it bring?
3. What concerns you about it?
4. Is digital transformation a 'global north' thing?
5. What type of capacities do you think the different technologies need?
6. Could you rank which capacities are easy to acquire, and which are hard to acquire?

References[1]

Douglas, S. (2022, December 4). *These are the World's fastest marathon runners.* Runner's world blog. https://www.runnersworld.com/races-places/a20823734/these-are-the-worlds-fastest-marathoners-and-marathon-courses/

McGinnis, D. (2023, February 2). *What is the fourth industrial revolution?.* Salesforce, The 360 blog. https://www.salesforce.com/blog/what-is-the-fourth-industrial-revolution-4ir/

Paffenholz, T. (2021). Perpetual peacebuilding: A new paradigm to move beyond the linearity of liberal peacebuilding. *Journal of Intervention and Statebuilding, 15*(3), 367–385. https://www.tandfonline.com/doi/full/10.1080/17502977.2021.1925423

Schwab, K. (2015). *The fourth industrial revolution.* Penguin books.

[1] All last accessed 1 May 2023.

CHAPTER 4

PeaceTech Drivers

Abstract This chapter examines how digital transformation of peacebuilding connects to digital transformation in closely related areas, such as humanitarian intervention and development. I also consider the connection with digital transformation of security and even war. I set out the main drivers of PeaceTech.

Keywords SomethingTechs • Humanitarianism • Development • Security • WarTech

4.1 Locating PeaceTech

Beyond business marketing, new technologies and capacities are impacting distinctively on other spheres of life. Some of these spheres are connected with distinctive aspects of business that are key to social ordering, such as financial services, or ownership of property. Others deliver 'public goods' such as how healthcare is planned for or delivered, how government interacts with us, or how policing takes place. Some examples of what I term 'SomethingTechs' are set out in the box below.

C. Bell, *PeaceTech: Digital Transformation to End Wars*,
https://doi.org/10.1007/978-3-031-38894-1_4

'SomethingTechs'

FinTech: financial technology, which consists in the use of innovative technologies applied to the financial industry. FinTech includes mobile payment apps, cryptocurrency based on block chain. (Fintech Weekly, 2023)

PropTech: 'all the tech tools Real Estate experts use to optimize the way people buy, sell, research, market, and manage a property. These innovative technologies are also known as Real Estate Tech, Retech, Realtech, CRE Tech depending on which lens you're looking through. However, at its core, prop tech always means robust alignment between real estate and technology.' (Ascendix, 2023)

GovTech: 'GovTech is a whole of government approach to public sector modernization. It emphasizes three aspects of public sector modernization: citizen-centric, universally accessible public services, and whole-of-government approach to digital government transformation.' (World Bank Govtech)

MedTech: a combination of medical technology and healthcare interventions.

ClimateTech: 'Technological solutions that mitigate the impacts of climate change and build resilient communities.' (Reichert, 2020)

WeddingTech: Is this a thing? New smart rings can now be purchased as wedding rings, that transmit couple's heartbeats to each other. Really! (Cassidy, 2023)

(For more SomethingTechs see Nathany, 2021.)

There are areas very close to that of peacebuilding, where technology is also playing a key role in innovation. Indeed, PeaceTech can be understood to intersect with these spheres of digital transformation, all of which intersect with each other. These are: tech use for humanitarian intervention, tech use in development intervention (including GovTech), and tech-based security interventions. (see Fig. 4.1).

The synergies between these cognate-Techs and PeaceTech are two-fold. First, the suite of innovation tools is virtually identical—it is often the same type of tool and same type of intervention that is used in each area. Second, the subject matter of each is close to that of the others. Those in the field often talk about 'the triple nexus', that is—the interlinkage between humanitarian, development and peacebuilding interventions and actors (see ICVA, n.d.). This triple nexus recognizes the ways in which

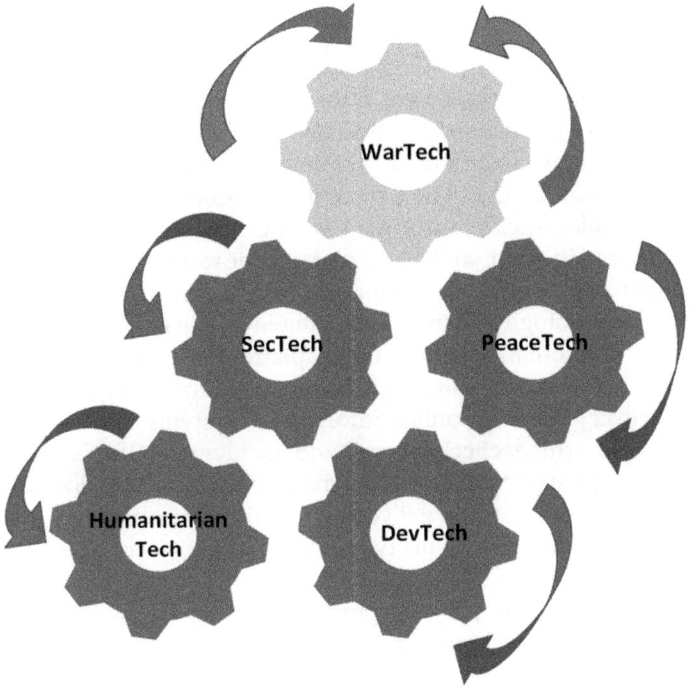

Fig. 4.1 Peacebuilding Gears

conflict causes humanitarian crisis, and longer-term development and social justice needs, that if not met continue to operate in a cycle with the conflict. PeaceTech applied to peacekeeping, peacemaking and building draws on and is connected to development and humanitarian digital innovation, with processes, tasks, and digital tools that overlap.

Also overlapping, is digital transformation in the security and war sphere. Military responses to prevent or address conflict involve many of the same tasks with the same difficult backdrop as peacekeeping and humanitarian intervention. For example: understanding where violence is taking place and responding to it, strategic communication with local populations, Early Warning Systems, and logistics of mobilizing projects involving people and goods in complex and violent geo-political environments. These tasks are carried out often using the same tools and techniques as PeaceTech.

We will examine these related fields further.

4.2 Humanitarian and Development Tech Initiatives

Humanitarian organizations have embraced digital transformation to support provision of humanitarian relief. Being on the relief frontline can also mean being on the frontline of negotiations with conflict actors. The International Red Cross/ Red Crescent, for example, must often negotiate forms of micro-peace agreement with armed groups to get its relief safely to people in need, and has a digital innovation unit to enable support aid delivery. Digital transformation for the Red Cross includes using a range of technologies: Artificial Intelligence, Chatbots, voice recognition, robotic automation, new digital platforms, crowd-sourcing, GIS, drones, open source software, and mobile apps. Increasingly, the logistics of relief delivery relies on online information systems that can track supplies, but also armed check-points, and incidents. ICRC's RCView—a platform described as 'a digital ecosystem' is used to 'visualize all aspects of a disaster response effort, delivering real-time information for decision making and coordination'. This type of development—critical to humanitarian responses to conflict—overlaps with the types of platform now used for 'situation analysis' in peacekeeping (see further Chap. 11).

MercyCorps, a development organization focused on humanitarian relief, has built-in digital transformation to its core ways of working. Funded by Cisco, it developed a five-year partnership 'centered on delivering humanitarian aid and development assistance faster, better and to more people around the world by accelerating digital solutions'. Cisco is a major business that 'offers an industry-leading portfolio of technology innovations'. It offers 'networking, security, collaboration, cloud management, and more' to 'help to securely connect industries and communities' (Cisco). Cisco has a strong corporate social responsibility ethos, and uses its capacities and philanthropy to support a range of partnerships such as this one, with non-governmental organizations, that we could broadly associate with humanitarianism and peace.

The Mercy Corps—Cisco digital innovation programme has supported development tasks such as: automated reporting systems to streamline operations; civic online forums that seek to improve inclusion of local people in development planning; using social media scanning to combat Covid-19 disinformation by targeting strategic communications at particular rumours; providing for digital cash and voucher assistance. These tasks overlap with peacebuilding ones when they occur in the same conflict settings.

4.3 CyberSecurity and SecTech

Increasingly war is fought not just conventionally but in cyberspace, and forms of cybersecurity are being developed to support actors trying to promote civicness. The point is illustrated by an interesting digitally focused Canadian non-governmental organization SecDev Foundation. To give a flavour, one of its initiative is 'SalamaTech Syria'. This project points to the reality that

> The Syrian conflict is the first protracted war to be fought on and through the internet. All actors use the internet to organize, plan, and share information; some use it to document human rights abuses and bear witness; others use it to propagandize, collect intelligence, sow fear, and win followers. Now, as the conflict drags on, many use it to maintain family and social connections, continue formal education, and learn new skills for the future.
>
> The Syrian social media space has been dominated by the voices of militant actors. Social media is used as a weapon of war. By contrast, the voices of Syrian non-violent actors have been drowned out by the noise of violence and extremism. To the outside world, the concept of Syrian civil society has been largely reduced to that of powerless 'refugees.' SalamaTech has been working hard to correct this. (SalamaTech Syria)

In response, SalamaTech has provided very practical tools to help Syrian civilians stay safe and stay connected. These include: emergency tech support to Syrians who have been arrested or had their accounts hacked; digital safety audits and 'real-time remediation' for Syrian civil society organizations; and Digital Technology First Responders who provide in-person and remote training to empower women and youth, to become active drivers of peace and development.

A board member and founder of SecDev Foundation is Rafael Rohozinski, is Principal of the SecDev Group, and CEO of Zero-Point Security, whose core cybersecurity work overlaps with the mission of SecDev the NGO such as the SalamaTech project. SecDev Group provides not just cybersecurity, but also wider 'thought leadership' in areas such as cyberwarfare. Rohozinski himself combines a diverse set of connections between security services, cyber initiatives, international organizations, diplomatic initiatives and Universities (Centre for International Governance Innovation). In Part II we will come to understand the PeaceTech ecosystem that he in a sense builds and is part of through these connections.

4.4 WarTech?

Aspects of providing security overlap with what we might consider 'WarTech'—'cyberwarfare' itself in a sense interlocks with the technologies used to combat it, as SecDev Foundation's work illustrates. Digital innovation has also transformed traditional forms of warfare in ways that change the relationships between combatants—for example the use of armed drones (forms of robotic device) by the US in places such as Pakistan, where they engage in bombing those suspected of 'terrorism'. Beyond this, digital innovation is applied to 'smart-bombs', and other forms of warfare machinery, that are taking warfare into an area where the distinction between hardware of guns and bombs, and the influence of thoughts and minds, are deeply entangled.

PeaceTech often relies on uses of technology that we associate with war. In the field of GIS, satellite and use of drones, actors such as peacekeepers are increasingly in a sense 'appropriating' what originated as WarTech, for peace process support, in a search for 'better intelligence' for peacekeeping missions. We will consider the implications further in Chap. 10.

4.5 Drivers of Digital Innovation: Value

Before we move on, it is perhaps useful to pause and think about why businesses adapt to embrace digital innovation, and what the drivers for PeaceTech might be. The new technologies outlined in the last chapter drive change in a number of different ways, illustrated by the fitness watch example, because they add value to the business. Value is the underlying driver of digital innovation in business, understood as creating a better more productive business with improved service provision and improved profits.

New technologies enable companies can to deliver a better product to their customer. For example, new improved fitness watches give people a range of options that their ordinary watch never could. Hence the label 'smart watches'.

New technologies can enable businesses to be efficient. They can help to streamline internal processes making businesses more agile and efficient. New data systems can help track where products are in a delivery supply chain to make delivery faster. Data crunching can help companies predict when there might be a demand for their product—for fitness watches say at Christmas and New Year, meaning they manufacturers can make sure they have sufficient stock, in the right warehouses to sustain timely delivery.

New technologies can increase business opportunities. For example, data analytics might be able to identify which types of people are regular customers, and where a customer base could be expanded to a new demographic, or new products sold to existing customers, for example where a fitness watch user might have a tendency to buy particular types of shoe.

In the SomethingTech areas set out above, the drivers of digital innovation will be a bit different from those set out above in the pure commerce field. For example, where governments attempt to engage in digital transformation it will often be in an attempt to improve services to the public—for example a planning portal may help people track planning applications; an App may help people pay public utilities bill. Innovative dashboards may improve transparency and responsiveness of government—for example by surveying people on future plans, or letting them see where their taxes have been spent. Efficiency of some government processes may be improved, for example, because electronic forms of bureaucracy can be automated reducing the need for people to be employed to enter data manually. 'GovTech', therefore has a distinctive set of drivers of change, that connect to a particular set of relevant digital transformation technologies.

4.6 Drivers of PeaceTech

What then are the drivers of PeaceTech, as digital innovation relating to peacebuilding? What value does PeaceTech add to the practice of ending wars? I suggest the following are the main drivers.

4.6.1 Creativity-at-work

PeaceTech has partly emerged because of a mutual alignment between people who approach life creatively. Different types of peacebuilding look very different. The practice of negotiating ends to conflict—say trying to negotiate a peace agreement—can look like high end level 'diplomacy' between governments and international organizations in which ordinary people get a bit lost. However, at the level of the everyday conflict, peacebuilding is often a creative enterprise in bringing people, ideas, activism and communication together to try to build a vision that would enable people to displace use of violence. Digital transformation has been driven not just by business and profit, but by creative industries such as gamers, artists, visualizers. There is perhaps a natural tendency of peacebuilders to creativity, and therefore a synergy between tech and peacebuilding as creative fields. Some examples illustrate.

Butterfly Works is an Amsterdam-based social design studio 'pioneering the use of co-creation and design thinking in international development'—interestingly with a predominantly female team. As part of a GIZ (German Agency for International Cooperation) peace initiative on Yemen, it worked to co-create games with Yemeni designers. Arabia Felix, a series of six mobile games designed to inspire users to strive towards peace, through quests, treasure hunts, puzzles and decision-making challenges (for the story more fully, see here; see also the game's Facebook page. The Games can be downloaded and played in both Arabic and English on Google player).

The project shows different forms of creativity at play: co-creation from Global North and South (albeit as a northern-led initiative); digitally connecting young people from different locations who could otherwise meet; peace games, that challenge war games; and a creative attempt to gently challenge attitudes. Within two years the games had 40,000 downloads. Arabia Felix by the way, means 'happy or flourishing Arabia, and in ancient geography was the comparatively fertile region in southwestern and southern Arabia that included Yemen. It contrasted with Arabia Deserta—barren Arabia, and Arabia Petraea—Stony Arabia. (Britannica) So even the name navigated the complex divided history of Yemen.

4.6.2 'Shiny' ('Now I'll eat you, so prepare your final plea')

People are attracted to 'shiny new' things and want to give them a go, to see if they produce shiny new results. There appear to be shiny new things to use 'out there', so why not try to apply them to innovate with regard to peacebuilding? PeaceTech exists partly because applying new tech tools to improve peacebuilding practices seems to make sense. A range of quite different actors have become interested to drive and support PeaceTech in part because it is a 'new kid on the block' (CMI, 2020). The move of a range of governments to support PeaceTech has been motivated by wanting to be at the front end of innovation, as well as out of conviction that new forms of digital innovation offer immediate improvement of peacebuilding practices.

Yet, a more general disruption of peacebuilding sees a push against 'supply-driven' peacebuilding interventions often from global north, rather than demand-led peacebuilding support that is responsive to the requests from activists in the Southern-based countries in which peace process predominate. Perhaps, like the villainous crab on the Disney cartoon *Moana*, who uses his shininess to gobble all the fish attracted by it, we should be cautious of 'shiny' as a reason to do PeaceTech.

4.6.3 It Is Lower Risk to Fund

Supporters of PeaceTech may have been drawn in because it enables them to 'do good' in new more effective ways. Philanthropy—that is money donated from business to do 'good things'—has often been a bit wary of supporting activities that can seem 'political' such as peacebuilding. Similarly, people we may think of as purely profit-focused, such as venture capitalists who invest somewhat experimentally in businesses they think might just make a big profit, or investment bankers that invest other people's money to make interest, and other tech-focused companies, may have business reasons to support PeaceTech. They will often have Corporate Social Responsibility (CSR) requirements, and sometimes also their own commitments and reasons to engage in some sort of social justice intervention alongside their wish to make money.

These financial entrepreneurs often support PeaceTech as a way of being seen to 'do good' and even trying to do good. They may also get involved because they can add value by connecting the businesses they invest in to support PeaceTech projects. The new EUI Global PeaceTech Hub, for example, is supported by Kluz Ventures, a private investment firm that is 'passionate about new technologies'. Kluz Ventures understands its investments to be about 'long term returns across private and public markets' but also articulates a vision to invest in companies that are in some sense changing the world in a good way (Kluz Ventres, About). Supporting PeaceTech is a way of connecting companies with the side of the angels (Nicolaïdis & Giovanardi, 2022).

We may feel that 'supporting peacebuilding' is a nice thing and not a bit political. But think for a moment about the conflict in Ukraine that is raging at the time of writing this book. Many people think that fighting this war is the only way to create 'peace'. Arguing for negotiations, appears to suggest that compromise with a country that has invaded your country is a good thing. That view is controversial. Yet, in most conflict countries wars are waged in the name of peace and justice, sometimes cynically and sometimes not. In fact, all sides in most conflicts claim that they have turned to war in pursuit of a just peace, and peace mediation must traverse conflicted concepts of what the war is 'about'.

Businesses can be reluctant to try to change conflict contexts, whether through philanthropic giving or corporate social responsibility, because conflicts are messy and complicated and have 'sides'. Deciding what is a good peacebuilding intervention to fund is not the sort of calculation businesses are well placed to make. Plus they may seek to do business with all of the actors in the conflict at some point down the road.

Supporting PeaceTech's provision of the technological tools for peacebuilding can feel a bit safer than supporting what people might do with them in complex conflict contexts. It will feel closer to their business 'tech' mission. But also, provision of tech tools, is detachable, in a sense, from what people do with those tools.

4.6.4 Evidence-Based Approaches to Intervention

Digital innovation offers the possibility of more evidence-based approaches to peacebuilding. While the early 1990s saw peace negotiations as somewhat of an experiment, over time the practice became more structured and complex. Given that the practice is over 30 years old and, as we shall see next Chapter (5), has a patchy record of success, there is a strong wish to develop peacebuilding policy with an evidential basis. Ongoing pressure on public budgets means that funding peace processes and peacebuilding brings increasing pressure to be rigorous in terms of only funding interventions that have a clear capacity to acheive a clear outcome.

The search for evidence-based policy, drives some PeaceTech initiatives, including our own. A broad range of research attempts to correlate what goes into a peace agreement with peace process outcomes; and indeed seeks to understand and measure the overall success of peace processes themselves. For example, data has been used to suggest that peace processes in which women are included, are more successful than those where they are not (Krause et al., 2018). As we will see further, using data to define and measure what might be the ingredients of success, is not simple.

4.6.5 *Global Southern-Based 'Needs Must'*

Although we might think of technological development as a global north dominated affair, in fact PeaceTech innovation has often been developed in the Global South to respond to pressing needs in conflict-affected states. Necessity is the mother of invention. For example, one of the much-cited PeaceTech initiatives is Ushahidi. The name comes form the Swahili word for 'testimony'. Ushahidi provides an online platform for using crowdsourcing to collect and geocode and map, information about incidents and events. It grew out of tech colleagues who worked in 2008 to establish a digital platform to monitor and map post-election violence in Kenya. The platform that emerged enables the rapid collection, management and analysis of crowdsourced information.

Ushahidi has now developed a business model that sustains its work. It invites donations, and receives grants for projects. It offers a basic platform for free, and an 'Enterprise plan' for bigger scale platform capabilities—a form of 'servitization'. It is a good example of what is called 're-usability' in design model, and the platform has now been used in other places for example, to ensure fair elections in the US, Kenya and Nigeria, documenting police brutality in Portland during Black Lives Matter protests, and helping women address sexual violence in Egypt.

Also located within Kenya and Nairobi are a number of other creative initiatives that have a digital focus, and operate collectively to position Kenya at the heart of PeaceTech. For example Build Up, a 'peacetech enabler' who we will look at more next Chapter, holds key trainings in Kenya with a presence there. Busara, a Center for Behavioural Economics, is a nonprofit organization that uses social and behavioural science, including innovative approaches to data and technology, to address problems that include conflict. For example Busara's project in Uganda, assessed the 'behavioural effects of conflict exposure', seeking to understand how exposure to conflict affected social preferences, including decisions to use violence.

Our own work relating to exploring a digital peace process for Yemen, in association with other partners, revealed multiple organizations within Yemen engaged in digital peacebuilding that collectively had interesting tech capacities. This included women's groups networking through WhatsApp, and groups such as Deep Root Consulting, with a strong interest and capacity in new technologies, as well as Butterfly Works discussed above in Chap. 4, and further in Chap. 8 below.

Similarly, in Syria an audit of use of technology by activists found extensive use and innovation (British Council & Build Up, n.d.). Initiatives, such as the SecDev SalamaTech, have emerged to provide layers of professional security expertise to these types of organic local initiative.

PeaceTech has therefore some potential to support local actors to take control of their own modes of production. It also offers mechanisms to adjust imbalances of knowledge between local actors and international actors: to render the local more knowable to internationals, and to enable locals to connect to and influence international agendas.

4.6.6 *Supporting More Inclusive Peace Processes*

As the Everyday Peace Indicators project of Chap. 2 illustrated, PeaceTech offers innovative solutions of scale for including the public in peace processes. It offers innovative ways of reaching hard-to-reach populations, and conducting surveys or polling on peace process options and drafts. 'Digital inclusion' for peace processes is a key PeaceTech development (see further, Hirblinger, 2020). Hirblinger defines digital inclusion in peace processes as meaning that 'the voice of conflict stakeholders is integrated into that peace process in the form of digital data' (2020, p. 10).

Examples include Facebook consultations in Myanmar ceasefire negotiations (prior to the current coup); digital platforms for negotiations which included capacity to upload submissions in Colombia; offline and online consultations in preparation of the Libya National Dialogue. In addition to providing digital tools to enable people to input to peace processes, forms of machine learning now have capacity to enable views to be more quickly parsed from electronic submissions, in ways that can be quickly fed to mediators. A project in Chile for example, used natural language processing to compare respondent's views on the priorities for the constitution, with the language of the constitution; a proof-of-concept study in Yemen, demonstrated how topics could be modelled on consultation responses (Arana-Catania et al., 2022).

4.6.7 *Covid Effect*

Covid-19 displaced many internationals from conflict zones who as they were relocated home. It also led to lock-downs, emergency laws, restrictions on association, and an urgent need for medical supplies. As in all areas, Covid-19 drove a greater uptake of digital technologies as things like online meetings became a necessity. Conflicts create some similar constraints to Covid—people stuck in places, international flights being shut down, and individuals being unable to meet safely in person. As I write, for example, emerging conflict in Sudan has led to rapid evacuation of most international staff, displacement of civilians, and people confined to houses, so key communications relating to any attempt to broker peace will have to happen remotely. Covid-19 digital innovation therefore remains useful.

4.7 Disruption of Peacebuilding Practice

A final driver of digital innovation is a response to the reality that peacebuilding practices and processes are in a moment of flux and even crisis. Conflict patterns are changing, and the global order that supported the evolution of peace processes and mediated ends to conflict is changing.

Digital innovation appears to offer some capacity to respond to this crisis. We now turn to consider disruption.

Questions

1. Where do you think digital innovation seems useful in humanitarian, development and security interventions?
2. What do you think are its risks in these areas?
3. Can war ever be a 'pro-peace' intervention?
4. Can you think of other drivers of PeaceTech?
5. How do you feel about the word 'disruption'?

References[1]

Arana-Catania, M., van Lier, F., & Procter, R. (2022). Supporting peace negotiations in the Yemen war through machine learning. *Data and Policy, 4*(e28). https://doi.org/10.1017/dap.2022.19

Ascendix. (2023, March 20). *What is proptech and how it changed the real estate industry*. Ascendix blog. https://ascendixtech.com/proptech-real-estate-definition/

[1] All last accessed 1 May 2023.

Cassidy, A. (2023, April 24). *The wedding tech now at the heart of couples' nuptials.* BBC online news article. https://www.bbc.co.uk/news/business-65322101

CMI. (2020, September 17). *Digital technologies and peace mediation—Can Finland drive peacetech development?*. Martti Ahtisaari Peace foundation blog. https://cmi.fi/2020/09/17/digital-technologies-and-peace-mediation-can-finland-drive-peacetech-development/

Fintech Weekly. (2023, March 12). *Fintech definition.* Fintech weekly blog. https://www.fintechweekly.com/fintech-definition

Hirblinger, A. T. (2020, September). *Digital inclusion in mediated peace processes: How technology can enhance participation.* United States Institute of Peace report, 168. https://www.usip.org/publications/2020/09/digital-inclusion-mediated-peace-processes-how-technology-can-enhance

Krause, J., Krause W., & Bränfors P. (2018). Women's Participation in Peace Negotiations and the Durability of Peace. *International Interactions, 44*(6), 985–1016, https://doi.org/10.1080/03050629.2018.1492386

Nathany, M. (2021, September 1). *Fintech, Medtech, Edtech, Regtech and all the other terms ending in 'tech'*. UCL Finance and Technology Review (FTR) blog. https://www.uclftr.com/post/fintech-medtech-edtech-regtech-and-all-the-other-terms-ending-in-tech

Nicolaïdis, K., & Giovanardi, M. (2022). *Global Peacetech: Unlocking the better angels of our techne*". European University Institute, Global Governance Programme working paper. https://hdl.handle.net/1814/74985

Reichert, E. (2020, October 8). *What is climatetech?*. Greentown labs blog. https://greentownlabs.com/what-is-climatetech/

CHAPTER 5

Double Disruption

Abstract This chapter examines how new patterns of conflict are disrupting both efforts to mediate ends to conflict, and the wider peacebuilding practices that support peace processes. I argue that the distinctions between conflict and peace have become very blurred. To be effective, PeaceTech practice must seek to add value to peacebuilding, but it must do so in current moment of crisis that relates to a rapidly changing conflict landscape. This landscape is one of double disruption—that is, disruption to peacebuilding from changing conflict dynamics, and disruption from the digital revolution and its impact on peace and war.

Keywords Peace process • Transition • Disruption

5.1 There's This Trick With a Knife I'm Learning to Do

There's this trick with a knife I'm learning to do. I love this title of a book of poems by Sri Lankan–Canadian novelist and poet Michael Ondaatje (1979). I can't explain why.

The phrase is really intriguing. It sounds ominous—what is he learning to do with the knife? Is he learning to cut and to hurt and be a harsher

C. Bell, *PeaceTech: Digital Transformation to End Wars*,
https://doi.org/10.1007/978-3-031-38894-1_5

nastier version of himself? It feels as if he could be cutting himself? Cutting something out? A good something or a bad something? Or could he be cutting free, or carving a beautiful wood sculpture, or experimenting with what a knife can do in a more artistic way, that subverts the darker side of what a knife can be?

I first heard the phrase from a peacebuilder called Ken Bush many years ago when we worked together in University of Ulster. He was presenting a paper on how we might decide what 'peace agreement success' was, and *who* should do the defining, so that we could measure delivery. He did not explain the title, but it captured how monitoring success in peacebuilding requires imposing a definition of peace to monitor against, when constructing what peace might mean in any country context, is itself the object of the peacebuilding effort. Ken presented at a small expert seminar I ran in 2008 that continues to inform our efforts to benchmark peaceful directions of travel in conflicted societies, by developing a Peace and Transition Process Tracker as described in Chap. 11.

I turn to the knife phrase because what we are doing with PeaceTech requires us to think about what peace is, what its relationship with conflict is and how technology might relate to both in ambiguous ways.

5.2 Disruption

The growing list of 'SomethingTechs' and their coining as SomethingTechs, signifies two things. First, a set of drivers of turn to digital innovation that are distinctive to different domains of application; and second, that new digital capacities often disrupt existing ways of doing business.

The SomethingTech label speaks not just to a connection between the 'something' and technology, but to how digital innovation transforms the something itself in ways that can have unpredictable outcomes for good and for bad. FinTech, for example, has enabled mobile banking that has shaped where ATMs and banks are located. It has also enabled new forms of currency such as bitcoin that float free from country monetary systems, and therefore can operate outside of normal regulatory frameworks. Or faster-than-light transactions whose speed changes the nature of speculation in ways that can destabilize financial institutions. All of these changes in a sense change what money is, how it is used, and have knock-on unpredictable changes to the financial sector, some of which seem good and some bad.

MedTech can include medical technology for hand-held pregnancy tests, or old tech such as ultrasound, but the term signifies advances that are transformative of how medical interventions take place. This can include, nano-computers being injected into blood streams to both detect and modify things that cause disease, or robotic surgical interventions or linked screens, enabling surgery to take place with doctors in one country and the patient in another in ways that globalize healthcare and the frameworks that govern it.

The word often used to describe this type of change is 'disruption'. What the SomethingTechs have in common is that they 'disrupt' normal ways of doing business by providing alternative ways of doing business. As the word 'disruption' indicates, there is something unpredictable about what then happens.

5.3 'Change Everything Except Your Wife and Kids'

We tend to think of disruption as a 'boo word', rather than a 'yay word'. On a closer look, however, whether it gets a boo or a yay might depend on what is being disrupted. If it is something bad being disrupted—like a cycle of violence, then we might think of disruption as a yay word. Mac Ginty (2022), for example, suggests that local peacebuilding is often an attempt to disrupt conflict, and also that conflict is sometimes disrupted by events such as a natural disaster. Interestingly the Tsunami of 2004, helped create a renewed peace process in the conflict in Aceh, Indonesia, but destroyed one in Sri Lanka, while the earthquake in Nepal led political parties to finally agree a constitution to consolidate the peace process after years of disagreement. If something good is being disrupted, such as an attempt to bridge polarized views, then we think of it as a boo word. Indeed, conflict itself is a form of disruption of the prior status quo.

In the business world, digital disruption is viewed by some as yay—it presents new business opportunities that they capitalize on, and by some as boo—it can appear that the new opportunities often arise because of capacity to circumvent fairer more regulated practices.

Disruption can be both good and bad for particular businesses. For those that adapt, new lines of work may emerge that are very lucrative. Samsung is best known for phones and electronics. However, it began in 1938 as a grocery store in Korea, trading noodles and flour. Who knew?

And yes: someone in Samsung actually said 'change everything…' to his senior executives: Lee-Kun-Hee, son of Lee-Byung-Chull who founded the grocery store. Lee-Kun-Hee masterminded its electronics division and the rise of the Samsung the electronics giant we know today.

Digital disruption, however, is also high risk for businesses—particularly if they stick to their old ways. Famously, Kodak who held the biggest market share in cameras and film for decades, dismissed digital innovation in both. By 2012, the unthinkable had happened: Kodak filed for bankruptcy. It is one of the most famous stories of failure to respond to disruption, although even digital cameras were ultimately somewhat displaced by smartphones.

5.4 PeaceTech and Disruption

Is PeaceTech disruptive? If so, how? There are a number of quite different possibilities, some yay and some boo.

PeaceTech could be adding value to peacebuilding enabling new or more efficient modes of disrupting conflict, and therefore better peacebuilding. The Arabia Felix games to support peacebuilding in Yemen mentioned in Chap. 4 and examined further in Chap. 8, for example, enable forms of communication between young people who cannot meet, regarding 'peace' in a country where even the word 'peace' is contentious between different groups.

Or, PeaceTech could be disrupting peacebuilding in a way that leads to unpredictable results, which means also some bad results. For example, remote connectivity of conflict parties might enable peace talks to take place because it deals with security and logistical issues of in-person meeting, but could it have knock-on effects for trust-building—something that seems to happens in a unique way in face-to-face human encounter.

So is PeaceTech a yay word, or a boo word, or somewhere in-between? EUI scholars have suggested a tendency to approach PeaceTech from two different converse perspectives, that captures an ambivalence (Nicolaïdis & Giovanardi, 2022, p. 10). The first perspective emphasizes human agency and views Tech as 'just another tool' that humans use in bad and good ways. The second perspective is 'tech determinative', and views the use of the technology chosen as determining the outcome in ways that the user did not contemplate. They suggest a kind-of middle ground perspective that views technology and politics as interacting to shape and reshape each other in complex and unpredictable ways—sometimes termed the study of 'technopolitics' (Cf., Fritsch, 2014). What then are the unpredictable outcomes of PeaceTech for peace processes?

5.5 Double Disruption

The question of whether and how PeaceTech disrupts traditional approaches to ending wars, has an additional complication. As alluded to earlier, peacebuilding as a practice of actively mediation ends to conflict by constructing peace processes finds itself in a contemporary moment of fundamental disruption.

Conflict is changing shape, and interventions to end it are struggling to respond. Peacebuilding in the sense of a practice of trying to end wars stands somewhat confounded. Digital innovation, I suggest, has played very little role in this more fundamental disruption, despite how it now stands tied up with it. If relevant at all, it is an accelerator rather than a cause.

To understand the current disruption of peacebuilding as active attempts to end conflict, it is useful to sketch out a short history of how peace processes and peacebuilding developed (see further, Bell, 2017).

5.6 A Potted History of Peace Processes

In the last three decades, peace mediation has been directed primarily at violent conflict within states. In its contemporary form, the 'peace process' in its current form came into being in the early 1990s. Peace and transition processes proliferated due to three main factors relating to the end of the Cold War.

First, a rise in intra-state conflict and associated peace efforts to resolve it. Data shows that conflicts within states reached a peak post–Cold War in the early 1990s, typified by the Balkans conflicts.

Second, alongside this spike in conflict, new possibilities for ending long-standing conflicts with geopolitical dimensions appeared to exist. Peace processes began to take shape in places like Central America that had previously seen conflict locked-in by the tensions between West and East and the geopolitics of the Cold War in ways that began to change.

Third, with the Cold War gone, increased international attention became focused on conflict *within* states, and new possibilities emerged for using tools such as peacekeeping that Cold War tensions had limited. Over time a new international architecture of support for intervention, mediation and implementation of peace agreements was built (see Bell, 2008, pp. 28-31).

A practice of ending wars through negotiation took hold, and typically involved the following common elements.

Face-to-face talks between states and their non-state armed opponents. These replaced mediation tactics that sought to work with 'moderates' to marginalize groups using armed violence. Talks focused on tying commitments to a ceasefire, to a revised more inclusive state structure involving elections.

Formalised peace or transition agreements. These saw armed opponents make public the commitments they had agreed to in formally written agreements. These agreements typically put in place elaborate implementation institutions involving a range of international actors in implementation roles as 'third parties', from joint monitoring commissions to international 'guarantors'.

Governed by human rights and humanitarian law. International norms relating to human rights and humanitarian law were viewed as relevant to what was negotiated. Over time the idea grew that they should constrain *what* was agreed between the parties, and also *the process* by which they were agreed.

Peace processes based on formal negotiated ends to conflict were surprisingly extensive, and surprisingly successful over time. Our own PA-X Peace Agreement Database indicates that since 1990 over 2000 peace agreements across all stages of a peace process have been signed in over 150 different conflicts. There is debate about the measurement of success and what it shows, but on one estimate over 70% of agreements were successful in ending violent conflict for over five years—a political science threshold of success (Suhrke & Samset, 2007; Krause, 2019). Between 1990 and 2012 deaths in conflict and other conflict indicators fell fairly steadily (Global Peace Index). Peace processes, therefore, were good at achieving reduced deaths in conflict—what we might term negative peace, and this is no small matter. However, they were less successful in building functional stable states that could continue to transact political relationships non-violently through political institutions, so as to deliver good public services and social justice. These sorts of outcome are often called 'positive peace'.

Over this same time-period, the international infrastructure to support peace processes proliferated and peace processes were increasingly internationalized and legalized. New UN Departments and units were created, for example, a Peacebuilding Commission, a UN Department of Political and Peacebuilding Affairs (DPPA), including a Policy and Mediation Division with a Mediation Support Unit, to mention a few. New international legal standards, such as the United Nations Security Council Resolution 1325 (2000) on Women, Peace and Security, started to further 'regulate' how peace processes should ideally be designed and what peace agreements should include.

States too adopted support of peace processes as key foreign policy objectives, and a concept called 'private mediation' was born which involved essentially diplomatic type mediation functions being produced by non-governmental organizations, notably the Centre for Humanitarian Dialogue, and Independent Diplomat.

However, from 2012 on, this way of doing business had begun to unravel, and deaths in conflict in Syria alone, reversed previous downward trends. Indeed, figures across different measurements of peace all started to reverse (World Bank, 2018, p. xvii).

As a result, the practice of using peace processes to end conflict is somewhat in crisis. Partly this reflects an internal crisis of peacebuilders. With contemporary peacebuilding practices over 30 years old, the failure to deliver positive peace, and instead deliver 'un-ending transition' of a 'no-war-no-peace' nature, has increasingly triggered serious introspection on the reasons for lack of deeper success.

Two issues have come to the fore. First, the question of 'inclusion' in peace talks and agreement outcomes seemed to be part of the problem. The focus on armed actors, rather than those engaged in building civic-ness, prioritized their needs above those of ordinary civilians who had always been committed to peace, and constituencies such as women that tended to work in non-violent ways. Empowering armed actors in the new political dispensation, created government mechanisms that over time proved difficult to make work.

Second, unease existed regarding peacebuilding being 'done from and by' the global north, 'on or to' the Global South. In other words, peacebuilding seemed 'supply-led' from the global north, more than 'demand-led from the Global South. As a result, peacebuilding organizations have mounted initiatives to try to respond (see for example, the Principles for Peace Initiative).

However, the crisis is not just one of apparent failure after a long period of success. It is more profound. The crisis emerges from a number of disruptive realities, related to how conflict patterns are changing in some of the most protracted conflicts—Afghanistan, Iraq, Libya, Sudan, South Sudan, Syria and Yemen. There are several elements to this disruption.

Change in conflict patterns sees multiple conflicts within countries operate to create a complex conflict system. The peace process model no longer seems to map-on to the new conflict dynamics. Peace process design has focused on achieving a deal between an authoritarian and violent state that was 'owned' by a dominant political grouping, and one or several major armed opponents. The peace process tried to bring them to a mediated solution that would encapsulate a new more inclusive political settlement. However, conflict does not look this way anymore. It is characterized by fragmentation, with multiple armed groups who come together and fall apart in strategic alliances. This was brought home to us when we began to find and collect 'local peace agreements': it was sometimes difficult to judge when a local agreement was a 'peace' agreement because it appeared to focus on alliance to stop fighting between two groups, so they could unite and fight even harder against others (See, Bell & Wise, 2022; Bell et al., 2021).

Second, conflict is also much messier in terms of whether it is 'within states', or 'between states'. The conflict in Ukraine illustrates. It is a conflict between two states—Ukraine and Russia. However, the conflict takes place almost entirely within Ukrainian territory. Previous agreements between the two countries addressed not just inter-state arrangements but also internal conflict in Ukraine, and internal issues were then used by Russia as justification for invasion in 2022 (see e.g. Minsk I Agreement, 2014). The dynamics are different in different conflicts, but as Burke's reflection on the conflict in Sudan illustrates, conflict within states is now characterized by the connectedness of local, national, transnational, and geopolitical inter-state conflicts, and armed actors that move easily across these levels to leverage their position (see Burke, 2023). This dynamic makes it harder to resolve conflict with an in-country mediated agreement.

Third, there is a break-down in the international consensus—fragile as it has been—that—put broadly—mediating ends to war within established international legal rules is a 'good thing'. While international organizations such as the UN used to have central responsibility, now a range of mediators—often neighbouring states—all intervene in overlapping, competitive ways, often with motives that are unclear (Carothers & Samet-Marram, 2015). Local armed groups 'mediation shop' over who will mediate, and non-rules-based mediators are often attractive to conflict actors (Lanz, 2021). Indeed 'peace mediation' itself is now a space of geopolitical contestation (see Peter and Rice, 2022).

These external challenges mean that a peace process model which looks for an state / non-state elite deal to end 'the conflict' often fails to map onto how conflict is conducted. Conflict in many states is better thought of as a complex conflict system involving local, national, transnational and even geopolitical conflict, that cannot be resolved by focusing on one level only.

Some 30 years on from its inception, a profound problem of managing enduring transitions now exists and is fundamentally disrupting both formal institutionalized peacebuilding and the efforts of peacebuilding non-governmental organizations.

To make matters worse, the new conflict dynamics are not what continues when peace processes fail: they seem, in part, to be a by-product of past peace process failure. Conflict fragmentation has been accentuated and propelled by peace process nation-state-building projects that have been tried and failed. New transitions and processes are overlaid on earlier ones, and new armed groups form as earlier ones are demobilized, because being armed seems to be the way to gain entry to the peace process.

Digital technology is tied up with this new world, as the practices of conflict themselves are constantly being transformed digitally, as the example of Syria and shows (as per the SalamaTech initiative). It would be wrong, however, to view the above dynamics as driven by the digital revolution, it is more an accelerant in particular through use of disinformation and cyberwarfare.

Yet, both digital disruption and peace-conflict disruption involve a form of 'blurring' in ways that are becoming increasingly interconnected. The digital revolution blurs the connections between people, things and computing, while the conflict and peacebuilding revolution blurs the relationship between conflict and peace. That is a lot of blur.

5.7 Conclusion

The label PeaceTech is an attempt to capture a distinctive domain of digital transformation—that of peacebuilding. PeaceTech aims to disrupt war, but also may carry consequences for disruption of peacebuilding that we should consider and try to manage. Yet both these disruptions occur alongside a more fundamental disruption of peacebuilding caused by the changing nature of contemporary conflict.

For me the commitment to peace means trying to find new ways of working in this newly fragmented conflict world. In one sense that drives my own instinct to explore what technology can offer to map, track and respond to the new forces of change that seem to be carrying us in a negative direction.

However, engaging in PeaceTech also involves asking: how do digital and peacebuilding disruptions entangle and what are the overall consequences?

What trick with the knife are we learning to do?

Questions

1. What is a 'complex conflict system'?
2. Do you see links between disruption of peace processes and peacebuilding, and disruption due to digital innovation?
3. Do you agree that digital innovation is merely an accelerator of the new conflict and peace context?

References[1]

Bell, C. (2008). *On the law of peace agreements: The new lex Pacificatoria*. Oxford University Press.

Bell, C. (2017). Peace settlements and human rights: A post-cold war circular history. *Journal of Human Rights Practice, 9*(3), 358–378. https://doi.org/10.1093/jhuman/hux025

Bell, C., Wise, L., Beaujouan, J., Epple, T., Forster, R., and Wilson, R. (2021). *A globalised practice of local peace agreements*. In C. Bell, J. Pospisil & L. Wise (Eds.), Local Peace Processes (pp. 7–14). The British Academy, London.

Bell, C., & Wise, L. (2022). The spaces of local agreements: Towards a new imaginary of the peace process. *Journal of Intervention and Statebuilding, 16*(5), 563–583. https://doi.org/10.1080/17502977.2022.2156111

Burke, J. (2023, April 30). *A War for our age: how the battle for Sudan is being fuelled by forces far beyond its borders*. Guardian online news article. https://www.theguardian.com/world/2023/apr/30/a-war-for-our-age-how-the-battle-for-sudan-is-being-fuelled-by-forces-far-beyond-its-borders

Carothers, T., & Samet-Marram, O. (2015). *The global market-place of political change*. Carnegie Endowment for International Peace report. https://carnegieendowment.org/files/global_marketplace.pdf

Fritsch, S. (2014). Conceptualizing the ambivalent role of technology in international relations: Between systemic change and continuity. In M. Mayer, M. Carpes, & R. Knoblich (Eds.), *The global politics of science and technology—Vol. 1. Global power shift* (pp. 115–138). Springer.

[1] All last accessed 1 May 2023.

Krause, J. (2019). How do wars end? A strategic perspective. *Journal of Strategic Studies, 42*(7), 920–945. https://doi.org/10.1080/01402390.2019.1615460

Lanz, D. (2021). Envoy envy? Competition in African mediation processes and ways to overcome it. *International Negotiation, 26*(3), 499–526. https://doi.org/10.1163/15718069-bja10039

Mac Ginty, R. (2022). Conflict disruption: Reassessing the peace and conflict system. *Journal of Intervention and Statebuilding, 16*(1), 40–58. https://www.tandfonline.com/doi/full/10.1080/17502977.2021.1889167

Nicolaïdis, K., & Giovanardi, M. (2022). *Global Peacetech: Unlocking the better angels of our techne*". European University Institute, Global Governance Programme working paper. https://hdl.handle.net/1814/74985

Ondaatje, M. (1979). *There's a trick with a knife I'm learning to do: Poems 1962–1978*. W. W. Norton and Co Inc.

Peter, M., & Rice, H. (2022). *Non-Western approaches to peacemaking and peacebuilding: State-of-the-art and an agenda for research.* (PeaceRep Report: Global Transitions Series). The Peace and Conflict Resolution Evidence Platform. https://peacerep.org/publication/non-western-approaches-to-peacemaking-and-peacebuilding-state-of-the-art-and-an-agenda-for-research/

Suhrke, A., & Samset, A. (2007). What's in a figure? Estimating recurrence of civil war. *International Peacekeeping, 14*(2), 195–203. https://doi.org/10.1080/13533310601150776

World Bank. (2018). *Pathways for peace: Inclusive approaches to preventing violent conflict.* World Bank and UN Report. http://hdl.handle.net/10986/28337.

PART II

Doing PeaceTech

CHAPTER 6

PeaceTech Ecosystem

Abstract This chapter examines who is involved in PeaceTech, in terms of the types of organisation involved, and their different incentives for engaging PeaceTech. I also examine how this 'PeaceTech ecosystem' structures what is produced as PeaceTech.

Keywords PeaceTech ecosystem • PeaceTech enablers • Funders • United Nations • Corporate Social Responsibility

6.1 Who Does PeaceTech?

Remember the opening stories in the book. Seán struggling to distribute peacebuilding funds to local groups, to shore up (or substitute for?) a failing peace process. Atem and Samuel designing an App to stop kidnappings and cattle rustling. Aker wondering how to address sexual violence. Nick, observing satellite earth images and seeing conflict unfold.

Let us return to the stories to observe who is doing PeaceTech, why, and what drives their digital innovation efforts.

6.1.1 Observe First, the Collective Story

This is a story where digital technologies not previously available are now central to the business of peacemaking activities, but often in an ad hoc,

C. Bell, *PeaceTech: Digital Transformation to End Wars*,
https://doi.org/10.1007/978-3-031-38894-1_6

unconnected, and experimental way. They involve a range of organisations: traditional peacebuilding communities; and also organisations who have some connection to peacebuilding even if it is not their main business. These last can include University researchers tracking agricultural developments, or private companies such as the satellite companies, who have become involved in PeaceTech intentionally or unintentionally say by putting their capacities open-source, or taking on a PeaceTech-related job.

6.1.2 Observe Each Story

Each story shows very different types and scale of peacebuilding actor with very different relationships to the conflict and any peace process. They show very different personal and organisational energies and incentives, and very different types of access to financial and technological resources for digital innovation, as the short examination of each below shows.

6.2 Local Peacebuilders

Local peacebuilders Atem, Samuel and Aker will have perhaps a lifetime commitment to address the social troubles around them in an attempt to improve their lives, and those of their community. They will engage with both conflict and peace process over decades, but may have limited resources to work with. They will have copious expertise in how the conflict 'works', often not really recognised as such. They will likely see the conflict less as a singular conflict but as a complex system in which types of conflict: armed-actor violence, gender-based violence, violence against children, and the structural violence of social injustice, all operate to reinforce each other in ways that are difficult to unravel and disrupt. They will often 'multi-hat' in different roles and organisations simultaneously, as peace and social justice entrepreneurs.

Local Peacebuilders will often understand the potential for conflict system mutations with a predictive and analytical capacity that outpaces the most advanced technology. For example, how armed actors will adapt into organised criminals who run drugs or people-trade along routes they once used for arms; or how programmes to demobilise armed actors send them home with weapons, increasing intimate-partner violence against women. This local peacebuilding expertise is vital to making sure a peace process works by creating a connectivity between projects of social justice that over time can extend and legitimise a narrower peace 'deal' into a social contract.

6.3 International Peacebuilders

In contrast to the local actor, the international actor such as Seán or Paul may in not ever be in the country 'properly' if at all. They may monitor and assess from afar, whether that is the relative safety of a gated community within a capital city, or outside the county altogether. Like local peacebuilders they will often be deeply committed, and passionate about peacebuilding, but ultimately they do it as a career choice rather than a life necessity born of their situation.

Those in-country may struggle to get a sense of a huge, wide diverse country they will never fully see or know. Their presence will be temporary, from less than a year to a maximum of around three years, although they may return for stints across a lifetime and career. They may be isolated to one part of it, with in-person interactions with local peacebuilders and conflict parties constrained. Those outside country will work with information about what is going on. This itself is the subject of digital innovation—virtual reality depicting conflict landscapes has been used to sensitise remote UN staff to local contexts they work on.

All of these people and their organisations will work with things called: log-frames (setting goals and indicators of 'success'), 'theories of change' (that define what they are trying to do), and even 'exit strategies' (that specify the end-goals for success that mean that the international organization may be able to leave, and take its staff and resources to another con flict situation). The need to square these bureaucratic demands with partial knowledge of hugely local complex conflict system, will often drive digital innovation, in particular regarding data.

6.4 Private Companies and Philanthropy

Less visible but present in our stories were private companies. These may involve an entrepreneur who is passionate about peace, or is from a conflict country. The business person may offer local peacebuilders the company's tech know-how, directly by setting up a philanthropic wing, or indirectly by a strong commitment to open source technology. Examples include SecDev Foundation and SecDev Group; and the Cisco support for MercyCorps, set out in Chap. 4. Individuals at the heart of these businesses may have originally set up in business for a peace-related purpose. Or they may view peace and security as inter-related. Their philanthropic contribution to PeaceTech may well be part of a broader commitment to 'do good', closely aligned to what they understand to be the social value of their own business. SecDev Foundation's SalamaTech, for example, built on the cyber-risk awareness of SecDev Group, to design its support to civilians in Syria.

Even without this type of deep peace commitment, businesses have a range of business incentives to engage in Corporate Social Responsibility (CSR) activities that may drive them to contribute to PeaceTech.

However, there can also be more profit-oriented business benefits to PeaceTech, beyond those of CSR. Not-for-profit innovation in the peacebuilding field, can build expertise for the company's for-profit business by offering a 'proof-of-concept' example of an experimental but potentially profitable technology. An offer of small-scale satellite use for 'conflict early warning', may enable its development and later purchase by, for example, a country's intelligence service, with the business losing control over exactly when and how its technology is used.

Other businesses may engage in PeaceTech as a paid element of their business offer, either as the entire offer or as paid-for PeaceTech application of a more general technology. These last may then have little interest in fully interrogating conflict and peace impacts, and have to develop forms of conflict-awareness 'on the hoof'.

Elon Musk for example, has used his Starlink Satellite system to provide mobile broadband to Ukraine. This is a digital innovation that can 'beam in' internet capacity in hard-to-reach places, such as Ukraine became after Russia invaded and particularly as it targeted Ukraine's telecommunications infrastructure. There is some ambiguity as to whether Musk's company was paid by the US government, and if so whether fully (Smith, 2022).

Even if the motivation was altruistic, being a lead provider of satellite-enabled internet in places with no cables is a significant business prize. Being able to demonstrate capacity in a context such as Ukraine has a proof-of-concept benefit that can assist future commercial take-up.

Musk, however, quickly encountered conflict-related dilemmas. News reports and his own tweets, have indicated that while he was happy for the internet to be used for civilian government, he was unprepared to have the mobile internet used to enable Ukraine's long-range drone strikes (Sabbach, 2023).

Musk may have been concerned to draw a distinction between supporting Ukraine's defence of civilians, and supporting Ukraine's pro-active war effort—particularly one that could escalate by attacking Russia on Russian soil. Enabling civilian tasks and military ones seem different. However, he may also have been concerned not to be seen to be actively involved in the conflict in ways that might draw him and his business interests in as targets. Both concerns, of course, are legitimate.

6.5 Universities

Universities also feature on the edge of our PeaceTech stories: remember Nick—a North American researcher in North America, and Samuel—an African student at a 'Norwegian University'. Both of these researchers—one a researcher on agriculture and one a peace and conflict researcher (double-hatting as local peacebuilder), had ways within their University system to gain skills or partnerships that enabled them to innovate with technology.

Our own PeaceTech work at the University of Edinburgh comes out of this type of relationship as described in the next chapters.

Universities often comprise the 'research and development' engines of PeaceTech, developing proof-of-concept work to support peacebuilding applications. However, they can also act as conceptual developers of the field of PeaceTech, and PeaceTech enablers, who seek to support students and practitioners to enter the PeaceTech world

A number of initiatives centred in North American Universities, have been central to building both technological capacity, and PeaceTech as a field of scholarly activity. These include:

Peace Innovation Lab, University of Stanford. This Lab has been at Stanford since 2008, initially as a class then a project within the Persuasive Technology Lab and then as its own Lab. It focuses on the connection between business, technology and peace, with a particular mission to 'catalyse a PeaceTech sector'. Their work lies at the intersection of behavioural psychology, technology, innovation and business.

Peace Innovation Institute (Hague). Produced as a spin-off from Peace Innovation Lab in 2018 in collaboration with the City of the Hague, the Institute provides a focus on the relationship between peace and business, or as they put it 'making peace profitable'! This Institute describes its mission as to 'catalyse a peace tech sector and industry' and 'create new frameworks and curriculum for the ethical and safe deployment of emerging technologies and innovation'. In particular, it is working to provide a 'Peace Data Standard' to allow organisations using technology to 'measure their peace impact in the background'. The idea is to try to address structural issues in capitalism by reconfiguring how corporate social responsibility is activated for peace by providing a credible way of measuring a company's peace contribution—a bit like 'carbon credits' in the environmental field (see Guadagno et al., 2018).

Beyond North America, similar initiatives exist.

University of Ulster has had an **InPeaceLab**, with activities relating to the relationship between peacebuilding and technology.

European University Institute (EUI) Global PeaceTech Hub, already mentioned, is recently formed but placed to play an important networking role for academics and practitioners, as the name 'hub' suggests. The Hub brings together EUI's School of Transnational Governance, TheGovLab, and the University of Lucerne's Institute of Social Ethics, and focuses on exploring PeaceTech as a globalising phenomenon.

PeaceRep Team, University of Edinburgh. We too work in particular to develop 'Peace Analytics', in the form of a new capacity to understand through structured and unstructured, quantitative and qualitative data, the ways in which peace is incubated, created and sustained, as set out in throughout this book.

6.6 PeaceTech Funders

All of the PeaceTech projects in our initial stories needed funding, whether it was funding for PeaceTech innovations, research monies for digital innovation, or funding for core work in which digital innovative practices were used. PeaceTech engages a broad array of funders engaged supporting PeaceTech that include:

- University research-grant-giving organisations
- Donor states
- International organizations and funds
- Businesses and private philanthropy

6.7 PeaceTech 'Enablers and Connectors'

A number of key PeaceTech organisations work as 'PeaceTech enablers'. These organisations seek to build PeaceTech capacity and ways of working, and develop and support good practice. There again are different scales of organixation here, but three key organisations with three slightly different missions are important and useful to understanding this type of role.

PeaceTech Lab. PeaceTech Lab and its CEO Sheldon Himelfarb have been at the heart of the development of PeaceTech as a concept and a tool. They are in a sense the foundational enablers. The lab began life as a Center of Innovation at the US Institute of Peace (USIP), in 2008, and became a non-profit in its own right in 2014. In its own words it 'drives action-oriented solutions by bringing a diversity of experts together: data scientists, social scientists, engineers, MBAs, global influencers, media ambassadors, and creatives' to 'collectively develop effective peacebuilding solutions'. This work has been incredibly diverse. PeaceTech Lab has programmes on digital challenges to peace such as misinformation and hate speech. However, it also runs a 'PeaceTech accelerator', that helps support PeaceTech start-ups—in particular with secure access to cloud computing but also by offering workshops on easy-to-use Tech for peacebuilders, as well as a Master's programme. It has also supported similar labs in other countries, see PeaceTech Lab Netherlands.

Build Up. An interesting connector organisation, in its own words Build Up is, 'a global non-profit that works beside local organisations, to identify and address emergent challenges to peace through interventions, research and training, that combine best peacebuilding practices, participatory methodologies and digital technologies'. This statement speaks to double disruption, in viewing new technologies as capable of responding to a shifting peacebuilding field, in which digital transformation may also be a threat. One of their key programmes relates to digital conflict, and the other to participation or inclusion in peacebuilding.

Build Up

- enables local groups to access technological capacity and funding for innovation
- supports innovation in peacebuilding
- provides tools that enable groups and individual to use technology even where they have few technical experts
- provides thought-leadership on the principles and values that should underpin PeaceTech.

Its work is critical to plugging some of the ethical gaps we address in Chap. 13 by providing guidelines for good practice.

New York University, Center for International Cooperation (NYU CIC). NYU CIC is a non-profit centre housed at New York University that focuses on policy connecting politics, security, justice, development and humanitarian issues. This organization has had a focus on data and worked as PeaceTech enablers, with a strong connection to the United Nations, who it works to support.

Types of Organization in the PeaceTech Ecosystem

- Peacebuilders—local and international—looking to increase tech savviness.
- Private company CSR/Philanthropy Wings
- Ecosystem-building enabler and connector organisations and networks
- Companies with relevant software
  - Companies focused on a peace impact
  - Companies for hire
  - Hybrid companies with a range of outputs and motives
- Individual tech experts: Visualizers, software engineers, data hard ware engineers
- United Nations (and other similar regional organisations)
- Universities
- Funders
  - State funders
  - University Grant funders
  - Entrepreneur funders
  - Not-for-profit funders

6.8 United Nations

The United Nations operates as a PeaceTech innovator, and PeaceTech 'enabler', by:

- Innovating to produce PeaceTech applications and connected digital innovation
- Enabling by supporting the wider infrastructure for PeaceTech to be engaged in by others externally

The UN seems to be the only possible location of a PeaceTech masterplan that could cohere initiatives across countries and contexts. However, in practice it has a lot of different PeaceTech spaces and initiatives that seem very scattered. This is because the UN is a bit 'like this'—big and departmentalised with organisations within organisations (remember Seán and Paul?). It therefore tends to work with broad policy directions and discrete organisational responses.

6.8.1 UN Policy Direction: Digital Transformation

Digital development has been set as a strategic objective by the UN Secretary General (essentially the CEO of the UN), and this is translated into departmental missions even if the exact mechanism of translation is not always clear. Indeed, it has been a bit chicken-and-egg: digital transformation in some departments preceded and drove the wider strategy, propelled by that Department's needs. A number of general and department-specific reports and policies therefore underpin particular areas of peace-related digital innovation (see box for key examples), giving the UN its own internal PeaceTech ecosystem.

Institutionally, the UN works to try to join up initiatives. The Innovation in the UN Quick Guide, is really a website of resources that tries to pull together a picture of where and how innovation is happening. Interestingly, the Guide begins by 'acknowledging innovation is complex, uncertain and somewhat disorderly'.

A UN Innovation Network (UNIN), attempts to cohere the work across the organisation, and to galvanise and connect to an ecosystem of technology, civil society, and academic partners outside the UN system, thereby leveraging innovation for the shared goal of peace.

UNIN subscribes to Principles for Digital Development, by humanitarian organisations, informed by early UN departments, and country and organisational initiatives (see timeline on about page).

Individual units within the UN, under this broad policy direction and driven by their own needs, have often their own digital transformation initiatives in the PeaceTech space.

UN Global Pulse is described as 'Secretary-General's Innovation Lab—a hub for experimentation to support and advance the UN Charter'. This in particular has developed Pluselab Jakarta (jointly between UN (Global Pulse) and the Government of Indonesia), and Pulselab Kampala (an inter-agency initiative established under the UN Resident Coordinator).

These Labs work in a sense as 'ecosystem builders', similar to PeaceTech Lab, by supporting projects and innovation. While largely development-focused, they connect to conflicts in their respective regions directly, and indirectly.

PeaceTech-Relevant UN Policy

Keeping Watch: Monitoring, Technology and Innovation in UN Peace Operations (Dorn, 2011)
Performance Peacekeeping: Final Report of the Expert Panel on Technology and Innovation in UN Peacekeeping (UN, 2014)
UN Secretary General's Strategy on New Technologies (UN, 2018)
The UN Secretary-General High Panel on Digital Cooperation Report (UN, 2019)
Data for Peace and Security (NYU Centre on International Cooperation, 2019)
Policy on Peacekeeping-Intelligence (UN, 2019)
Strategy for the Digital Transformation of UN Peacekeeping (UN, 2021).

Digital transformation strategies are now in place across peace-related departments, as we turn to.

6.8.2 UN Digital Innovation Cell, UN Department of Political and Peacekeeping Affairs

The Digital Innovation Cell is a unit within the Department of Political and Peacebuilding Affairs, established in 2020 that is a sense is most central to PeaceTech. This department houses most of the UN's political work on peace processes and in particular the Mediation Support Unit (UN MSU), which supports peace negotiations. The innovation cell is 'an interdisciplinary team dedicated to helping the Department and its field presences to understand and explore, pilot, and scale new technologies, tools, and practices in conflict prevention, mediation and peacebuilding'.

UN DPPA MSU has also conducted a report into Digital Technologies and Mediation in Armed Conflict (UN, Centre for Humanitarian

Dialogue, 2019), as part of developing a Digital Toolkit (UN DPPA, Centre for Humanitarian Dialogue. (n.d.)) for mediators and these are available as an online resource.

The Toolkit describes three main technologies that are used by peacemakers:

- social media
- geographic information systems
- data analytics

It also notes technologies of interest: blockchain and GIS systems—in which the UN has a distinctive capacity. The toolkit also identifies four main tasks that digital innovation assists:

- Conflict Analysis
- Engagement with Conflict parties
- Inclusivity
- Strategic communications

Two other aspects of the Innovation Cell's work deserve mention as critical to the ecosystem. First, the provision of an open access Peace and Security Data Hub, modelled on the UN's Humanitarian Data Exchange—itself also a useful PeaceTech resource. These are essentially data repositories which work to curate relevant global data and make it easily accessible on CKAN, an open source data management system. Second, a Futuring Peace initiative aims to 'encourage interdisciplinary approaches such as futures thinking and speculative design and their practical limits to peace processes in a world of increasing complexity'. These two initiatives work in an 'enabling' capacity to create a wider infrastructure and community for PeaceTech.

6.8.3 Peacekeeping and Political Missions

Peacekeeping—a vital components of third party support for peace agreements—has seen further digital innovation initiatives. In 2021 a new *Strategy for the Digital Transformation of UN Peacekeeping* was published (2021), however digital transformation was already underway.

A digital interface—the ***Situational Awareness* Geospatial Enterprise (*Sage*)** Computer IT system (Manning, 2018) now supports Mission reporting in select countries, using the Ushahidi software discussed earlier. The system provides for incident reporting by peacekeepers, and for 'situational awareness', and has diverse forms of data feeding into it. This tool is part of an attempt to provide Peacekeeping 'intelligence', to support safe and effective operational capacity, and can now ingest a huge amount of data, including that collected from intelligence technologies that are themselves experimental for the UN (for example, tethered balloons, see Druet, 2021).

More recently, a distinct system called the Comprehensive Planning and Performance Support System (CPAS) aims to support 'adaptive management' by peacekeeping missions, by providing a data basis drawing on formal datasets and mission-specific data and reporting, to support better planning and decision-making (see further De Coning & Brusset, 2018). We will return to these in later chapters.

6.8.4 Other Peace-Related Departments and Digital Innovation

All of the key UN organisations whose work connects to peacebuilding also have digital transformation initiatives. The UN Refugee Agency—UN HCR that has responsibility for those displaced by conflict also has an Innovation Service, which includes a programme on digital inclusion of refugees in planning (UNHCR Digital Inclusion). UN Women has an innovation strategy, focused across its work. It has supported the PeaceFem App which we have been involved in creating, as described in the next chapter. The UN Office of the Commissioner for Human Rights, which coordinates its human rights work, and works critically conflict-affected states, has a Hub for Human Rights and Digital Technology including a useful resource page. UNICEF working for children's rights also has a digital transformation mission and addresses the impact of digital technology on children.

6.9 The Ecosystem

The above panoply of initiatives and actors describes what has been described as a PeaceTech ecosystem—coined by NYU CIC. The ecosystem refers to the diverse range of actors and institutions building a

PeaceTech concept and practice (Panic, 2020). The metaphor of an ecosystem refers to 'complementary dynamic environments in which innovative approaches are implemented'.

It is possible to set out this ecosystem in lots of detail that attempts to map all the main PeaceTech projects globally. Indeed NYU CIC and EUI have done just this in interactive actual mapping of diverse projects. The EUI interactive mapping sets out 170 PeaceTech projects. The NYU CIC map is connected to an Ecosystem report (Panic, 2020).

Nearly all the PeaceTech reports produced spend time mapping and illustrating PeaceTech to try to capture what it comprises. They produce long lists of interesting examples. By the time reports are published, however, the world they describe is already out of date. Collectively, they reflect an ecosystem that is constantly changing and populated by eclectic actors and initiatives that come and go. The NYU CIC and EUI mappings are online and interactive and ongoing, in part to enable mapping a fluid PeaceTech world, with maps that can be changed over time.

The NYU-CIC report suggests five elements are important to building the PeaceTech ecosystem in the future:

- Building trust through human-centred approaches
- Capacity building
- Innovation
- Providing principles and frameworks
- Building community and partnership

6.10 A Word About Ecosystems

Rather than doing organisational/initiative mapping—the existing ones are ongoing and excellent—I have focused more on thinking about the types of organisations involved and why they might be involved. Not just, 'who' is doing PeaceTech, but why and how?

I am interested in how the ecosystem is produced and what it in turn produces.

The word ecosystem is interesting here. We think of an ecosystem as 'just there'. Yet, the whole idea of an ecosystem is an attempt to talk about both agency and natural development and how they come together—say, to create a garden.

We know that things we do and don't do affect a garden's ecosystem—like putting slug pellets or not putting slug pellets on our vegetable patches. Other changes to the garden ecosystem happen randomly—like a major frost that destroys some plants but not others. Yet others are produced by legal regulation—preventing people from using certain pesticides. The ecosystem will also have boundaries that are often artificially created and sustain the particular form of life there—whether it is by the garden wall, or our labelling of a particular habitat as being 'its own ecosystem'.

Ecosystems, like life itself it would seem, develop stochastically. This is a great word that means 'partly by design and partly due to random elements.' In other words, we only control so much.

6.11 Conclusion

It is worth asking—what does the PeaceTech ecosystem sustain, what does it not sustain, what could we re-balance if we could? Are the motives of those in the ecosystem aligned? Does that matter?

These seem important questions for understanding how to access and navigate the ecosystem. My functional account of the types organisations involved in the PeaceTech ecosystem set out above, starts to tell a story of how complicated it can be to figure out how to work on a new digital strategy in the peacebuilding field.

I now turn to give examples of how we provided two PeaceTech tools, by way of illustrating how PeaceTech emerges in practice and connects with this ecosystem.

Questions

1. Do any of the types of organization in the PeaceTech ecosystem surprise you, and why?
2. Are there any types of organization missing?
3. What do you think this ecosystem would be good at producing? What might it struggle with?

References[1]

De Coning, C., & Brusset, E. (2018). *Towards a comprehensive results-based reporting and performance assessment framework for UN peacekeeping operations.* Norwegian Institute of International Affairs research report. https://nupi.brage.unit.no/nupi-xmlui/handle/11250/2496840?locale-attribute=en

Dorn, A. W. (2011). *Keeping watch: Monitoring, technology and innovation in UN peace operations.* United Nations University Press. https://digitallibrary.un.org/record/708466?ln=en

Druet, D. (2021). *Enhancing the use of digital technology for integrated situational awareness and peacekeeping-intelligence.* Thematic Paper for the DPO Peacekeeping Technology Strategy. Not published. https://peacekeeping.un.org/sites/default/files/20210430_-_sa-pki_technologies_research_brief_final_clean.pdf

Guadagno, R. E., Nelson, M., & Lee, L. L. (2018). Peace data standard: A practical and theoretical framework for using technology to examine intergroup interactions. *Frontiers in Psychology, 9*(734). https://doi.org/10.3389/fpsyg.2018.00734

Manning, N. (2018). *Keeping The Peace - The UN Department Of Field Service's And Peacekeeping Operations Use Of Ushahidi.* https://www.ushahidi.com/about/blog/keeping-the-peace-the-un-department-of-field-services-and-peacekeeping-operations-use-of-ushahidi/

NYU Center on International Cooperation, Netherlands Ministry of Foreign Affairs, & UN Peacebuilding Support Office. (2019, July). *Data for peace and security: Report of the practitioners workshop on harvesting best practices and building a community of practice.* Center on International Cooperation, New York University. https://cic.nyu.edu/resources/data-for-peace-and-securityreport-of-the-practitioners-workshop-on-harvesting-best-practices-and-building-a-community-of-practice/

Panic, B. (2020, October). *Data for peacebuilding and prevention ecosystem mapping: The state of play and the path to creating a community of practice.* Center on International Cooperation Report, New York University. https://s42831.pcdn.co/wp-content/uploads/1662/65/data_for_peacebuilding_and_prevention_-_ecosystem_mapping_-_october_2020.pdf

Sabbach, D. (2023, February 9). *Fury in Ukraine as Elon Musk's SpaceX limits Starlink use for drones.* Guardian online news article. https://www.theguardian.com/world/2023/feb/09/zelenskiy-aide-takes-aim-at-curbs-on-ukraine-use-of-starlink-to-pilot-drones-elon-musk

[1] All last accessed 1 May 2023.

Smith, A. (2022, October 5). *SpaceX was paid by US government to send some Starlink terminals to Ukraine despite claiming it wasn't.* Independent online news article. https://www.independent.co.uk/tech/spacex-ukraine-elon-musk-starlink-government-b2055491.html
UN. (2014). *Performance peacekeeping.* UN expert panel on technology and innovation in UN peacekeeping final report. United Nations. https://peacekeeping.un.org/en/final-report-of-expert-panel-technology-and-innovation-un-peacekeeping
UN. (2018). *UN Secretary General's Strategy on New Technologies.* New York, United Nations. https://www.un.org/en/newtechnologies/images/pdf/SGs-Strategy-on-New-Technologies.pdf
UN. (2019). *The age of digital interdependence.* UN Secretary-General high-level panel on digital cooperation report. https://www.un.org/en/pdfs/HLP%20on%20Digital%20Cooperation%20Report%20Executive%20Summary%20-%20ENG.pdf
UN. (2021). *Strategy on digital transformation of UN peacekeeping.* UN peacekeeping online strategy article. https://peacekeeping.un.org/en/strategy-digital-transformation-of-un-peacekeeping
UN, Centre for Humanitarian Dialogue. (2019, March). *Digital technologies and mediation in armed conflict.* United Nations Peacemaker and Centre for Humanitarian Dialogue Report. https://peacemaker.un.org/sites/peacemaker.un.org/files/DigitalToolkitReport.pdf
UN DPPA, & Centre for Humanitarian Dialogue. (n.d.). *Digital technologies and innovation toolkit 1.0.* UN Department of Political and Peacebuilding Affairs and Centre for Humanitarian Dialogue online digital toolkit. https://peacemaker.un.org/digitaltoolkit

CHAPTER 7

Doing One Thing

Abstract How have we operated broadly as part of the PeaceTech ecosystem, and what have we learnt about how to do PeaceTech? Often big projects start by 'doing one thing'. I offer two stories relating to how we produced 'single use' tools, focused on doing one thing and doing it well.

Keywords Ceasefires • Women mediators • Covid Ceasefire Tracker • PeaceFem

7.1 Journeys and Single Steps

The stories that follow illustrate how often PeaceTech develops in response to specific problems. As we saw last chapter, the PeaceTech ecosystem evolved from this approach, and in turn supports PeaceTech as an eclectic set of digital peacebuilding interventions, more than a holistic digitally transformed field. In contrast, WarTech, has developed to digitally transform many practices of war—utterly. Is PeaceTech as an eclectic practice a strength or a weakness?

C. Bell, *PeaceTech: Digital Transformation to End Wars*,
https://doi.org/10.1007/978-3-031-38894-1_7

7.2 Ceasefires in a Pandemic

When the pandemic came upon us, as researchers with some PeaceTech capacity, we tried to respond. We had always tried to be digitally savvy not just in what we researched, but in how we organised as researchers, even in simple ways. Two years before the pandemic, influenced by how well our Yemen partners were able to work remotely, we had moved to online ways of working as much as possible. We were motivated by our own environmental concerns not to jump on planes or waste time travelling unnecessarily. When the pandemic hit, we looked startlingly prescient.

We immediately started thinking about how the pandemic might play-out in the countries we were working in (see Bell, 2020, for initial thoughts). In deeply divided societies experiencing violent conflict, basic public services such as healthcare are often complicated to deliver. How they are delivered can create distrust, or can build trust. Governments may lack a will to treat all people equally, or lack capacity at all, with unfairness exacerbating conflict. Armed groups may occupy areas and control who enters and exits them, and impede access to vital health provisions. Checkpoints between lines of control can be difficult for citizens to cross. On top of that, conflict itself causes massive health needs in an ongoing way. People are killed and physically and mentally injured; health infrastructure such as hospitals are degraded; and Doctors, who are often internationally mobile, may be difficult to find.

7.3 UN Secretary General's Global Ceasefire Call

With the global health threat of the pandemic and a world struggling to respond, the health threats of conflict seemed in a sense more unnecessary and preventable. It was therefore unsurprising that close to the start of the pandemic, the UN Secretary General (UNSG) publicly called for 'a global ceasefire in all corners of the world to focus together on the true fight—defeating COVID-19'. In the days and weeks that followed over 180 countries, the UN Security Council, regional organisations, civil society groups, peace advocates and millions of global citizens all endorsed the Secretary-General's ceasefire call.

The question was: would it make any difference? Would people go on ceasefire?

There was some precedent for anticipating ceasefires might follow. Getting humanitarian aid, including access to vaccines, often involves what are sometimes called 'de-confliction' agreements (a form of humanitarian agreement). These agreements can involve micro-spaces such as when and how at truck will pass through a check-point and with what permission and protection. Or a ceasefire may operate at a larger geographic area operating across a local area (see Haider, 2022; Dorith et al., 2021).

In any short ceasefire a window of possibility is created. The ceasefire may be agreed to cover a specific moment in time, or apply only to a specific task, but it may somewhat 'disrupt' the conflict, shifting its landscape. People can see what life without the conflict is like, and their response can influence armed actors who claim to represent them, to consider moving from conflict. Armed groups can take risks, and find new political opportunities open to them, including forms of international recognition, that give them confidence to move from violent pursuit of their goals. However, armed actors also fear even temporary ceasefires: armed activity is often 'held together' by 'operations'. Particularly for those who operate as non-state armed actors to fight state security forces ceasefires can start in a sense to demobilise them.

7.4 Rapid Ceasefire 'Data'

We already collected information about ceasefires as part of our ongoing agreement data collection efforts. Soon a group of practitioners who mediate ceasefires, monitor them, and generally advise parties on how to reach and sustain them, came together to exchange information on how the UN Secretary General's call was being implemented and how to support the ceasefires, under the auspices of the United States Institute of Peace (USIP). The group involved peacebuilding organisations, individual mediators, mediators from the UN Mediation Support Unit (MSU), and researchers with expertise on ceasefires. Collectively the group had direct contacts into a large number of active conflict situations.

Ceasefires are commitments by those involved doing the fighting, to stop fighting, temporarily or permanently. They can also be called truces or armistices. They involve armed actors committing to each other, often through signed documents also endorsed by other international actors, to stop fighting. These agreements often need to be detailed. 'Stopping fighting' needs defined. Does it involve all forms of fighting, or do they need to be listed specifically: shooting bombing, but what about things like kidnapping, or 'recruiting' (which can often be forcible and connected with kidnapping). Or rape and use of sexual violence? Does the ceasefire need to include things like 'moving troops' and 'moving heavy weaponry' as well as actual violence? What will it take to ensure that people stick to the ceasefire: demarked zones that armed actors pull back to? Some sort of monitoring commission? Who will be on the monitoring commission, armed actors, citizens, international actors?

Explore Ceasefires
You can explore further how ceasefires work in our peace agreement data, by searching on 'ceasefires' at the PA-X website. For an interesting project on both written and unwritten ceasefires see the ETH Zurich ceasefire dataset of also one of the collaborators in the 'ceasefires in a time of Covid-19 tool'. For our ongoing analysis of ceasefires see our key findings, and policy recommendations.

The group exchanged information on pandemic ceasefires in a sense generating 'data' on what was happening with ceasefires. Surveying country experts is a recognised form of data collection. While not set up to provide a comprehensive survey, collectively the group had up-to-date information as experts and mediators connected to many of the conflicts and to multiple ceasefire initiatives. Researchers in the group who were already engaged in documenting ceasefires, with established methods of unearthing them, could add to this, such as ETH Zurich's Govinda Clayton, and ourselves at PeaceRep Edinburgh. Triangulating this information gave a comprehensive understanding of what type of ceasefires were happening, what were not, and what the nature and impact of the ceasefires were.

7.5 The Covid Ceasefires Tracker

To support the group's thinking, and to make information more widely available we suggested building a small online interface for recording and exploring them. This was to become the Ceasefires in a Time of Covid-19 Tracker. Originally, the aim was to pull together all the information we had, to create a small dataset, to enable easier ongoing monitoring and public information, and perhaps even engage people in contributing ceasefire information.

We were able to offer to create the interface because we had designed a previous database to have a structure that could easily be repurposed and reused—the Amnesties, Conflict and Peace Agreement Database providing open access to Professor Louise Mallinder's data.

7.5.1 Creating a Dataset

However, having information about Covid ceasefires and constructing a coherent dataset was more complicated than we had anticipated despite a level of ceasefire expertise. It is not possible to simply ask—'is there a ceasefire, yes or no'. We found many initiatives being reported as ceasefires that were armed group 'no-first-strike' policies. These may look similar to a ceasefire, but technically involve a unilateral commitment not to undertake armed action if none is taken against you. Yet, discussions also revealed that sometimes one group's 'no-first-strike' policy, can cause another group to reciprocate positively with its own no-first-strike policy. Issues such as these meant that defining 'what is a ceasefire' and classifying them, needed thought, something we engage in a lot as regards agreements!

The process revealed substantive research insights (Wise et al., 2021). Different groups were calling ceasefires for different reasons. Some were unrelated to Covid-19 or the UNSG's call, and had been reached because of a particular moment in the conflict, perhaps in a country not much affected by Covid at that point. Some armed groups who were not very active, in low-level conflicts, declared a ceasefire as a way of reminding the world 'we are still here, we are still fighting for our cause'.

Ceasefires in a Time of Covid-19 Tracker
An open access tool that tracks ceasefires and related events, such as commitments to move towards a reduction in violence, or subsequent ceasefire breakdowns, which have occurred during the Covid-19 Pandemic. It is a collaborative project between PeaceRep Edinburgh, the Peace Research Institute Oslo (PRIO), the Centre for Security Studies (CSS) at ETH Zurich, Conciliation Resources, MeiatEUr (European Forum for International Mediation and Dialogue), and the United States Institute of Peace (USIP), with contribution also from the UN MSU in the UN Department of Political and Peacebuilding Affairs. The data is available: (a) on a timeline, which can be filtered by region, country and declaration type; (b) through a search tool that displays information in entry boxes, and (c) on a map where it can be triangulated with Covid-19 infection data. A formal write up of the tracker is in The Lancet, where it received interest from medical professionals in the field (Allison et al., 2020).

Interestingly, this detail also meant that we did not call the tracker the 'Covid Ceasefire Tracker' even though we use that name as shorthand. As some ceasefires were not responsive to Covid, and sometimes it was hard to tell what the motivation was, we felt 'in a time of Covid-19' was more accurate.

To make the different types of ceasefire more visible and searchable, we then categorised ceasefires as: unilateral; unilateral-reciprocated'; bi-lateral; multilateral. We also found that when ceasefires were declared they were often declared for specific durations of time—e.g., three months, at the end of which time armed actors sometime 'extended' the ceasefire. We registered ceasefires as 'temporary' if a clear end date was stated, but did not classify any as 'permanent' (because, how long is permanent?).

We registered ceasefires as unilateral where they were made by one conflict party, and bi- or multi-lateral if they included some element of agreement between armed actors. If a unilateral ceasefire was positively responded to by a (unilateral) ceasefire from opponents, we marked these ceasefires as unilateral-reciprocated, which meant that people could see that there was a de facto 'bilateral' element to the arrangements, even though made unilaterally.

To present the full picture we included a category also of 'Update' to include ceasefire extensions or terminations, so that viewers could find out if the ceasefire was still formally in place. We also included 'related events' as part of the picture of what was in force—for example when a government or group rejected the unilateral ceasefire of another group. The UNSG ceasefire call itself was included as a 'related event'.

7.5.2 *Iterative Design and Co-creating with End Users*

When we presented the interface back to the group it generated discussion, and someone suggested—a timeline rather than a searchable tool might be more useful to end-users, and maybe a map. We had capacity to do both. For some time we had used a little timeline tool from NorthEastern University, Knight Lab, US, designed for open access re-use, for our main peace agreement data. It is available for 'no-code' use, so that it timelines can be created without coding skills. However, they also give access to the code to customise and adapt the tool. We could therefore simply share Knight Lab's simple google doc tables, for people to input data. This created a quick and easy mechanism for cross group collaboration.

However, we also developed computer code to customise the timeline for our version, and a mechanism to import and refresh anytime a new ceasefire happened, or an existing one terminated. The customization enabled different ways of moving through the timeline, and exploring it by country, or by type of ceasefire. We also used our visualization capacity to put the data onto maps. We worked to create toggle mechanisms on a map, to explore types of ceasefire, or regional patterns.

At each point in design, we went back to end-users—mainly those in the support group who were the perfect model of our end-user, but also others in country field missions who are part of our own practitioner 'ecosystem'.

We were not, however, the only project producing Covid data and interfaces. Countries were all trying to match health capacities with need, and as a result health dashboards proliferated and saw increasing innovation. Elsewhere in our University social scientists explored the phenomenon of 'dashboarding' (see Falisse & McAteer, 2022). We all became a connected through University funding modalities, but also because we had found ways to work together previously meaning our work could draw on a wider knowledge base. This wider research infrastructure supported us to situate our work in wider questions of how data and visualization connected to outcomes.

7.5.3 *Reuse and Repurpose: Future-proofing All Tools*

For our main PA-X Peace Agreement Database we have been developing a thing called an API, or 'Automated Programme Interface'. That is a mechanism whereby you make your data structure public and 'readable' by others elsewhere. An 'open API' means that others can automate pulling your data into their platforms. APIs provide a good solution to the barriers of institutional ownership of data (the fact that people want their data on their own website). It means that you can have your own website with your institutional branding, but that data can be brought together by a range of people with their data, independently of long and complicated legal agreements, and without any loss to your ownership.

John Hopkins University was at that point providing some of the world's best infection data on Covid supporting world-wide monitoring. They made their API public with clear terms and conditions for how you could use it. We could therefore 'pull in' their data onto our ceasefire map, which we did in 'bubbles' that showed how and when ceasefires called overlapped with infection levels. We thought this was interesting to do, although it did not in the end yield any startling insights. To be honest, we did not mind because it helped us learn how to use APIs, and learn to overlay data of different types and create user-friendly ways to toggle between views (see further, Bhattacharya et al., 2021). This was a capacity we wanted as part of our wider 'peace analytics' ambition.

7.5.4 Funding

Originally, we started working on this project out of our interest and wish to be relevant to attempts to end conflict, and support pandemic relief. However, over time, we started to get funding for this and other work, from a mechanism called the Covid Collective (CC) that brought together a range of practical research projects across disciplines and institutions. The CC was fantastic as it gave us a wider set of researchers and end-users to engage with. This funding also supported longer-term collection of the data than we could otherwise have managed. We kept collecting data until March 2022. At that point we felt that there was no real relationship between ceasefires and a pandemic that had largely eased so we brought the data collection to an end. Interestingly, John Hopkins also stopped collecting Covid 19 infection data from 10 March 2023.

7.5.5 Ceasefire Tracker Outcomes: Quick Evaluation

The Tracker was useful to enable a wide range of people to learn quickly what was going on as regards ceasefires during Covid. It was the most detailed and accurate data that existed, and more detailed and accurate than news reports of ceasefires where we found often to be wrong.

It played a role in supporting particular ceasefire efforts. Some of this impact continues, as we all learnt more about ceasefires in the process, and in particular added analysis to understanding the long-term effect of short-term ceasefires. As double disruption means that conflict are less able to be resolved in a 'comprehensive peace accord', we are currently considering how various types of humanitarian agreement create 'islands of peace' through initiatives such as temporary ceasefires, that might unwind aspects of a conflict that cannot be resolved through a comprehensive agreement, including in Ukraine (Wittke, 2023).

Remote information, such as our data, played a particular role in a pandemic, where international actors were less present in country than at other time. The Tracker remains useful to informing ceasefire construction more generally, and we have been able to use it to consider when and how 'health ceasefires' work and do not work, by bringing this data together with other historic cases of 'vaccine ceasefires' (See Russell et al., 2021). Long-term there is little to no cost to keep in place an historic dataset and tool that has ongoing relevance to conflict resolution.

7.5.6 *Doing PeaceTech: Covid Tracker Lessons*

The project indicates the different elements that the project had to have to be successful:

Data collection and creating a dataset. Technical data collection had to be triangulated with ceasefire expert information, and analysed to understand and classify ceasefires into a dataset.

Focus on end-users. Thinking about why people might want to look at the data: in this case primarily because they would want to understand whether anyone was responding to the pandemic ceasefire call, and whether other ceasefires were being agreed during the pandemic, even if not technically 'in response'.

Analysis of the data. To understand what was going on: how and why ceasefires were agreed. Here again the connection to a group of experts was invaluable because it supported understanding ceasefires that helped us categorise the data in ways that made sense of it, and then give access to data capable of providing answers to practitioner questions.

Visualising. We had to design a visualization of the data that was intuitive to the same types of experts we were engaging with. To do this we needed capacity to work with visualisers, and database designers. This involved writing clear 'specifications' in language that everyone understood, and ongoing liaison with visualisers through iterative design processes.

Data ownership. We had to deal with the attribution of ownership. Here the data interface was produced at University of Edinburgh, but the group had co-created the data. We enabled joint ownership by making the ceasefire tracker able to be i-framed into any website, so that anyone in the group could 'own' the outcome institutionally. The joint ownership of the product was then acknowledged through use of logos rather than needing legal agreements, although getting organisational permissions still required a level of bureaucracy.

Past 'future-proofing' as design. The project was also enabled by previous technical work and 'reusing and repurposing', assisted by the ways in which we had designed past interfaces to be able to be re-customised for other uses.

Low-code speed versus bespoke capacity. Moving fast was enabled by using cool 'no-code' tools from other projects, and from the fact that other projects had made their APIs open access with clear terms of use for having permission. APIs pulled through updated data in an automated way without us having to invest further time and work to update manually.

Funding. The fact that we received funding was also useful. A relatively modest amount enabled us to extend data collection and spend some time analysing it in ways that are useful for future pandemics or temporary ceasefires.

7.6 The PeaceFem App Story

The PeaceFem App also arose out of collaboration in a practice-based project. The project was called 'Enhancing Women's Leadership for Sustainable Peace in Fragile Contexts in the Middle East and North Africa (MENA) Region', funded by the German Federal Ministry for Economic Cooperation and Development (BMZ) and the German Agency for International Cooperation (GIZ).

The 'Enhancing Women's Leadership' project brought together several project partners, including ourselves, under the auspices of UN Women. Its central purpose was to enable peace processes to be more successful and more inclusive of women, and more reflective of their needs and demands. You can see a fuller explanation of the project and what it achieved in Iraq, Libya, Syria and Yemen here.

As one element of this project, we sought to make data and knowledge on gender inclusion more accessible to mediators and to women—and of course to women mediators! We have really good data on peace agreement provision on women in the PA-X Peace Agreement Database in what we call PA-X Gender. This data serves as an example of what can be achieved in peace processes, and acts as guidance or inspiration to support drafting for those seeking to have peace agreements deal with specific gendered issues.

Women and mediators find previous drafts on gender useful, but also want to know 'how did those provisions get there'—what did women do to get their needs written into peace agreements? And 'what happened next'—was the agreement successful, were the provisions implemented, and was the situation of women improved?

Answers to those questions are not simple and not easily quantifiable. However, another of the partners in the project Inclusive Peace, a 'think-and-do' tank focused in particular women's inclusion, in peace processes, had some answers. It had produced a set of country case studies that documented both the actions that women had undertaken to try to influence peace processes, such as 'mass mobilisation', and 'being at the negotiating table', and some of the outcomes. We were also aware that another project (Towards Inclusive Peace), whose work we used a lot, led by Jacqui True at Monash University, had also designed case studies with a quantitative methodology for assessing gender provision strength, and implementation of provisions. To supplement our data we reached out also to collaborate. The full story of how we brought all this data as a piece of research and what we learnt, is told by Laura Wise (2023).

7.6.1 *PeaceFem—What Is It?*

The result was the PeaceFem mobile App, which can be used on Android and iPhones. It illustrates women's inclusion in peace processes around the world. PeaceFem provides information about strategies women's rights advocates have used to influence peace agreements, information about the enabling and constraining factors that shaped the space for influence, and the gender provisions in the peace agreements that resulted and information as to how well they were implemented.

7.6.2 *Doing PeaceTech: PeaceFem Lessons*

For my 'how to' purposes of storytelling, the following were the lessons of PeaceFem, and they overlap with those of the ceasefire tracker.

End-users. The project grew out of a need from and connection with end-users, and a wish to have a small but very instantly accessible way to support women in peace mediation, in particular in the Middle East.

Data interoperability and literacy. A key initial issue was what case studies to focus on, and whether we had data on all the issues across those case studies. In other words, what did our data collectively allow us to do? What gaps existed? To what extent did 'where' we could data match across case studies, match with the peace processes that were useful for women to have information about.

Iterative design process, and complexity of contracting. On this project we needed to bring together end users, two other data producers, an App-design team, a visual designer, and UN Women who were the funder and commissioner, together with our expertise in data matching and conceptualising how the App could work. At University of Edinburgh we brought our peace agreement data and expertise in digital innovation, including how to write technical specifications, and knowledge of the issues to be traversed technically and legally.

All of this was quite complicated in practice. UN Women contracted all the partners, and the App company who were based in India. However, we led the design process and were their main point of contact for the work. So contracting the work, and implementing the work were done by different organisations. This affected capacity for iterative design. We had a good working relationship with the App company staff who were very competent. But it was difficult for them to price App development tasks in ways that would allow for an element of iterative design. It was also difficult for us to work just through specifying rather technically, rather than 'co-creating'.

While excellent technical experts, the App company had no 'domain' expertise in the subject matter, and distance and contracting meant there was little opportunity to build knowledge across their team and ours (although we do feel we all ended with good relationships). This meant the process was more 'back-and-forth' and demanding that our usual one. An additional complication was that UN Women also had their own 'designer' who in essence was to provide a new 'skin' (that is new set of fonts and colours) for the prototype provided by the App company. In the peace and conflict field things like colours can be complicated politically. This added a layer of complexity in a three-way relationship related to the usability of the App, albeit one that improved the end-product.

The University of Edinburgh team did an initial 'product design' of the types of relationships between the data that would be needed, and the type of App interface that would make those relationships easy to explore. We looked at other App design and where and how they enabled navigation, including for very different purposes, such as language Apps, to think through what types of ways they enabled data to be searched, and navigated.

Licencing arrangements to use the data. The three research organisations providing data—ourselves, Inclusive Peace and Monash University, all had to sign licencing agreements with UN Women, who technically 'own' the App. For this this was complicated as our Intellectual Property includes not just our coding and country data, but the design of the relationships between it, which were built into the App. So getting the right licence took time across partners, even though everyone's data was already open access and there was good will for it to be made available and used in this way. None of us could risk inadvertently creating an accidental intellectual property obstacle to continuing to develop and use our own underlying data in the future.

Languages. It was critical that the App was available in Arabic as well as English. This meant getting translation and we have found that Arabic translation needs really proofed by local language speakers to see if it really works. It also meant that the App design and navigation had to be one that worked not just reading left to right but right to left. Having Arabic speakers on our team was really helpful. The content of the App needed translated—but also the 'rubric' of the search terms, and this was something that was easy to forget.

Future-proofing. All the partners wished to extend the App to include more case studies over time. We made sure technical specifications included provision of a 'back end' that was user-friendly to load new data. This meant thinking through all the components of a new country entry that would need uploaded, such as the country map.

In practice, the App attracted a lot of interest beyond the Middle East, so we recently updated it. This involved adding new languages. We had budget restrictions so added French, which at least makes the App more accessible in areas of Africa where English is not spoken, and also Indonesian, and Burmese to make the App more accessible in conflicts in Asia. We had no further money for translations, so we worked to future-proof the back end to enable new languages to be uploaded in the future without further App design.

We found that personnel within UN Women changed over time, so that relationship had to be built over again with people that were less familiar with what the project was about, and how to commission the work from the App company, or even what the previous licencing arrangements for all our data was. This type of complication is common when working with international organizations, and points to the importance of documenting the project as you go, across those involved.

In terms of developing the App further, we are limited by what is appropriate for App to do. It cannot provide a comprehensive data interface and information, it can only make short-form information accessible. This is also important to keeping the download size usable for women with limited data download capacity.

7.6.3 PeaceFem Outcomes: Quick Evaluation

PeaceFem is downloaded by women all over the world and can be used online and offline. Many of the Middle Eastern peace processes it was designed for, sadly did not progress. While some still contain possibilities for agreement, it is also likely that women will struggle to be heard as the focus is on deals between armed actors. The App is perhaps most useful in providing information quickly, that can be useful to people drafting clauses, or thinking about how issues can be dealt with in a peace agreement. It also works more generally as a 'bill board', for both the types of activism that women used, and the types of provisions they were able to influence. While App gives basic information, it contains clear links to underlying detail of the case studies and partner websites. Women can use the App as an entry point for a deeper dive into comparative material. The App connected to the wider 'Enhancing Leadership' project that had 'regional and global convenings' of women mediators and peacebuilders regularly, which brought women together across countries to learn from each other, in what was in-effect a large global end-user group.

7.7 Work Flows

To what extent do the Covid ceasefire and PeaceFem projects give an indication of a digital innovation 'work flow'? I would suggest it is the following:

Identification of a problem. In our experience we always in a sense co-identified issues that digital innovation might help with, with people in the field. This seems to me the only way it can be done. It does not work to say 'we have a tool, how can we use it'. Neither can one be vague about what the digital tool aims to do, such as 'we want to help end conflict during the pandemic'. A more specific question such as: 'how can we collectively monitor ceasefires during Covid and make the data available', is a better statement of a problem that digital innovation can help with.

Identify to what extent you have information or expertise to address that problem. How good is your data, is it the right data, do you trust it, is that reasonable, and how could you improve it? Do you need to form new collaborations? In particular:

- What relationships of trust do you have with others who seem to have relevant pieces of information or data to bring to the table and can you find a way to collaborate?
- What are the 'ownership' and legal difficulties with bringing that data together poses? Are these solved by licences, and do you have organisational capacity or support to do that? Are they solved by simpler non-legal agreements on how the data will be presented and used and who will be acknowledged and thanked?

Identify the end-users and establish mechanisms of feedback. For us and our partner organisations this is an ongoing process.

Work iteratively (again!). Improving digital tools over time, based on feedback from end-users leads to better results. This requires thinking about whether and how your relationships with technical providers have been established and will be paid for over time.

Try to locate yourself into a wider ecosystem on the very specific subject/practice area, as well as within 'PeaceTech'. In our case, it was vital for both PeaceFem and the Covid Ceasefire Tracker, to be in a wider research and practice set of relationships with people in the areas of gender and peacebuilding, and ceasefire mediation. It was also valuable to be part of a wider research community beyond the peace and conflict community, interested in how dashboards, their visualisation, and 'things to do with Covid' were being developed at that time.

7.8 Using the PeaceTech Ecosystem

Business analysts seeking to understand 'what works' in digital transformation have noted that trying to implement digital transformation across your business requires a set of commitments to embrace change, which often includes spending money differently, and even staffing organisations differently. In the business world, most transformation project fail. We will examine the reasons further in Chap. 12.

For us the main challenge was: it can be really hard to get even apparently simple digital transformations to deliver and be useful!

Knowing you need different forms of expertise, finding the right experts and bringing them together, enabling them to have a conversation across very different types of expertise with very different language, and actually producing a good and useful PeaceTech product, is in fact very difficult. In our experience as 'PeaceTech entrepreneurs', there are real obstacles and challenges at each stage. The projects I described above nearly fell at all of the little hurdles of inter-organisational conversation, licencing, contracting, and just because turning qualitative and quantitative data into a small usable tool, is conceptually quite difficult.

I always felt that 'doing one thing well' was what we did best. But I felt that this was a sign of our limitations, and reflected where we were on the learning curve. In fact, having now worked to embrace change by re-training somewhat myself, I have been encouraged to learn that the advice from the most ambitious digital innovators in the world is often to begin with a distinct problem to which digital innovation appears to offer a smart solution, and begin there. Do one thing, do it well, and move forward from there.

The idea of a PeaceTech ecosystem as set out in the last chapter is a valuable one as it operates to build a sense of community across what are quite disparate enterprises. In so doing, and in PeaceTech enablers bringing people together in actual networks, the ecosystem has a reality that can be very valuable for finding people and initiatives that inspire, and even practical support. But it can also at times feel a bit remote. It seems to operate at a super high-powered level that can feel a bit competitive. BIG INITIATIVES can look impossibly impressive, whether they deliver anything immediately useful or not. Listen carefully though, and a lot of things are 'proof of concept'—that is, showing that something can be done, but not quite delivering that 'something' as a final usable product (we too have done this by the way, and perhaps even sounded impressive).

Ecosystem builders themselves can appear impossibly well-connected. You wonder will they be bothered with you and are you really needy enough, or is your idea good enough, to ask for their time and energies. There can also be a slight feeling of—who to reach out to—sometimes everyone seems to be offering 'PeaceTech Central' or claiming to be 'the one' to deliver the coordination the field needs and centralise its resources,—to frame and map PeaceTech the best, to provide the network to end all networks.

Or maybe this is just me!

Yet in practice, various PeaceTech networks all co-exist, collaborate and are proliferating.

Perhaps the best advice is: don't expect to feel connected to the big and apparently connected PeaceTech world 'out there'. Focus any PeaceTech initiative focus on the problem you are trying to solve. Build the connections you need when you need them, and, inevitably, these will be with those engaged with similar problems to you. Actively draw on the ecosystem when useful, and seek to connect what you have done back into the ecosystem. Be prepared to be in multiple networks, to the extent you have time.

In practice, you will probably need to create your own immediate ecosystem—your own little garden as it were. You may even need to build mini-ecosystems around particular projects, experimentally, and responsively. Sometimes getting from the 'nearly there' to the 'usable there' will take years of further development and work. Some projects will falter, but the failures will enable other projects. Other projects will deliver and thrive.

Questions

1. How convinced are you by 'one good thing' projects?
2. Can you see other lessons from the stories?
3. HAVE YOU DOWNLOADED PeaceFem? You know you want to.
4. HAVE YOU EXPLORED the ceasefires tracker? Did you realise all this was going on in the pandemic?

References[1]

Allison, J., Badanjak, S., Bach, B., Bell, C., Bhattacharya, D., Knaussel, F., & Wise, L. (2020). An interactive tracker for ceasefires in the time of Covid-19. *The Lancet Infectious Diseases, 21*(6), 764–765. https://doi.org/10.1016/S1473-3099(20)30932-4

Bell, C. (2020, March 24). *COVID-19 and Violent Conflict: Responding to predictable unpredictability*. Just Security blog. https://www.justsecurity.org/69340/covid-19-and-violent-conflict-responding-to-predictable-unpredictability/

Bhattacharya, D., Badanjak, S., Bell, C., Knäussel, F., Wise, L., Allison, J., & Bach, B. (2021). Designing an interactive real-time web-mapped dashboard to visualise conflict ceasefires data over COVID-19 infection rates: Facilities and the way ahead. In *IEEE global humanitarian technology conference article* (pp. 200–207). https://doi.org/10.1109/GHTC53159.2021.9612457.

Dorith Kool, L., Pospisil, J., & van Voorst, R. (2021). Managing the humanitarian micro-space: The practices of relief access in Syria. *Third World Quarterly, 42*(7), 1489–1506. https://doi.org/10.1080/01436597.2021.1896359

[1] All last accessed 1 May 2023.

Falisse, J. B., & McAteer, B. (2022). Visualising policy responses during health emergencies. Learning from the COVID-19 policy trackers. *Convergence, 28*(1), 35–51. https://doi.org/10.1177/13548565211048972

Haider, H. (2022, April 14). *Humanitarian access issues linked to peace processes: Advantages, disadvantages and examples.* Institute of Development Studies, K4D Helpdesk report 1123. https://opendocs.ids.ac.uk/opendocs/handle/20.500.12413/17397

Russell, I., Wise, L., & Badanjak, S. (2021). *Breathing space: Vaccination ceasefires in armed conflict* (PSRP Research Report). Global Justice Academy, University of Edinburgh. https://peacerep.org/publication/breathing-space-vaccination-ceasefires-in-armed-conflict/

Wise, L. (2023). *From protests to paper: Using PeaceFem to analyse women's inclusion in peace processes.* The Peace and Conflict Resolution Evidence Platform. (Forthcoming).

Wise, L., Badanjak, S., Bell, C., & Knäussel, F. (2021, March 22). *Pandemic pauses: Understanding ceasefires in a time of covid-19.* Political Settlements Research Programme research report. Global Justice Academy, University of Edinburgh. https://peacerep.org/publication/pandemic-pauses-understanding-ceasefires-in-a-time-of-covid-19/

Wittke, C. (2023). *Creating islands of agreement and civility' through humanitarian negotiations: A conflict management and disaster-mitigation strategy in Russia's war against Ukraine* (PeaceRep Report). Conflict and Civicness Research Group, London School of Economics. https://peacerep.org/publication/islands-of-agreement-conflict-management-russia-ukraine/

CHAPTER 8

PeaceTech as Hack

Abstract In this chapter I consider PeaceTech innovation comprising 'demand-led' digital support for discrete peacebuilding activities. This is PeaceTech as a digital 'hack' designed to support traditional peacebuilding tasks. It involves the 'doing one good thing' approach. I examine whether a 'digital hack' to peacebuilding tasks is a form of responsiveness to peacebuilding needs, or an unambitious fiddling-round-the edges sort of response to 'double disruption'. I ask 'what is going on *really*'?

Keywords Hacktivism • Modularization • Retrofitting • Adaptive peacebuilding

8.1 Task-Based Digital Innovation

The stories in the last chapter focused on delivering a PeaceTech application focused on a single area and objective. The ecosystem appears to focus on incubating scattered PeaceTech hacks for tasks, in part perhaps because peacebuilding involves a diverse set of practices. PeaceTech appears as a messy tapestry of examples, and multiple accounts of 'PeaceTech' begin with mapping, because it can be difficult to paint a coherent picture of PeaceTech. The label PeaceTech suggests there is a whole that is more than the parts. But is there? Does PeaceTech as a 'thing' really exist?

C. Bell, *PeaceTech: Digital Transformation to End Wars*,
https://doi.org/10.1007/978-3-031-38894-1_8

This chapter examines PeaceTech as ad hoc digital peacebuilding-support, and consider how it supplements low-or-no tech practices, to create greater peace process reach and traction. I call this PeaceTech as 'hack', because it tries to make peacebuilding practices more efficient and effective through task-specific Apps, online methodologies of consultation, improved security of communication, or technical fixes for peace agreement implementation tasks.

In the following chapters, in contrast, we will consider PeaceTech bundles of work that have ambition to be 'of scale' and offer themselves as solutions at a system cross-conflict level. However, this chapter asks—is once-off applications in fact the main and best contribution of PeaceTech?

8.2 Peacebuilding Tasks

At the beginning of our PeaceTech journey, we asked experienced peacebuilder Andy Carl to map PeaceTech as a field and his work continues to influence ours and this book. He did not start with technologies, or interventions of scale. He noted that PeaceTech solutions could appear very 'supply side' driven—solutions produced for which no need has been articulated. Working from a more 'demand side' perspective, Andy set out a list of peacebuilding tasks and needs. His framework has a broad application to all forms of peacebuilding, but it is useful to showing how key tasks undertaken to create and sustain a peace process can be the subject of digital experiments in-country (for further examples focused on inclusion, see Hirblinger, 2020). I set it out here in modified peace process applied form.

Understanding (Analysis and Sense-making) Using Innovative Data-Driven Approaches

- Conflict and situation analysis to inform peace and conflict prevention and management response strategies
- Understanding and seeing trends and patterns
- Media monitoring and news aggregating
- Public perceptions, views and opinions analysis
- Early Warning and conflict and security risk monitoring (including maps and satellite image analysis),
- Processing and translating big data
- New data generation

Learning (Knowledge and Skills-building) Using Innovative Communication Technologies, Data and Interfaces

- Informing stakeholder's peace process strategies, tactics and decisions
- Conflict and peace-related data sets and analysis
- Comparative learning
- Knowledge-sharing
- Informing of the strategic learning needs of primary parties in negotiations

Enabling and supporting mediation digitally through data, online meetings and virtual reality

- Enabling virtual meetings
- Facilitating consultation feed-in
- Improving mediator access to comparative data
- Helping mediators understand conflict contexts
- Reaching hard-to-reach communities
- Providing for education

Strategic communications and enabling participation in peace processes (with conflict parties, and wider society) using digital innovation

- Encrypted channels of communication for digital mediation
- Strategic Public Communications on peace processes and agreements
- Alternative and safe (virtual) space(s)
- (online) Digital Dialogues
- Digital platforms for engagement
- Enabling collaboration

Influencing and educating through digital means

- Influencing Behaviour and Personal choices through gamification and online information
- Promoting ideas, values, attitudes and behaviours through same
- Mobilising tjrpigj sa,e
- Countering abusive, coercive and militarised uses of digital technologies
- Immersive Environments

- Pro-Peace and Pro-settlement (positive) digital communications
- Resourcing? (encouraging business community to value and invest)
- Collecting Data and Countering Hate Speech and Rumours

Accountability and transitional justice using online mechanisms

- Online advice, counselling and resources
- Online memorialization and 'visiting'
- Listening and promoting understanding through online tools
- Promoting digital engagement with transitional justice mechanisms

Countering cyber-attacks, rumours and disinformation
Managing (and organising)

- Project planning
- Evaluating Peacebuilding

Interestingly, 'PeaceTech enabler' organisations often also start with tasks, and match possible 'methodologies' enabled by digital innovation. ConnexUs, which describes itself as a 'social network' and involves a collaboration between Build Up, and peacebuilding NGO Search for Common Ground, for example, provides an interactive web-based Digital Peacebuilder's Guide. It is a terrific resource, worth exploring for inspiration. It provides a choice of 'goals' and each goal is linked to a set of digitally enabled tasks, which links to a 'digital peacebuilding approach', that includes a good description of the digital tool or technique, what the skills needed are, and examples of each in action.

The Guide is a great 'ecosystem' intervention that supports digital design and capacity. The list of tasks overlaps with Carl's. It includes tasks such as 'advocacy awareness' that have analogue methods, and some digital peacebuilding techniques that have no analogue counterpart—digital information hubs, or games, that can be used for peacebuilding. You can use it to find real world examples of the types of digital innovation in the list above.

8.3 'One Thing' Digital Technologies

There are a number of digitally transformative technologies that come into play in 'once-off' PeaceTech applications, as some examples illustrate.

App-isation. Seldom discussed as a game-changing technology on business courses (although the underpinining mobile technology is so-discussed), the capacity to put small programmes into simple 'Apps', that is forms of programme that can be used simply and easily from a mobile/ smart phone, opens up PeaceTech solutions that are easy use in conflict contexts. These tools also have a data-gathering function. KoboToolbox, for example, provides a survey/data collection tool for challenging settings. KoboToolbox can be used online or offline, and synchronises in brief moments of connectivity, enabling also transfer off local mobile phones. It provides those collecting data with pre-programmed automated ways of creating statistical graphs and forms of descriptive analytics regarding the results of any survey.

Another interesting example is **eyeWitness to Atrocities**, provided by Lexis-Nexis and International Bar Association. This is an App that provides a mobile camera capacity to human rights defenders to document human rights abuses. The App uses meta-data and ways of storing and recording that enable verification but also storing in a trusted chain of custody, in ways that are designed to meet robust fair trial standards relating to management of evidence. The App can be 'disguised' on phones, where issues of human rights defender security requires.

Gamification. A range of self-managed deliberation tools provide forms of gamification or deliberation that aims to bridge polarization on contentious issues relating to the peace process. **Sole Self-organised Learning Environment, Colombia**, for example, has used a self-organised learning environment platform in Colombia to engage people in answering big social questions, with a view to peacebuilding. Also in Colombia the **Atrévete online deliberative platform**, was designed to support a deliberative process to address controversial peace process issues (see Restrepo, 2018).

Virtual Reality. Virtual and augmented reality has played a role in enabling visualisation, and forms of gaming. The UN DPPA Futuring Peace initiative already mentioned, has experimented in a number of countries in a number of different ways with using virtual reality to connect a range of people, including mediators, to situations in-country (UN DPPA, 2021).

Big Data. Big data from varied resources plays a key role in informing understanding and mediation efforts, and can be garnered from social media platforms, and large-scale surveys. Forms of machine learning, can enable information from say, peace process submissions, to be parsed into subjects very quickly, and brought together with other data points such as Twitter/X or other social or online media analysis.

Data visualisation. Date interfaces and dashboards, and interactive maps, enable ways of participative interactive visualization of information about peace and conflict situations, and also enable access to resources. For example, the Syria-Carter Centre Syria conflict mapping project has used analysis of open-source information related to the Syrian conflict, together with consultations with people in-country, to document and map over 200,000 conflict events in Syria. It also maps changing relationships between thousands of armed groups and changes in the lines of control between them. This information is used to provide mediators and humanitarian responders with up-to-date analysis of developments in Syria.

8.4 Peace Tech Value-Added

What does PeaceTech as Hack, offer to peacebuilding? In the business world digital transformation projects are driven by the concept of literal 'value'—what they add to the business profits by adding efficiency, speed, or automation of tasks that reduce staff costs. If you look at the lists above, the digital methods change the core peacebuilding practices add value in a number of ways.

Remoteness and capacity. Hacks offer a capacity to work more remotely from the people being interacted with, and therefore with staff and budget efficiencies, but also provide capacity to navigate lack of safe travel, or dangers in face-to-face meetings.

For example, in Ukraine in 2014, a **Donbas Dialogue Platform** was created to provide a way for those who looking for nonviolent resolution of the conflict in the Donetsk and Lugansk regions, to interact and share ideas across divided communities. In Northern Ireland, **INCORE, CAIN** have provided a database of physical memorials to victims across the country, with geolocations and photographs. The memorials database is also available in 'App' form, enabling not just those who may want to visit the memorials, but others moving around Northern Ireland, to explore memorials. However, the resource also enables relatives of victims who may not be able to visit memorials due to it being unsafe to visit them, or because they are living abroad.

Scaling up and out. Hacks offer a capacity to reach and incorporate the views of more people because of greater systematic capacity to survey, greater capacity for automation of survey and responses, or because innovation reaches new constituencies who are remote physically or disengaged from formal processes. Twitter/X analysis, for example, can reveal social attitudes (at least of twitter/X users), and inform how to influence audiences, or what forms of disinformation need combatted. These are new peacebuilding tasks that digital transformation in a sense enables and creates.

In a peace process, digital innovation can improve the reach of consultation, for example, in Libya, an interactive website in Arabic established in 2017, relating to the UN's National Action Plan for Libya. A key element of this Plan was the organization of a National Conference and a preparation process. The website enabled people to engage with the process and submit views (see further UN DPPA, 2019; Lanz & Eleiba, 2018). **Everyday Peace Indicators**, and SMS to reach remote communities, already mentioned, provides another example.

Appeal to new constituencies. Hacks also may extend peacebuilding's reach, to children and young people, and in particular young men who are the recruitment ground of armed groups, but also possible next-generation peacebuilders. Butterfly Works, Arabia Felix games discussed earlier, are an example.

Scientific method. Hacks offer an apparently more 'scientific' method for reaching people and obtaining information, because of capacity to quantify communications and responses, or perceptions and attitudes surveys, made in peace processes, rather than give impressionist or personally biased information as to 'what people think' (although of course other biases exist).

New mechanisms of influence. Hacks offer new and different ways to influence. Digital developments such as 'gamification' of peace that aims not just to engage people in questions of peace, but in a sense to get into their mind, to shape their attitudes towards particular situations, or to change ideological positions. During peace processes, digital innovation can improve strategic communication, or help to counteract disinformation or counter-messaging. For example, PeaceTech Lab has developed **Hate Speech Lexicons** in different languages that understand overt and coded vocabularies of hate speech, across dialects, to enable hate speech in social media to be identified, monitored and combatted in conflict areas.

New Systems of Support. Digital interfaces, offer new mechanisms for institutional support. For example, in Sudan the **Conflict Sensitivity Resource Facility (CSRF)** aimed to support a range of international actors and interventions to have a 'conflict sensitive' approach, so that they coordinate to supported a struggling peace process (at time of writing, disrupted by conflict). It works by providing guidelines, research and a space for 'critical reflection' on conflict sensitive practice. The interface provides an interactive map of Sudan, designed to support aid workers and peacebuilders.

8.5 'Ad hoc-ery'—Good or Bad?

Ad hoc digital peacebuilding is responsive to people just wanting to do 'one good thing'. But is it sustainable? Is ongoing experimentation or 'hactivism' good or bad? Does it deliver on the promise of digital transformation in the peacebuilding field? And—perhaps most crucially—does it address the wider disruption of peacebuilding in a positive way?

Some practical concerns arise, such as whether some of the technology invented for 'one purpose and context', can be re-used and re-purposed. Or can a business model can be developed to sustain the initiative? Even a cursory glance at PeaceTech initiatives indicates the number of experiments and software innovations that have disappeared into the mists of time. Perhaps that does not matter if a very context-specific, time-limited use was intended. But, at least, questions should be asked about use of resources, efficiency and what constitutes good design practice.

To evaluate the impact of PeaceTech hacks, I suggest there are three different ways of understanding the relationship between PeaceTech 'task-focused' experiments, and the practice of peacebuilding, that speak to the nature of the contribution.

8.5.1 PeaceTech as Retro-fitting

When you have an old house and you want to say, add wall and roof insulation to bring it up to the energy efficient standards of new houses, you will be 'retro-fitting'. Retrofitting is the act of adding something more technologically advanced than previously existed, long after the building has been built, to make it more efficient.

PeaceTech as hack in a sense 'retrofits' digital innovation to standard tasks, as a colleague alerted me to (on retro-fitting see Walker, 2023). In nearly all of the examples above, what is offered is a new digitally enabled way of doing something better—such as, building trust, improving communication, monitoring outcomes, that was part of past peacebuilding practices. What the technology offers is a better more efficient way of doing something that used to be done another way—a form of value.

8.5.2 *PeaceTech as Modularization*

However, sometimes what PeaceTech seems to offer a more radical modification of peacebuilding practices than the retrofitting analogy captures.

Many of the communication, participation and inclusion examples seem to offer not just better efficiency but a new form of 'adaptive peacebuilding' responsive to peace processes needs (De Coning, 2018). Adaptive peacebuilding focuses less on achieving pre-defined peacebuilding outcomes, and more on dynamic support to complex political processes where unexpected things happen.

Desai and Lang, examining the development work of PulseLab Jakarta, have suggested that we should think of digital innovation, less as 'retrofitting' and more as 'modularization' (2022). Modularization is an idea, at the heart of contemporary business practice, that a standard base machine can be customised in multiple ways by the attachment of different modular components in different combinations. Adding different components can change what it is that the machine is and does: a phone can become a top-spec camera; a drone can become a weapon.

Modularization in business has the advantage of creating a flexible production system that enables multiple customised configurations while reducing what is re-fabricated each time. It reconfigures production processes from Engineer-to-Order to Configure-to-Order operating models; in other words, from 'building-from-scratch' to 'assembling-from-parts' production. The advantages are: less effort to customise; reduced costs; and reduction of internal complexity in fabrication machines by standardising components, and reducing the number of variants to design. Modularization therefore brings businesses flexibility, agility and cost savings.

What does 'PeaceTech as modularization look like? How does it shift the 'production process' of peacebuilding, and what advantages might modularization bring in this domain?

PeaceTech as modularization is in a sense set out in the ConnexUs way of looking at things. The ConnexUs Guide asks—what are you trying to do, and rather than retro-fitting a standard new 'thing' to that practice, it points to a new way of bolting digital innovation onto the practice, depending on your skills, resources, and capacities, in ways that make you differently agile, flexible, and efficient in the practice. However, the bolting on also customises the practice to be something different than it was before, different in scale, in reach, in responsiveness.

Often the digital module added to peacebuilding task achieves several things at once. Peace gaming, for example, can build trust and civicness between young people, but without them having to travel and meet each other when that is not possible. The ways in which they game provide further data—for example how moves are made that can be fed back into algorithms that tell us something about what builds trust and how an individual's choices change over time. The gameification of peacebuilding can reach huge numbers—in the case of Arabia Felix, 40,000 kids—a population that would have taken a massive resource for any organization to reach using analogue methods. Similarly, surveying online can deal with issues of security and access in complex field situations; and using online automated ways of processing surveys, enables many more people to be surveyed, and their opinions weighted mathematically in an instant, without embedding huge data team in a UN Mission. Modularization therefore brings the capacities of scale, remoteness, and behavioural influence already mentioned.

But of course, the question is whether all of these things are always better? Further, these same digital techniques can be bolted on as modules to attempts to destroy peace processes and employ logics of war. Bolting the same tools to war-making tasks, leads to more agile, flexible and efficient ways of pursuing war, that change what we even constitute to be war—for example cyberwarfare itself.

Does this matter? Most tools can be used for good and ill, as we discussed in Chap. 2. It does, I think. Enabling modules that can be used not just for peacebuilding but for war-making, or as we will see in the next chapters, vice versa, puts us in a curious fake-real space where war and peace themselves are intertwined in new ways.

For example, a key dynamic of double disruption is the attempt to game peace processes by claiming to be involved in conflict resolution by countries and militarized actors at the international level. The ability to articulate peace to be war and war to be peace, and to fuel this with disinformation, when coupled with peacebuilding's potential increased 'virtual' nature, leaves 'reality' somewhat suspended across the board. However, virtuality may have upsides as well as downsides. Hirblinger argues that some of the 'non-tangible' outcomes digital technologies are not fake but part of a 'a *subjunctive* sensitivity for future worlds that 'could' or 'should' be' (2023, p. 113).

8.5.3 Hacks as Experimental Response to Disruption

A related, even more provocative idea as to 'what is really happening' is suggested by David Chandler's work in the development field (2017). Chandler suggests that a kind-of unravelling of certainty as to 'big development interventions', reflects a new recognition of the profound political difficulties of achieving structural change. He suggests that in the absence of believing in structural interventions, the experimental once-off-hacks that digital innovation offers are attractive. He uses the term 'hacktivism' and an analogy with 'life hacks'. Big issues cannot be solved, but experimental 'hacks' that offer small improvements may make a big difference. You can't cure the pain of human existence, but you may be happier if you make your bed in the morning, sort of thing.

Chandler seems both attracted by a move, as he sees it, from the certainty and hubris of international development interventions, but also says that the move to 'hacks' is also a move to accept a socio-economic status quo, given an inability to change it.

Does this have resonance in the peacebuilding field? If the 'big peace process' is no longer possible in the world's most protracted conflicts, and logics of war, and political marketplace are prevailing over logics of civicness, then supporting local people to 'do their own thing', including in a remote way by providing digital resources, is perhaps the only sensible intervention. It is interesting, is it not, that Seán in Chap. 1 was working for the UN, but on local peace—not something that could perhaps be immediately recognised as a 'threat to international peace' that the UN was set up to address. Yet, local agreement-making makes sense as a strategy for unravelling a complex conflict system in the new double disruption context: particularly if no other peace process is possible. However, does it essentially admit defeat to a national conflict status quo?

8.6 Conclusion

Is the 'hacktivism as status quo' charge fair? Not entirely. Perhaps I am wrong, but Chandler himself seems a little conflicted as to whether experimental responsiveness to particular development challenges, given the difficulties of structural change, is to be welcomed as less hubristic and more practical, or rejected as pro-status-quo. Plus, any problem with 'ad hocism', lies not in the digital technology's impact, but in the scattered, overlaid, un-strategic practices of peacebuilding itself. Was it already a set of hacks, and if so was that bad?

On the whole my view is that, if a conflict system as in a system made up of related conflicts, rather than a singular conflict, exists and needs to be unwound, then perhaps it is time to ask ...

How do local actors try to build peace from nothing? What activities of international peacebuilders support this? How do local people engaged in 'civicness' attempt to widen and deepen elements of a peace process into something capable of having nation-wide impact. What would it mean to really leverage PeaceTech to support these activities?

Could digital innovation be more ambitious and help cohere them into an incrementalist vision of piece-by-piece 'conflict unwinding' that was understood as a strategy where the sum would be more than the pieces? I think there is something in how hacks can be made to add up.

Questions

1. Which analogy for how PeaceTech do you think works best?
2. What are good and bad about 'life hacks'? Do these same things apply to PeaceTech 'hacks'?
3. Should PeaceTech try to be more systematic? How?

References[1]

Chandler, D. (2017). Securing the Anthropocene? International policy experiments in digital hacktivism: A case study of Jakarta. *Security Dialogue, 48*(2), 113–130. https://doi.org/10.1177/0967010616677714

De Coning, C. (2018). Adaptive peacebuilding. *International Affairs, 94*(2), 301–317. https://doi.org/10.1093/ia/iix251

Desai, D., & Lang, A. (2022). From mock-up to module: Development practice between planning and prototype. *Law and Critique, 33*, 299–318. https://doi.org/10.1007/s10978-022-09326-1

Hirblinger, A. T. (2020, September). *Digital inclusion in mediated peace processes: How technology can enhance participation*. United States Institute of Peace report, 168. https://www.usip.org/publications/2020/09/digital-inclusion-mediated-peace-processes-how-technology-can-enhance

[1] All last accessed 1 May 2023.

Hirblinger, A. T. (2023). Building a peace we don't know? The power of subjunctive technologies in digital peacebuilding. *Peacebuilding, 11*(2), 113–135. https://doi.org/10.1080/21647259.2022.2154957

Lanz, D., & Eleiba, A. (2018, December). *The good, the bad and the ugly: Social media and peace mediation.* Swiss Peace policy brief. https://www.swisspeace.ch/assets/publications/downloads/Policy-Briefs/aa3fc8830f/Social-Media-and-Peace-Mediation-Policy-Brief-12-2018.pdf

Restrepo, E. M. (2018). Online technology as a pathway for citizen deliberation and depolarization. *Perspectives on Global Development and Technology, 17*(3), 239–263. https://doi.org/10.1163/15691497-12341477

UN DPPA. (2021, July 12). *Virtual reality bites: using technology to bring post-conflict situations to life.* United Nations Department of Political and Peacebuilding Affairs online blog. https://dppa.medium.com/virtual-reality-bites-using-technology-to-bring-post-conflict-situations-to-life-bd5cb98ce3f6

UN DPPA, Global Pulse. (2019, January). *E-Analytics guide: using data and new technology for peacemaking, preventive diplomacy and peacebuilding.* Department of Political and Peacebuilding Affairs, UN Global Pulse United Nations University Institute on Computing and Society E-Analytics Guide. https://www.unglobalpulse.org/wp-content/uploads/2019/04/e-analyticsguide2019.pdf

Walker, N. (2023). *Europe's constitutional retrofit.* Global Constitutionalism, forthcoming.

CHAPTER 9

Conflict Early Warning Systems

Abstract Conflict Early Warning Systems, or CEWS, are our first example of a sustained systematic PeaceTech intervention happening across multiple institutions and contexts globally. These initiatives use technology to provide state-of-the-art conflict CEWS, either at a country-wide level or even globally. CEWS have a hinterland in intelligence practices. As regards their use as PeaceTech, the idea of better 'early warning' is linked to 'conflict prevention'. We examine CEWS and their limitations.

Keywords Early Warning Systems (EWS) • Conflict Early Warning Systems (CEWS) • Knowledge foundry • CEWS gaps

9.1 I Predict a Riot

Once during what was called 'the troubles' I walked up a street in Northern Ireland with international visitors. As we got near the city centre, I noticed that lots of young men were lurking in an unusual way, around the sidewalks. I realised that while none were wearing balaclavas or other disguises, hats were being pulled lower, and scarves higher. There were very few whose faces I could see. But it was more the way they were behaving. There were looks between them. They were all 'waiting' and I felt a sort of feverishness in the air. Suddenly I was on high alert. I looked up into

C. Bell, *PeaceTech: Digital Transformation to End Wars*,
https://doi.org/10.1007/978-3-031-38894-1_9

the town and realised a march by 'the other side' was taking place and the young people could be expected to oppose it. We were right on the interface between divided communities and I suddenly knew: 'I predict a riot'. It would not be serious, but could injure people. I knew that police—who I could see up the street and were clearly prepared, could fire plastic bullets if things escalated. The chance that my guests would be hurt was slim, but I did not want to take it.

I told my guests, 'let's go back'. Some were quite upset with me, when I told them I would explain later. There was trouble as it turned out. No-one got seriously hurt, but it was better not to be around it. Interesting to me, my guests were really surprised at my decisions and the explanation I later gave. They kept asking 'but *how* did you know that was going on?' The told me they had not seen anything untoward and were most surprised. For my part, I wondered how they could not see what was so obvious.

Now I realise I could have answered: I was alerted by my in-built, highly sophisticated, Conflict Early Warning System.

9.2 Conflict Early Warning Systems: What Are They?

It was not a hunch that triggered my anticipation of conflict; it was my expert local knowledge of conflict put together with observed data. This knowledge came from a life lived in conflict, from having been in similar situations before, coupled with wider political understanding of conflict triggers. This combined to produce an 'instinct' that was predictive. You will have had similar instincts in similar situations, and re-examination may show they were based on knowledge and rationality, despite being experienced in the moment as 'a feeling'.

I called my reaction an in-built Conflict Early Warning System (CEWS), and boldly claimed it to be 'highly sophisticated', because it is impossible to parse out all the relevant data sources I unconsciously drew on, and the life-long underlying expertise that informed what looked like an unscientific 'hunch'.

Nowadays we think of CEWS as technological, data-driven and scientific. CEWS have been a holy grail of conflict analysists. Technology such as we examined in outline in Chap. 2, promises a capacity to deliver a science of early warning drawing on infinite and varied data, at speed, to provide automated systematic predictions of conflict. Can it?

Often times the local person's highly sophisticated 'hunch' will be better, and in practice CEWS often rely on hybrid forms of knowledge across 'data analytics' and 'human expertise'.

9.3 From EWS to CEWS

Early Warning Systems or EWS provide early indications that something concerning is happening, based on assessing physical events on the ground, and predicting their consequences. They are used widely to monitor weather and natural disasters and climate change: a confluence of natural events can indicate that a major event might be imminent, such as a storm or earthquake. We usually think of EWS as both systematic and automated, and therefore scientific in some way. Yet they mostly depend on human responses to be effective. In the conflict area, they have started to be called 'Conflict Early Warning Systems' or CEWS, the term we will now use, and other definitions can be seen in the box.

Early Warning System: A warning system that can be implemented as a chain of information communication systems and comprises sensors, event detection and decision subsystems for early identification of hazards. They work together to forecast and signal disturbances that adversely affect the stability of the physical world, providing time for the response system to prepare for the adverse event and to minimize its impact. (Waidyanatha, 2010)
Conflict Early Warning Systems: Systems to alert people to the risk or onset of militarily violent conflict. Their specific purpose is, 'to identify and trigger actions to reduce the onset, duration, intensity, and effects of multiple forms of political violence'. (Muggah & Whitlock, 2022, p. 1)
World Bank: A process that (a) alerts decision-makers to the potential outbreak, escalation and resurgence of violent conflict; and (b) promotes an understanding among decision-makers of the nature and impacts of violent conflict. (Defontaine, 2019)
Hague Centre for Strategic Studies: A CEWS warns specifically for the onset, occurrence, escalation or resurgence of various forms of political violence. (Sweijs & Teer, 2022)

9.4 Who Do CEWS Alert?

CEWS aim to produce a response in a range of different actors (not necessarily all targeted by a single system).

Humanitarian agencies. These can be alerted to the possibility of humanitarian consequences of conflict such as death or injury, hunger, new health needs or mass movements of people.

The diplomatic community. This community may be alerted to support local crisis interventions, and forms of diplomatic or military or humanitarian intervention, or to plan to evacuate their own nationals. Anticipatory diplomatic responses may be particularly important if the nature of the conflict is such that it could trigger ever wider international conflict, for example if it breaks out along a border, or involves allies of a powerful geopolitical power, such as Russia, China or the United States.

Local communities. Civilians can be alerted to move out of harm's way, to operationalise their own community responses to violence, assisting those in flight, or even conducting forms of mediation. As my story at the chapter's start indicates, local actors may in fact have had even 'earlier warning' of the conflict than technological CEWS provide.

Military actors. Armed actors can be alerted to produce a range of military responses across quite different types of 'army'. Responses can be framed as counter-aggression, self-defence, community defence or civilian protection. We may think of some of these responses as peaceful and some as conflict, so again, CEWS may be 'modular' and part of both PeaceTech and WarTech.

Are CEWS then PeaceTech or War Tech? They are focused on 'conflict prevention', which as noted earlier, can be an important aspect of peace process implementation. However, they are really 'Conflict Early Warning *and Response*' systems, and responses can also be military, focused on security, or war—as Nick's story illustrated. Arguably, their origins are in SecTech or WarTech, adapted as module to peacebuilding, rather than vice versa.

9.5 CEWS in Practice

We have already encountered CEWS as PeaceTech in earlier chapters.

Ushahidi. Do you remember Ushahidi in Kenya, in Chap. 4?: the platform that initially began as a response to the violence around the Kenyan elections in 2008? This created a Kenyan CEWS, and now provides a soft-ware platform designed to collect and put together the information necessary to other CEWS. This platform has developed over time from 'a simple WordPress blog with dots on a map into an entire ecosystem of software and tools built to facilitate the work done by human rights advocates, journalists, election monitors and those responding to disaster and crisis'. It now enables data collection from multiple sources: SMS, Custom embedded web surveys, email, smartphone Apps, Twitter/X, and allows bulk data imports from CSV files. This data can then be presented in a range of ways.

Hala Systems, 'Sentry'. This system in-essence triangulates sensors in the ground, with crowd-sourced information about attacks, with tracking of flight paths of aircraft from open source material, to provide information on attacks in Syria. It employs technologies that have overlap with Ushahidi, such as smart phone Apps for reporting sightings of planes, but also uses remote-sensing, and AI algorithms to triangulate and verify information. It communicates back warning through an 'insight portal' with situation awareness, collaboration tools, and geospatial analytics, not just to 'inform' a range of actors, that they may need to take action quickly, but to '*integrate* civilians, local responders and global stakeholders' (emphasis added).

The Sentinel Project provides a CEWS. It uses data analysis to alert people to a 'situation of concern'. It has produced a 'conflict tracking system' that is publicly available (https://thesentinelproject.org/2015/02/11/the-sentinel-project-launches-conflict-tracking-system/). The focus is on identifying risk of genocide, and conducting 'operational process monitoring' regarding a possible evolving genocide. However, the project states an ambition for two more CEWS-type tasks: first a vulnerability assessment that would be able to identify country characteristics and all the actors within a 'situation of concern' to identify vulnerability to attack of key communities. Second, in the case of a predicted genocide, a prediction of severe it is likely to be (building upon information from the vulnerability assessment), and what the most likely perpetrator courses-of-action are—all designed to support responses. In practice, this work is still in a form of inception.

Strata. A 'sister' project at University of Edinburgh is an 'Earth Stress Monitor' developed with the UN Environmental Programme (UNEP). This monitors not just climate impacts, but also security vulnerability. It is not strictly an EWS or CEWS, but does use algorithms to show 'hot spots' where multiple risks coincide and people reside, and so points to places to pay close attention to. In marrying conflict and climate risks, the tool points to the need to understand multiple forms of conflict and climate risk together.

Beyond these examples, there are multiple diverse CEWS: this is a fast-proliferating field, often driven by research projects and non-governmental organizations. It is also a key focus of governments, and regional and international organizations often for their own intelligence and operational purposes. The following list provides links to other examples, although is not exhaustive (for good and recent overviews see Hegre, 2022; Sweijs & Teer, 2022).

Atrocity Forecasting Project (AFP), Australian National University,: aims to enhance forecasting of mass atrocities, performing in essence a 'Research and Development' function for CEWS (Butcher et al., 2020).

Conflict Forecast (CF), an FCDO-funded project that forecasts 'outbreaks of political violence and escalations into internal armed conflict' (Mueller & Rauh, 2018, 2022a, 2022b).

The Comprehensive Planning and Performance Assessment System (CPAS), a UN system for supporting adaptive management in UN Peacekeeping missions. An example of a long-term foresight tool as it supports long-term assessments as to how missions are going and how to improve them, rather than immediate 'early warning'.

Preview, German Government, includes a 'conflict forecasting component, see description here (Bressan, 2021).

The Violence Early-Warning System (ViEWS), provided by the Uppsala Conflict Data Programme: generates monthly predictions of the number of fatalities in impending state-based conflict 1–36 months ahead, and probabilistic assessments of conflict (Hegre et al., 2019).

UN Situational Awareness and Geospatial (SAGE), United Nations: a computer based reporting system that supports an event database including enabling UN peacebuilding and peacekeeping operations and staff to categories incidents in real time (see Druet, 2021). It is powered using the Ushahidi software, but is able to ingest a very broad amount of data including data that is structured, unstructured, quantitative, qualitative and visual.

Volatility and Risk Predictability Index (VRI), ACLED: tracks conflict surges, as part of the ACLED conflict data suite of datasets. (ACLED)

Vigil Monitor Ltd, a company that works with the XCEPT research programme to use satellite imagery to understand the drivers, dynamics and direction of conflicts, discussed more next chapter.

9.6 Variation in CEWS

It is interesting to note that the examples all have different approaches to:

- the purposes and drivers of the CEWS
- the decision-makers they seek to reach
- the time horizons over which they seek to influence change
- the methodologies and technologies for gathering, processing and presenting EW information
- the geographic scope the CEWS covers, from specific countries or areas within them, regions, or 'the world'

Let us examine further.

9.6.1 How Early Is the Early? Variation in Time Horizons

CEWS operate to warn on different time scales, and these link to the different 'prevention' tasks they aim to serve.

Nowcasting: warning about the emerging and ongoing. Ushahidi in its original incarnation, offers an example of a 'what's happening right now', system. It was designed to warn people of where they should go and not go in the moment. Hala works somewhat that way too with a focus on enabling civilians to protect themselves. But of course a wider range of more structural responses to violence may also be enabled—in the case of Ushahidi's initial work in Kenya, community responses to violence, or mothers making sure teenagers and kids did not go and join in. International Crisis Group has a Crisis Watch, conflict tracker, that it talks of as a 'nowcasting' tool because it tells people what is unfolding and may require a response.

Nowcasting may be so 'now' that it does not support timely intervention. Other purposes are also claimed for some of these now-focused CEWS, in what can seem like a form of hedging. Hala notes that its system is not only about warning but is also about 'accountability' after-the-fact, because it documents attack details that can potentially provide a basis for any international assessment of human rights violations and war crimes in the future. Other initiatives such as Sentinel, for example, and Vigil Monitoring that we will look at next chapter, similarly claim to really be about post-hoc accountability, although they offer a CEWS dimension.

Medium Term Adaptive management—warning about the risks of conflict onset. Other systems, aim to more link to wider preventative strategies, some that try to anticipate and produce responses aimed at further down the road, operating perhaps more at regional and organizational level. UN's CPAS that focuses focusing on adaptive management in peacekeeping missions has more this type of function, with SAGE providing more immediate incident response-support. Interestingly, although both are UN peacekeeping innovations the systems do not operate simultaneously in all missions and seem to operate as two different platforms.

Futures horizon-scanning—warning about long-term risks and conflict trajectories. Longer-term approaches to CEWS aim to anticipate conflict dynamics down the road. This type of system shifts the methods from immediate assessments of how conflict is unfolding, or even medium-term adaptive management, to help 'scenario plan' as to how to address some of underlying structural drivers of conflict that may need strategies for change. This type of approach is often embedded in governmental and international systems such as SAGE, Preview and CPAS.

Do-It-All (DIA) Systems. This is my term and reflects that increasingly CEWS are being brought together with all possible tools to address instability, to try to provide all of these CEWS functions, and also support quick access to good practice guides to support responses. For example the US is developing an Instability Monitoring and Analysis Platform (IMAP) to enable policy-making in line with evidence. It aims to make open access data and technology widely available through US government departments, 'to inform U.S. strategies, policies, and programs on conflict prevention and stabilization'. While DIA Systems sound attractive in terms of efficiencies, they run counter to the 'do one good thing' approach, and risk making so much data and analysis available that the right information at the right time remains difficult to access.

9.6.2 Who Are the 'Decision-Makers'?

Different CEWS are used by different organizations and therefore differ with regard who they reach as 'decision-makers'. For example, Ushahidi and Hala aim to reach ordinary citizens. However, Hala's system also requires consideration of how information should be verified and documented for any future domestic or international criminal law process, meaning that it also responds to professional needs, say of lawyers. Some systems are specifically organizational, such as the UN's SAGE and CPAS for peacekeeping operation support, or the US's IMAP.

Muggah and Whitlock have drawn a distinction between 'first mile CEWS' that are people-centred and bottom up, and 'last mile' that focus on threats and top down (2022, p. 8). They use this spatial reference to indicate proximity to people affected (first mile), and proximity to international responders (last mile). These are two different sets of decision-makers, whose time needs are different, and whose response capacities will be different.

9.7 Digital Innovation and CEWS

Questions of purpose, timing and decision-makers to be supported, tie into the types of digital innovation that is employed.

9.7.1 Innovation in Data and Data Analytics

It is difficult to generalise about the data used in CEWS as they vary as examples have illustrated. Contemporary CEWS that aim to operate at scale, tend to use predictive data analytics. While statistics or 'descriptive analytics' tell us what a situation is, predictive analytics try to use a range of techniques of analysing data to predict what might happen next.

The data in CEWS can be quantitative data about conflict, or qualitative about structural conditions such as poverty, that we think generate conflict. It could be expert data, gleaned from reports, or from expert surveys, or crowd-sourced data, such as reporting by people, as in the Ushahidi example. Or remote-sensed data such as Hala uses. Or social media data. Amongst these data are a number of 'old-fashioned analogue' types of methodologies—such as asking experts—whether local or academic or political—their opinion. For example, International Crisis Group's Crisis Watch works entirely on the basis of expert analytical assessment but visualises it on an interactive map. However, this is the exception. The multiplicity of possible data for CEWS, creates the possibility of millions of data points—in other words 'big data'.

9.7.2 *Innovation in Data Gathering Tools*

Digital transformation has also re-shaped the 'data gathering tools', as has already become apparent. SMS surveys, or tools such as KoboBoxTool enable large scale survey and analysis of information, all with a level of online-offline capacity and security. Webscraping of news stories, or Twitter/X feed, all now feed into CEWS. A range of innovative tools operate within missions to enable people to log incidents in ways that automate their integration into the analysis and visualization of the CEWS. Druet's detailed description of SAGE provides an example of just how diverse the types of data drawn on can be (Druet, 2021).

9.7.3 *Innovation in Statistical Techniques*

Also rapidly evolving is development of new analytical techniques for CEWS purposes. These are often difficult to follow and assess. Well established statistical methodologies of prediction continue to be used, the area has increasing methodological experimentation.

The Global Urban Analytics for Resilient Defence (GUARD) project of the Turing Institute, uses 'spatial interaction' theory, and links such as, number of people killed at major road junctions and onset of conflict, for predicting conflict. Guo, Gleditsch and Wilson, the project's creators, have brought deaths in conflict data, such as that mentioned earlier of ACLED and UCDP, all geocoded in space, to overlay it with other quantifiable information relating to political dynamics, and set it on a map, to attempt to predict where conflict will occur (2018).

9.7.4 *Innovation in Technology of Communication of Risk*

Other digital innovations have focused on connecting the CEWS information to decision-makers. For big data and systems, these often involve dynamic interactive dashboards or interfaces, such as the platforms of SAGE, Sentinel and CPAS. Some will be built using software such as Microsoft PowerBi, others using conflict-tailored software such as Ushahidi. Knowledge foundries, discussed below, are another innovation.

9.8 What Does It Take for a CEWS to Work?

On 14 April 2012, when the Titanic hit an iceberg, Thomas Andrews from Ballymena Northern Ireland and who had designed the Belfast-built ship was on board. When he heard the extent of the damage, he knew categorically that the ship would sink. He also likely knew there was insufficient lifeboat capacity to save all those on board. This was data. A signal was sent immediately to nearby ships. One, the SS California was only five miles away and saw distress flares. However, it did not respond. Two inquiries—a British one and a US one—found that had it responded, all those lost could have been saved. Another ship, the Carpathia, was 58 miles away and arrived three hours later—after the Titanic had sunk. It saved the lives of over 700 people but over 1500 people had already perished in the sea.

Those in charge of the SS California either misinterpreted Titanic's signal as not signalling imminent distress, or decided not to risk travelling through icebergs. Earlier the SS California had stopped amidst the ice field and sent a warning to other ships nearby—another EWS. However, miscommunications on the Titanic, meant that this warning did not reach the bridge, and the ship powered on to its fate—another EWS gap. Andrews, who in fact is my distant family relative, went down with the ship. The SS California was in the end sunk by a German Submarine in the First World War.

Advance information—or early warning—of icebergs existed, and was communicated at two points, once by the SS California, which if heeded could have prevented the ship's course into an iceberg, and another by the Titanic to the Carpathia, that could have resulted in a more successful rescue operation. But the seriousness of both communications were not fully appreciated, not fully communicated to the people with decision-making power, or not taken seriously by them when it was, and so did not trigger the necessary decisions for action.

The Titanic example points to 'EWS Gaps'. In the conflict field, similar CEWS gaps of communication and action exist, but are even more likely because conflict risks are very difficult to quantify. Also, forms of response, such as use of force, are themselves high risk and often unlikely to be used until conflict is actually unfolding, if at all. Research has also shown that 'who' communicates the risk in terms of how senior they are, and how much they are valued in the organization, is as important to how seriously a warning will be taken, as the reliability of the information—statisticians may carry little weight with army generals (De Meyer et al., 2019, p. 273).

For a CEWS to work as a peacebuilding measure, it would need to do the following:

- Provide a very early indicator that violence is escalating, or is about to escalate, that is reliable and trusted
- Get that information to people that are in a position to influence whether violence develops or not
- Connect to those people's mechanism of decision-making for intervening to stop the violence
- Produce responses that are effective in preventing conflict

If any part of the chain breaks, the CEWS is unlikely to be preventative. Certain things need to be in place for each stage to be successful.

Reliable Analysis of what predicts conflict. Knowledge of what causes conflict is limited. There is consensus about factors that are linked, but no real academic consensus on how and when they combine to 'cause conflict'. Conflict events such as killings or bombs might indicate that more conflict is on its way, but may not. Similarly, 'disagreeing about the sovereign status of a region' might cause conflict, or 'poverty' might cause conflict, but neither of these things predict conflict, because there are many instances where disputed status of a region, or poverty, do not cause conflict. Any predictive analytics capable of providing a CEWS, will find it difficult to decide what factors to explore correlations between, and what predictive conclusion to draw from them.

Even where good analysis exists, it may not be easily to combine possible relevant conflict triggers into a predictive methodology. Often political analysis of what causes conflict will have to be translated into some sort of algorithm that works with quantifiable data. A wrong calculation will lead to inaccurate prediction. Plus, one might be sceptical (I am, could you tell?!), about explanations for conflict that do not factor in the unpredictable factor of: human agency. Without going into the many deep and complex debates, it seems clear, to me at least, that some sort of complicated combination of structural conditions and the agency of armed actors, determines whether conflict results. It feels like a leap of faith, that probabilistic data based on quantifiable drivers of conflict, would produce good prediction.

Appropriate and accurate data. Knowing what to measure, and how to compute the measurement, can still leave a difficulty of what measurements to use. Even if we know what factors can be used to reliably predict violence, we need capacity to monitor and collect data on those factors. This is not simple.

Deaths in conflict, for example, would seem critical to conflict prediction in an immediate sense, and in principle deaths in conflict seem quite a certain thing to measure. However, counting such deaths is a massive, complex and even political undertaking. It requires both defining what is 'in conflict' (does it include the person who took a heart attack when they heard about their relative's death or not?). It also requires a methodology for actually counting the deaths in question. For example, both ACLED and UCDP measure 'deaths in conflict', but they define conflict in different ways and use very different methods to 'count'. UCDP defines conflict in terms of warring groups that have a publicly stated 'incompatibility' (or dispute) and uses two verified news sources to count deaths in desk-based review. ACLED counts different types of violent death—through protests, or shootings, using a network of in-country experts. This means, for example, that for UCDP cartel drug violence in Mexico is not conflict, and for ACLED it is. Both methodologies are thorough and valid, but the methodologies are different and will produce different results (see further Raleigh et al., 2023). Both may be built into CEWS, but unless transparently so, we may not know exactly how they are used to provide any predictive analytics, and therefore may not easily be able to assess how the hidden biases of either might affect the prediction.

If we move from 'deaths in conflict' to a range of other conflict-relevant data, such as the level of corruption in a country, the levels of relative poverty, or something like 'the belief your situation can improve',—all possible measures of conflict likelihood, then whether reliable data exists, or could be collected, becomes even more challenging. Moreover, apart from deaths in conflict data, most other relevant data is 'slow data'—produced annually and tracking slow-moving processes of change. Whether data is 'fast' or 'slow' affects the type of conflict prediction it is useful for.

Good communication of risk to decision-makers that have capacity to respond. In the field of conflict, a more common gap arises in the lack of political will or capacity to respond. In Srebrenica during the conflict in Bosnia Herzegovina, what has since been called a 'slow genocide' occurred over months, and eventually atrocities were committed in sight of UN Peacekeepers. Yet nothing was done to intervene, due to a range of factors that constrained the political will of peacekeepers on the ground and their political bosses back 'at home'. There was no will for engaging Peacekeepers in fighting genocidal military chiefs, or to use aerial bombing, or other forms of intervention (for an account of the unfolding of the 'slow genocide' see the chilling record in the International Court of Justice Application of the Convention on the Prevention and Punishment of the Crime of Genocide (Bosnia and Herzegovina v. Serbia and Montenegro), 26 February 2007).

If any one of these issues gaps arises, the CEWS will be rendered ineffective, or worse—counter-productive.

9.9 New Generation CEWS: Hocus-pocus Tech?

There are signs emerging of a new generation of CEWS that promise to overcome the warning-response gap by connecting data to more rapid and on occasion automated decision-making.

These are systems that claim to apply deep machine learning and Artificial Intelligence (AI) 'to generate increasingly parsimonious assessments that are, crucially, then matched to a range of possible real-time decision options elucidating their inherent risks and payoffs' (Muggah & Whitlock 2022, p. 4). In other words, to link automated predictive analytics with automated decision-making responses.

A range of 'knowledge foundry' systems now claim to be able to absorb and crunch a massive range of structured and unstructured data. For example, Palantir who are listed in NYU CIC's 'PeaceTech' ecosystem mapping, are one such company, and already have provided services to the US/NATO in Afghanistan as well to multiple police forces (we return to them next chapter).

When I say 'purport' to do this, a key issue is that often exactly how this works is not entirely clear, including: what data is being fed in; whether there are fire walls between data given for different reasons and projects; how the algorithms are used to make determinations; how and when they trigger an automated response; and when human decision-making interacts with automated response. Customising these systems to particular contexts is also very expensive work—so much so, that Palantir have often not made a profit. Founded in 2003, its first profit-making quarter was reported in February of 2023 (Capoot, 2023). The phrase 'connect to real time decision-making', also rather glosses over what those decisions might be.

Further innovation appears on the cards. Palantir, for example, aim to 'take AI to the edge'. By that they mean—off the cloud and into machines such as drones or remote-sensors. Remember the cloud/edge distinction? The push for faster analytics, means trying to embed Artificial Intelligence at the level of the machines themselves so that analysis will link even faster to automated response. This, for example, could mean having the algorithms calculated in drones, planes, submarines and satellites who communicate directly with each other to process information and do calculations and make decisions faster than cloud computing would allow.

In the words of Palantir this innovation involves a '"cascading chaotic process that has to be standardised"—this sounds a little scary. Taking AI to 'the edge' also involves stripping it down so that it can work in low-code environments with things like battery energy sources that are not limitless, so not everything is possible at the edge, that is possible in 'the cloud', posing the question: what might go missing and will be able to evaluate how that affects the process? (see further Palentir Edge AI).

The future direction of CEWS, for better or worse, seems to involve, innovation in:

- Types of data collection tools and diverse types of data that can be incorporated
- The data science of prediction
- The ways of communicating that data back to end-users in ways that enable and support decision-making
- Creating connected automated data collection and decision-making, in ways that are deeply decentralised and happen between pairs of machines, using 'stripped back' Artificial Intelligence

9.10 Predicting Peace—Peace Early Warning Systems?

In conclusion, what about 'predicting peace'. It is striking how bad social scientists, peacebuilders and militaries are at this. Interestingly, they are often more doom and gloom than is warranted. There are no 'Peace Early Warning Systems', nor much talk of them, although Crisis Watch puts peace talks on its crisis map, and the United Nations Development Program (UNDP) 'Social Cohesion and Reconciliation Index' (2015), both arguably moving in this direction. Does it matter that we do not have PEWS, or are they just a nice idea but not necessary or useful? I think it matters.

If you are a civic actor in Yemen, it might be important to know what type of 'peace' might emerge, if Saudi Arabia negotiates secretly with Houthis, regarding the fate of your country and life? It might be important to a UN Resident Coordinator's job, to know if the country's landscape is going to change and he or she will suddenly be managing a peace process rather than a country office. It might be important to react quickly with forms of confidence-building measure when a ceasefire is called, or even help one on its way. But more than all that, it might be important to 'see' more clearly the projects of civicness in play, to understand the possibilities, constituencies and conditions that are conducive to change. Why do we map conflict events, but neglect mapping dialogue processes, or mediation efforts even after-the-fact when risk of damaging them is over, or even where peace processes are 'active', or might 'break out'?

Questions

1. Have you had an instinct in a situation of what would happen, that you can now examine and see was rooted in knowledge and rationality?
2. How much do you 'believe' CEWS can be effective?
3. Which use of CEWS, nowcasting, medium or long term, seems the most useful?
4. Why do we map conflict and create multiple CEWS, and not map peace dialogue, or have even one PEWS?

References[1]

Bressan, S. (2021, June 29). *Crisis early warning: Berlin's path from foresight to prevention.* PeaceLab Blog. https://peacelab.blog/2021/06/crisis-early-warning-berlins-path-from-foresight-to-prevention

Butcher, C., Goldsmith, B. E., Nanlohy, S., Sowmya, A., & Muchlinski, D. (2020). Introducing the Targeted Mass Killing Data Set for the Study and Forecasting of Mass Atrocities. *Journal of Conflict Resolution, 64*(7–8), 1524–1547. https://doi.org/10.1177/0022002719896405

Capoot, A. (2023, February 13). *Shares of Palantir pop as it reports first profitable quarter.* CNBC Online news article. https://www.cnbc.com/2023/02/13/palantir-q4-earnings-2022.html

[1] All last accessed 1 May 2023.

De Meyer, C., Franco, C., & Otto F. (2019). *Warning about war: Conflict, persuasion and foreign policy*. Cambridge University Press. https://www.cambridge.org/core/books/warning-about-war/2B8E3B55370AF392411BBDDD33DDD0B9

Defontaine, K. (2019, February 15). *Setting up early warning and response systems to prevent violent conflicts and save lives*. World Bank Blog. https://blogs.worldbank.org/dev4peace/setting-early-warning-and-response-systems-prevent-violent-conflicts-and-save-lives

Druet, D. (2021). *Enhancing the use of digital technology for integrated situational awareness and peacekeeping-intelligence*. Thematic Paper for the DPO Peacekeeping Technology Strategy. Not published. https://peacekeeping.un.org/sites/default/files/20210430_-_sa-pki_technologies_research_brief_final_clean.pdf

Hegre, H. (2022). Early-warning Systems for Political Violence: How Should We Define our Prediction Targets?, in *Taking Stock of Early Warning for Atrocity Prevention. Report from the 2021 Sudikoff Interdisciplinary Seminar on Genocide Prevention*. Washington, DC, United States Holocaust Memorial Museum (10–12).

Hegre, H., Allansson, M., Basedau, M., Colaresi, M., Croicu, M., Fjelde, H., Hoyles, F., Hultman, L., Högbladh, S., Jansen, R., Mouhleb, N., Muhammad, S. A., Nilsson, D., Nygård, H. M., Olafsdottir, G., Petrova, K., Randahl, D., Rød, E. G., Schneider, G., Von-Uexkull, N., & Vestby, J. (2019). ViEWS: A political violence early-warning system. *Journal of Peace Research, 56*(2), 155–174. https://doi.org/10.1177/0022343319823860

Mueller, H., & Rauh, C. (2018). Reading between the lines: Prediction of political violence using newspaper text. *American Political Science Review, 112*(2), 358–375. https://doi.org/10.1017/S0003055417000570

Mueller, H., & Rauh, C. (2022a). The hard problem of prediction for conflict prevention. *Journal of the European Economic Association, 20*(6), 2440–2467. https://doi.org/10.1093/jeea/jvac025

Mueller, H., & Rauh, C. (2022b). Using past violence and current news to predict changes in violence. *International Interactions, 48*(4), 579–596. https://doi.org/10.1080/03050629.2022.2063853

Muggah, R., & Whitlock, M. (2022). Reflections on the evolution of conflict early warning. *Stability: International Journal of Security and Development, 10*(1), 1–16. https://doi.org/10.5334/sta.857

Raleigh, C., Kishi, R., & Linke, A. (2023). Political instability patterns are obscured by conflict dataset scope conditions, sources, and coding choices. *Humanities and Social Science Communications, 10*(74), 1–17. https://doi.org/10.1057/s41599-023-01559-4

Sweijs, T., & Teer, J. (2022, February 21). *Practices, principles and promises of Conflict early warning systems*. The Hague Centre for Strategic Studies Report. https://hcss.nl/report/practices-principles-and-promises-of-conflict-early-warning-systems/

Waidyanatha, N. (2010). Towards a typology of integrated functional early warning systems. *International Journal of Critical Infrastructures, 6*(1), 31–51. https://doi.org/10.1504/IJCIS.2010.029575

CHAPTER 10

Peace and Space

Abstract Geographic Information Systems (GIS), geocoding and remote-sensing, are a second key digital innovation that offers systematic-scale transformation of both conflict and peace efforts. Satellites are one form of 'remote-sensing' (remember the fitness watch GPS?), and the images they produce comprises geo-spatial data, that can be part of a 'Geographic Information System' or GIS. This chapter examines the use of GIS, in conflict prevention and peacebuilding, focusing on the importance and challenges of 'mapping peace'.

Keywords Geographic Information Systems • Geocoding • Remote-sensing • Space

10.1 War and Peace

Then... In 1502 Leonardo Da Vinci was working as a military engineer, a job he took aged 30 and was to hold for 17 years. While we remember him as an artist-scientist, he considered himself skilled in the art of war and contributed multiple technical drawings of weapons. In the middle of a period of Italian Wars between 1499 and 1504, evolving around city-states, Da Vinci found himself in the Italian town of Imola with his boss at that time—Cesare Borgia a nobleman, cardinal and, after retirement, a

C. Bell, *PeaceTech: Digital Transformation to End Wars*,
https://doi.org/10.1007/978-3-031-38894-1_10

soldier for hire. Borgia had 'taken' Imola in a war campaign of 1499 along with the city of Forlí.

While in Imola, Da Vinci was tasked with helping Borgia learn more about the town's layout. He created his 'Plan of Imola'—a kind of bird's-eye map of the town, using cutting-edge of surveying techniques, and artistic imagination (all maps are 'representations'). It looks remarkably like a satellite photo, with a 3D effect, and compared with early aerial photos, is highly accurate. The map was significant, as it moved cartography forwards, and led to maps being viewed not just imaginative art, but as information. The plan of Imola can be viewed online, along with the many other birds eye view maps he was to go onto create, both because he was asked to and because he had ingenious engineering projects he wanted to explore. Videos also help explain the Imola Plan's genesis. Da Vinci's plan was an early example of 'WarTech'.

Now… Today, Planet Labs offer Dove 'satellites for peace'. Their name is interesting, as their website explains:

> In the aerospace industry, satellites are typically referred to as "birds". From the ground, it looks like they are flying across the sky as they travel along their orbits. There's also a tendency in the aerospace industry to think of these satellites as birds of prey; satellite missions like FalconSat and Kestrel Eye bring to mind a circling hunter ready to swoop down and strike. Not so fun.

Dove's mission is,

> to utilize space to help life on Earth, and that attitude permeates everything we do. These are peace-bringing satellites, enabling commercial, humanitarian, and environmental applications at a scale that has never been attempted before. We call our satellites "Doves" so that the message is loud and clear. **Do good, foster peace, and take better care of our planet.** We're focusing on applications such as deforestation monitoring, disaster response, improvements in agriculture, the list goes on. (Emphasis in original)

This is a PeaceTech mission in the broadest sense, overlapping with development tech, humanitarian-tech and climatetech. Planet Labs' 'unique selling point' is that they launch millions of tiny satellites in groups they call 'flocks' into space. When I say tiny, the satellites measure around 10 x 10 by 30 centimetres—not much more than two volumes of the print version of this book put together. I first encountered this company in the

PeaceTech world, because Alex Lee, has created Vigil Monitor Ltd, which uses these satellites to address conflict atrocities (a form of 'early warning') has worked for a sister research project to ours, XCEPT, that focuses on cross-border conflict.

10.2 New Capacities

Images such as Da Vinci produced are now produced by satellite. Dove satellites indicate the ways in which satellite technology that was once hugely expensive and the preserve of militaries, governments and big business, is increasingly available to ordinary users (see further Card et al., 2015). A wide variety of open source platforms for earth data, and an active community of innovators who collaborate on its use for research purposes, now enable PeaceTech satellite use. Strata, for example, who we met last chapter, have built their platform using Google Earth images that are open source. The Strata partnership that includes a small dynamic Edinburgh-based company called Earth Bloxs provides a no-code way for educationalists and others to customise google spatial technology and build it into their interfaces. Incidentally, this is modularization in practice. Earth Blox' business model is one of engineering-as-assembling: it helps people to add satellite imagery to their practice as a module, by reducing the level of expertise needed to 'bolt it on'.

10.3 Embracing Failure: To Boldly Go

At the end of the last chapter, we explored Chandler's view of 'hactivism', as a marriage of experimental digital approaches to development tasks, and 'embracing failure' as regards larger-scale structural development interventions. Interestingly, Planet Labs came up with the idea for Dove satellites by an embracing failure approach to experimental design.

Satellites are normally fairly large and cost a lot of send up into space, and therefore developing and launching them is a high-risk venture financially. Planet Labs founders asked themselves—what if we sent up hundreds of tiny satellites? Then the failure of some would not affect the success of the overall coverage of the network as a whole. The company model is therefore to launch dozens of simple satellites into low orbit, in the knowledge that a percentage of failure can be weathered, with the network remains intact.

This 'low tech' approach to satellite aims to 'disrupt' traditional satellite provision, by providing an amended technology at a different scale of cost. As with other PeaceTech companies, Planet Labs has yet to make a profit, although its growth continues (see Planet Lab News). In a quirky aside, some of the Dove satellites are adorned with Star Trek artwork, in a partnership with the Roddenberry Foundation (of Star Trek creator Gene Roddenberry).

10.4 Geographical Information Systems, Geocoding, and Remote-Sensing

Geographic Information Systems (GIS), geocode and remote-Sensing, are a second key digital innovation that offers systematic-scale transformation of both conflict and peace efforts. Satellites are one form of 'remote-sensing' (remember the fitness watch GPS?), and the images they produce comprises geo-spatial data, that can be part of a 'Geographic Information System' or GIS.

A Geographical Information System is "a computer system that analyses and displays geographically referenced information. It uses data that is attached to a unique location." United States Geological Survey.

Data to do with place can be recorded as geocoded points or areas, so that they can be located with reference to each other, for example, on a map. Geocoding is assigning geographic coordinates to location data, and is not the same as mapping. A map is one of a number of visualizations of spatial data, albeit a common one. Geocoding can also combe data using AI. Google maps, for example, shows all addresses using both a map and a 'street view' obtained by photographing streets and locations. Its street view is produced not by satellite but by 'google street cars' and sometimes walkers with backpacks (!), that have special mobile cameras on the roofs and packs, that take 360 degree images. AI then helps overlay the photographs on top of each other, and blurs out car licence plate numbers and faces to create the street view image (on terminology see further, Farquhar, 2023). Although, as I view my house and car, I wonder when we consented?

As our opening story about Leonardo Da Vinci illustrated, the connection between war and geo-spatial data is strong and historical.

Contemporary conflict event-data is all geocode. We have already seen multiple uses of GIS in Early Warning Systems that often use maps to analyse where conflict is and point to conflict patterns. Is there a further capacity for GIS to support peace and transition processes, beyond alerting to conflict-renewal?

10.5 Space, Conflict and Peace

Let us digress a little. Conflict happens in real places. It seldom sprawls out evenly across countries and communities, but centres on areas that have people or important infrastructures or both. Like many forms of violence, wars map onto other social realities. They take place more in particular places: in borderland spaces between different communities; in poorer parts of the country; in areas in which minorities are present. These places reflect conditions of 'structural violence', that also have a spatial dimension. The Turing Institute initiative described last chapter, revolves around the idea of a link between war and 'big roads'.

The spaces of actual conflict sit alongside a more conceptual less 'plotable' space. For example, I lived in North Belfast in an area that was majority Nationalist or Catholic on half mile triangle of three roads that had seen over 25% of all the killings during the conflict. Kids played on the streets and did not leave their area because of an invisible 'sectarian geography' that meant they felt at risk if they entered a Protestant neighbourhood just a block away. Anderson has evocatively called identity groupings as 'imagined communities' because they involve communities of the mind, where differences between people are often created as much as real (Anderson, 1983). These imagined communities inhabit imagined spaces that create a physical geography that those who live in them are acutely aware of and must navigate.

Researchers, including ourselves, have argued that space requires more consideration in peace and conflict research. The ideas are useful for understanding the relevance to peace processes, pointing to the following ways in which 'space matters' to both war and attempts to produce civicness (Björkdahl & Buckley-Zistel, 2022).

People are involved in 'spatial practices' through which 'spaces are created, transformed, or dissolved in relation to peace and conflict'. In Colombia, for example, persistently across the conflict communities have tried to create 'zones of peace'. These are specific 'territories in which local communities have attempted to persuade armed actors to abide by certain rules to mitigate the effects of the armed conflict locally' (Idler et al., 2015, p. 1).

Spatial dynamics constitute particular spaces as significant. Peace processes and agreements often reconstitute what comprises 'the nation state', new international borders, new administrative districts, or federal regions, of even 'entities' (Bosnia Herzegovina!), with new interfaces and technologies. Conceptually, the disruption of peacebuilding sees the global, the local, the national and the transnational all blur; and space such as North-South, centre-periphery, also become important.

Stopping armed conflict involves combining logistics with maps. Ceasefires, for example, involve lines of control, buffer zones between armies, no-fly zones, areas from which withdrawal must happen. In Syria and Yemen, as already noted, often 'micro-confliction' local agreements attempt to create peace between communities, or to let humanitarian access through, navigating and creating realities such as check-points, that people must pass through. They can set up new ways of managing relationships in particular areas—check-points, airports, or borders.

While a space and peace research agenda is largely a future one, GIS, geocoding and visualizing that data is well developed with particular reference to conflict-events, and provides a basis for pursuing it using digital methods.

10.6 Geocoding

10.6.1 Conflict Data

Conflict patters and datasets are tracked spatially, and geocoding plays an important role in literally 'mapping' conflict patterns. ACLED and UCDP conflict event data is all geo-located in ways that mean it can be connected across datasets—we explore how we have connected this to peace agreements in the next Chap. 11.

However, while conflict events such as killing happen in actual point locations, conflict as a system is perhaps better thought of in terms of 'zones'—that is geographic areas. This involves a different type of mapping. In Ukraine, for example, multiple attempts have tried to 'map' in an ongoing way, zones of control as battle fronts advance and retract (see, PA-X Tracker Ukraine Interactive Map, for an example).

10.6.2 *Reporting*

Conflict and peace data, also can involve geo-located news, Twitter/X and other social media, or other forms of crowd-sourced reporting. Google has a source called GDELT, that geo-locates news stories—both the source of the story, and the location reported on, with coding relating to conflict and peace events, and sentiment (whether positive or negative) (see further, Gardner & Bell, 2022). Other forms of social media, and crowd-sourcing have techniques of geolocation although there are also ways of evading it.

10.6.3 *Geocoding Spatial Imagery*

Satellites and other remote-sensors geocode data, and are important to early warning mechanisms and 'post-hoc accountability' mechanisms, as we have seen. With the increase of climate change and increased concern to be able to track its conflict-impacts, satellite imagery can often map both, as our story of Nick at the start of the book, and Strata earlier illustrated.

However, satellites are not the only things that capture images from 'space'. Drones can also be involved, or even tethered balloons with arrays of cameras. We tend to think of these as WarTech, but they can be attached to peacebuilding—modular-style. In 2017, for example, UNICEF launched an initial drone corridor for what it and UN Peacekeeping prefer to call 'Unarmed Arial Vehicles' or UAVs—to distinguish what modularizing for war turns the drone into! The corridor was to test their humanitarian and developmental use, with a particular focus on their ability to deliver vaccines in Africa's Malawi (UNICEF, 2017). The UN humanitarian agencies and international organisations are searching for more ways to mount 'good' drones, and along with tethered balloons with cameras, they now play a role in giving Peacekeeping forces a new form of surveillance and with it a new 'intelligence' capacity. Drones or UAVs, have been used by peacekeeping operations in Democratic Republic of Congo (DRC), Mali and Central African Republic—all situations of hugely fragmented national conflict (UNICEF, Office of Innovation).

10.6.4 Geo-coding Peace?

Much less explored is how we might geo-code ‘peace’. This is something we have been thinking about, and tried. In a sense, the geo-coding of Covid 19 ceasefires described in our Tracker, was an attempt to geo-code peace.

We have also produced a map of our peace agreement data, which shows what peace agreements are in particular countries, and also reveals regional patterns in their content (Visualising Peace: Time and Space). The map lets you also explore the relationship between space and time—a concertina button enables the viewing of peace agreement and issue geography over time.

A second example, where we have ‘mapped’ peace, involves Ukraine. Here we produced a ‘map of maps’ that would layer different type of conflict event data, but also data about location of say—nuclear or other power plants, that seemed particularly to be targeted by Russian attacks, or were the location of fighting that posed substantial risk of catastrophe.

On this map we also mapped types of dialogue or mediation. We collaborated again with the EHT Zurich to use data they had collected in the first few months of the war, on attempts to negotiate ‘humanitarian corridors’. We represented the corridor mediations as arrows between beginning and end points on the map. It was more difficult technically, to plot and represent the *actual* route of the corridor. The exercise also made us realise that it would also have been useful to collect more information about the ‘type of route’ involved in the corridor—whether a road or a railway route, or other.

However, this mapping, arising as it did at a point where no mediated peace process seemed desirable or possible, visually illustrates just how much micro mediation was in fact ongoing. It provides a surprisingly ‘alternative’ story to the ‘no negotiations’ story that is told about the interstate conflict as a whole. We have produced new analytical research, that explores whether ‘islands of peace’, might be a strategy for unwinding aspects of the conflict, in an ongoing context in which immediate resolution seems unlikely, including an assessment of risks (Wittke, 2023).

Other deals, have a less easy way of pointing to the ‘to’ and the ‘from’. For example, a grain deal in Ukraine focused on how the 10% of the world’s grain that comes from Ukraine might get out through ports, to the countries that depend on it. What is the geolocation of this agreement? It is in a sense from Ukraine to the rest of the world. In practice, however, it had to transit through Ukraine's neighbours. The deal soon was opposed by Poland and Hungary as countries who found that transit regime set up by the grain deal led to large amounts of grain arriving in their countries and stayed there, to the determinant of their farmers. These objections have required further 'deals' to address, not least because they threated the EU consensus on support to Ukraine (Greenall, 2023).

In a move from 'geolocation', we are now attempting to map dialogues in both Ukraine and in Myanmar, using actor-network mapping. In both places 'grand bargain' negotiations with militaries seem undesirable and impossible for civilians, but multiple forms of dialogue between different permutations of armed and civic actors exist. This initiative responds to a view of peacebuilding that tries to work with the 'double disruption' dynamics, and views conflict as a system that needs to be unwound piece-by-piece, by understanding the 'peace systems' that focus on particular pieces of the conflict.

Our peace agreement data, as we will see next chapter, also includes a collection of 'local agreements'. These also pose challenges for map representation because the agreements do not exist in a 'point', but establish peace in an area. Our analytical research has identified three different types of areas that different local agreements deal with and also 'create':

- borderlands between communities
- 'peace roads' that enable security for those who are travelling through, and
- forms of 'peace zone', such as cities, towns or villages, where armed actors and civilians come to a local political settlement

How should these areas be represented on a map? Some of the edges say of a peace zone or borderland may be as much conceptual as much as actual, and deciding on the relevant zone may also mean deciding what the agreement was 'about' in ways that impose an a-contextual meaning on it. So when does mapping create and reinforce zones, rather than just reflect them? As Thrift writes,

> space formations such as borders, territories, battlefields, or buffer zones are produced by the practices of agents with particular agendas in mind. They are the outcome of a series of highly problematic temporary settlements that divide and connect things up into different kinds of collectives which are slowly provided with the means which render them durable and sustainable. (2003, p. 95)

All mapping involves choices of this complicated sort. Some choices are born of the difficulty of mapping a three dimensional world on a two dimensional page. The choices also have political import (for example, historically maps of the world have shown colonial countries as many times bigger than the countries they colonised when they were much smaller). The problems of geo-locating peace have possible solutions. We have researched the types of tools and standardised codes that can be used to map countries, administrative regions within them, and even polygons in which local agreements might operate (see Farquhar, 2023). However, which one is 'best' might depend on the end-user and their purpose in mapping. Ideally, the choice would be locally elaborated.

10.7 Risks of GIS

As Nick's story illustrated, GIS have distinctive risks, which are again due to the way they can be understood as modules that can be added not just to peacebuilding practices, or climate monitoring, but to practices of war.

Geo-locating people, or ceasefire zones, by mapping them, or mapping the movement of people, and even matters such as location of the Internet Service Providers that people use for PeaceTech, can all be used for war. We consider these risks and what to do with them in Chap. 13.

10.8 Conclusion

We began this chapter with the story of Da Vinci in 1502, and Dove satellites over five centuries later. One is a story of WarTech, and one a story of PeaceTech. But which is which?

We still revere Da Vinci as the epitome of the renaissance—a period associated with a civilising shift to art, culture and knowledge. We do not much see his drawings of complex killing machines, or think of the renaissance as also the age of the invention of gun powder. However, some suggest that Da Vinci perhaps travelled with Borgia merely to have a job and be able to produce art; they point out that the multiple drawings he did for weapons show uncharacteristic dysfunctionalities and could not have worked. They muse that perhaps these were the deliberate act of a secret pacifist.

As regards, Dove, we discussed earlier Elon Musk's SpaceX programme, and Starlink satellites (which have the Falcon and Kestrel names Planet Lab counterposes 'Dove' to). SpaceX, are now involved in a five year partnership with Planet Labs, to launch the miniature Dove satellites into space (Bradshaw, 2020). This has efficiencies for Dove, but sits uneasily with SpaceX's larger ambition being commercial flights to space—something that has huge negative environmental impacts. Relationships of philanthropy, business, war and peace, increasingly entangle in ways that make it difficult assess and predict their consequences.

Questions

1. What peace and conflict spaces can we map, and what ones can we not map?
2. What are the dangers of mapping?
3. Are you excited by the potential of satellite and other forms of aerial imagery for peace? If so, why? If not why not?

References[1]

Anderson, B. (1983). *Imagined communities: Reflections on the origin and spread of nationalism*. Verso.

Björkdahl, A., & Buckley-Zistel, S. (2022). Space for peace: A research agenda. *Journal of Intervention and Statebuilding, 16*(5), 659–676. https://doi.org/10.1080/17502977.2022.2131194

Bradshaw, T. (2020, June 9). Planet Labs to expand earth imaging as rocket-launch costs fall. *The Financial Times*, Online news article. https://www.ft.com/content/1070bb0e-4899-48b9-9321-c4571f74c8ac

Card, B. L., Raymond, N. A., & Baker, I. L. (2015). Conflict-related displaced population camps commonly visible in high-resolution satellite imagery.

Farquhar, A. (2023). *A primer on geocoding for peace and conflict studies*. [The Peace Analytics Series]. The Peace and Conflict Resolution Evidence Platform. https://peacerep.org/publication/geocoding-primer

Gardner, R., & Bell, C. (2022). *Global realignments: Understanding peace process interventions through news*. (PeaceRep Report: Global Transitions Series). PeaceRep: The Peace and Conflict Resolution Evidence Platform, University of Edinburgh, Edinburgh. https://peacerep.org/publication/global-realignments-peace-process-interventions-through-news/

[1] All last accessed 1 May 2023.

Greenall, R. (2023, April 17). *EU rejects Ukraine grain bans by Poland and Hungary*. BBC. Online News. https://www.bbc.co.uk/news/world-europe-65292698

Idler, A., Belén Garrido, M., & Mouly, C. (2015). Peace territories in Colombia: Comparing civil resistance in two war-torn communities. *Journal of Peacebuilding & Development, 10*(3), 1–15. https://doi.org/10.1080/15423166.2015.1082437

Thrift, N. (2003). Space: The fundamental stuff of geography. In S. L. Holloway, S. P. Rice, & G. Valentine (Eds.), *Key concepts in geography* (pp. 95–107). Sage.

UNICEF. (2017, June 29). *Africa's first humanitarian drone testing corridor launched in Malawi by Government and UNICEF*. Press Release. https://www.unicef.org/press-releases/africas-first-humanitarian-drone-testing-corridor-launched-malawi-government

Wittke, C. (2023). *Creating islands of agreement and civility' through humanitarian negotiations: A conflict management and disaster-mitigation strategy in Russia's war against Ukraine* (PeaceRep Report). Conflict and Civicness Research Group, London School of Economics. https://peacerep.org/publication/islands-of-agreement-conflict-management-russia-ukraine/

CHAPTER 11

Peace Analytics

Abstract This chapter examines data analytics for supporting peace and transition processes—what I term 'peace analytics'. It tells a story of our development of the PA-X Peace Agreement Database and a new Peace and Transition Process Tracker. The story illustrates issues of 'data-interoperability', data literacy and returns to the theme of how peace analytics can support 'adaptive' peace process support.

Keywords Adaptive peacebuilding • Peace analytics • Data interoperability • Dashboarding

11.1 Searching for Political Imagination

In Northern Ireland, during the conflict and as the peace process emerged I worked, with others, to support human rights issues being addressed in the agreement. As a 'multi-hatter' I was also involved in a 'Women into Politics' programme in Northern Ireland, aimed at supporting women in all political parties to engage in the peace process, and to form a women's party if they wanted (they did, and did!). This programme operated in women's centres across the country.

With the arrival of the peace process, we wondered how the peace process should and could improve human rights, equality and inclusion. Many

C. Bell, *PeaceTech: Digital Transformation to End Wars*,
https://doi.org/10.1007/978-3-031-38894-1_11

of the human rights issues had underpinned the conflict, or become part of how it was waged. The conflict lasted 30 years—at that point most of my life. We had a series of suggested reforms even during the conflict. But what could and should we expect to change 'all at once' if there was a peace process? How could human rights issues be leveraged into a mediation process that would assume a central focus on sovereignty issues, and what form of drafting would capture commitments in ways that could support effective implementation?

Instinctively I, and others, looked to see what people were doing in other peace processes. How had issues like police reform, removal of emergency law, or release of prisoners been addressed? When and how did human rights issues enter processes? What types of argument were persuasive? How had mediation design enabled those arguments to be made? When and how had women influenced a peace process? What had they asked for? How might that experience benefit women in Northern Ireland?

11.2 Emergent Peace Analytics

I began to look for information about other peace processes. Often Northern Irish scholars and activists looked to countries with historic or solidarity connections for comparison, such as to the Israel-Palestine conflict, or apartheid South Africa and to a lesser extent to Sri Lanka. Their processes often did not 'fit'. I looked to see if there were any other peace processes with peace agreements. To my surprise, I found a lot more than I expected, many of which I was only vaguely aware.

I collected peace agreements—increasingly obsessively! I worked to understand the conflicts and peace processes they grew from. These days were—amazingly—before the internet was fully part of our lives. To get agreement texts I wrote to both armed groups and governments. I was often surprised that they sent them in quick response—many were quite proud of the agreements they had negotiated. Other times I had visited the country to assist in mediation or met someone from it, and got hold of texts. In yet other contexts, pioneering individuals had made compilations of documents that were readily available in country, although hard to find abroad.

As the internet took off, some agreements appeared on the web only to disappear. I learnt to download upon finding, and worked to verify content. Some countries over time developed detailed web resources. The Israeli Ministry of Foreign Affairs, for example, put up all the Oslo Accords between Israel and the Palestinian Liberation Organization (PLO). Many are still there now, although reorganised and harder to find.

I began to develop a definition and list of peace agreements. I tried to stay neutral as to how long the agreement had lasted, or the form the agreement took as a 'treaty' or a signed text, or an interim constitution, or UN Security Council Resolution (which sometimes are modes of documenting agreement, Bell, 2006), provided it had been formally agreed. I also collected agreements regardless of whether they were successful or failed. My first 'census' was published in 2000 as an appendix to my first book 'Peace Agreements and Human Rights' (Bell, 2000).

11.3 PA-X Peace Agreement Database

Over-time this collection resulted in the PA-X Peace Agreements Database. This is a census of all peace and transition agreements from 1990 (when the Cold War ended and the contemporary practice largely began), to current day. It comprises over 2000 agreements found in 150 peace processes. A much different more expansive resource than that I initially contemplated and embarked on (see Bell & Badanjak, 2019)!

It includes agreements at all stage of a peace process classified into:

- ceasefire agreements
- pre-negotiation agreements that involve 'talks about talks'—who is going to come to the table, with what status, what agenda, and what pre-conditions met
- partial framework agreements, that address multiple issues but do not purport to be a final agreement
- comprehensive agreements, that purport to offer the main promises necessary to end the conflict
- implementation agreements, reworking agreements to include new actors or address new issues

Each is searchable by name, entity (where relevant), country, region, peace process, and stage. PA-X has over 250 searchable topics with extracts of the text, covering all the critical issues in peace negotiations. It enables both quantitative and qualitative research on actors and issues included. PA-X is best understood as a number of datasets, with a range of functions.

PA-X has a fully elaborated codebook and manual, and exists as a machine searchable corpus of texts (which enables machine learning—more on that later); and search results that can be exported as pdfs, or csv files of the topics included in a spreadsheet, or a timeline.

11.4 Peace Process Data

PA-X is not, however, just a database of agreements. I was interested, of course, in whether and how particular issues were included and the terms in which they were drafted. However, I was also interested in 'peace and transition processes': how mediation processes were designed, what parties were included at what stages, and how this shaped the issues deemed relevant to resolving the conflict. PA-X is best thought of as a peace and transition *process* database that enables peace processes to be traced and compared over time.

Agreements provide an important window into peace mediation trajectories and outcomes. They do not capture the sum total of what is important in a peace process, but they document the public commitments that the parties to the conflict made with a view to ending the conflict, at least for a moment of time. They therefore provide an interesting documentary trail that offers a basis for comparing peace processes, including what actors get to the negotiation table, and when, and how that influences the agendas for change adopted there.

As we visualized our data in process form –we began to be able to see and to communicate the long nature of peace processes as iterative. They moved forward and backwards, with new agreements re-shaping what had come before. This I suggest changed the mediation field. It helped researchers and practitioners to think about approaching negotiations, not as leading to a final agreement, but as ongoing complex processes of change over time (see eg Paffenholz, 2021). You can explore our 'messy' peace process interactive visualisation to see what the forwards and backwards movement of peace processes looks like (for an account of the process of production see, Bell et al., 2022).

Peace mediation trajectories globally, mirror ongoing implementation challenges in Northern Ireland. There an Agreement had been signed and included significant human rights and equality provisions. While we had seen it as an end-point in the conflict, we were soon taken aback in how difficult it was to get parties to stick to their promises and implement. It was interesting to compare to other peace processes, and see that an agreement is often the beginning of a new phase of negotiation, and even the peace process 'proper', rather than its end.

There were also other motivations for creating peace process data. I wanted to create a 'census' of peace agreement practice with capacity to trace processes over time, and produce descriptive statistics that would also enable multiple ways of using other data to track implementation.

Finally PA-X was driven also by trying to preserve an archive. If I had wanted these documents and found them difficult to collect and parse through, then others could benefit from my work. Plus, I cared about the documents surviving for history, as artefacts themselves.

11.5 PA-X Extension

Over time, we have created or incorporated other 'interoperable' datasets to build a broader picture of peace processes. Interoperability means that the data can be used together in ways that make sense. PA-X includes a 'gender database', that includes a 'deep dive' into gender provisions in peace agreements—this is the dataset that underpins the PeaceFem App described earlier. We also created PA-X Local, including agreements that refer to small geographic areas in broader armed conflicts, such as Atem was working on in Chap. 1.

We have linked an Amnesties, Conflict and Peace Agreement (ACPA) dataset, developed by Professor Louise Mallinder of Queens University of Belfast as part of PeaceRep. This is another 'process' dataset—amnesties are not events as they do not arrive in a single moment but are elaborated in processes that unfold through agreements and often legislation. By working to combine PA-X amnesty data with Louise's earlier amnesty project, and expanding it, we had a basis for a distinctive set of data and could couple data with a capacity to create a user-friendly interface for exploring it, and ensuring interoperability with the peace agreement data.

Amnesty data is important because amnesties remain controversial in peace mediation and often pose a stumbling block to agreement. Amnesty is often the price of reaching peace with armed actors, but forgiving and forgetting sells out victims and 'accountability' in ways that can undermine peace agreement implementation down the line. The amnesties data helps to move beyond assertions that amnesties are either all good or all bad, by illustrating the many options for their design and evolution over time. In so doing, it illustrates innovate ways to square the amnesty-accountability circle.

11.6 Data Interoperability

We have also worked to create interoperability with other datasets, that we either have partnered with, or have worked collaboratively in PeaceRep to develop. This includes: Constitute, a database of the world's Constitutions, a new International IDEA Database in Constitution-Building Processes in Conflict-Affected States, and detailed perceptions surveys that have been carried out in the field by local researchers in South Sudan, Syria and more recently Ukraine, that will be integrated with PA-X through a new Peace and Transition Process Tracker.

In the area of gender, we have created data interoperability with qualitative and quantitative data on implementation of gender commitments, to create the PeaceFem App as described in Chap. 7. We have also worked to create interoperability and a relationship between our agreements data and UCDP, Correlates of War, and ACLED conflict data. Again, these efforts to inform the development of the Peace and Transition Process Tracker described below.

11.7 Research and Development for Peace Analytics

Emergent peace analytics illustrate how research and development is driven in the field by collaboration between institutions involved in similar enterprises. Over time, others also became engaged in similar peace agreement collection efforts to our own, and other peace agreements collections emerged, for different purposes, with different parameters and ways of categorising and organization. USIP provided an early Peace Agreement Digital Collection, which survives as a 'library' in which some things are deposited and not others, around the same time as my census. UN Peacemaker—designed for mediators, started to publish agreements in the early 2000s, as part of a wider set of resources to support mediation. UCDP started collecting peace agreements that related to the conflicts and armed actors that it includes in its conflict data. This led to a collection that by 2021 had reached 375 agreements (Davies et al., 2022). The Kroc Institute for International Peace Studies, Peace Accord Matrix (PAM) at the University of Notre Dame, created data focused on the implementation of 34 'comprehensive agreements' over a ten year period. ETH Zurich, has recently released a ceasefire dataset, of lateral, verbal, written and non-implemented ceasefires from 1989 to 2021.

As these projects emerged, we worked to support these projects, sharing data and methodology, learning regarding modalities of creating interfaces, and often swapping agreement texts. In turn we benefited from how they developed their data, and reciprocal collaboration as their projects developed. Collaboration in the early days helped to bridge moments when the work was experimental and not always understood or supported. I remember once offering Stina Högbladh at UCDP a peace agreement she hadn't been able to find, and she said 'you know this is a little Christmas present for me'!

All of these projects have had close relationships with the mediation field of practice. It is worth noting that, like the deaths in conflict data described last chapter, each agreement dataset remains different in its purpose and scope, and therefore the scope of the collection, the classification and topic modelling approach are all different. Collectively the agreement collections have developed a 'state of the art' in how peace processes and agreements are traced and understood.

Collectively this work has built a foundation for data analytics in the peace building field, although none of us would have put it that way. Let me call it 'peace analytics'.

11.8 'Peace Analytics'

Peace Analytics is a third emergent area where there is ongoing digital innovation and capacity to produce impacts of scale across conflicts, in how peacebuilding is understood and supported. See the box below.

> **Data analytics:** The science of using raw data and computational analysis for use of discovery, communication and interpretation of patterns in the data, so as to inform about how real-world phenomenon operate in practice.
> **Peace analytics.** This use of data pertaining to peace and conflict related issues, for use of discovery, communication and interpretation of patterns in the data, so as to inform conflict resolution and peacebuilding practice.
> **Data.** 'Organised information' whether quantitative (numeric), qualitative, pictorial or text.

We have seen examples of peace analytics and relevant data in many examples in this book. For example, CEWS are data-driven, and increasingly integrate quantitative data with other forms of data. While CEWS focus on predicting and responding to conflict, peace analytics aim to support and resource peace and transition processes, although tasks and some of the data, intersect.

Peace analytics as it develops has some capacity to plug already-mentioned gaps, such as mapping peace or dialogue or civicness, and perhaps even predict its onset. However, challenges remain, as illustrated by our experience.

11.9 Challenges of Data Development

11.9.1 Software Choices

A key obstacle to developing a new dataset is finding the right software to use to produce it. The software is vital to how simple or hard the 'back end' of data input will be, and how user-friendly the front end will be. My earlier attempts at a database had been frustrated by using ready-made database programmes that tend to be the software installed on University computers, that did not quite 'fit' what we were trying design. They soon became difficult for people working with them to use in part because 'workarounds' to make them fit required training on systems that were not intuitive. I also very soon wanted to customise the data in ways existing software did not easily allow. My collection had massively grown to well over 1000 documents, and it was clear that direct topic-based access to the language of texts was very useful. As time progressed it felt much simpler to design a dedicated interface for coding agreements that staff could be more easily use and that would offer capacity to alter data structures or change one's mind over coding.

11.9.2 Staffing and Environment

A first breakthrough was finding the right team in University of Edinburgh's Information Services, to deliver a specially designed database with dedicated back-end and front end interfaces.

Soon, I needed to think about research staff skills. Both how to get the right skills, and also how to make laborious tasks more doable. I expanded my team to include a political scientist who was highly expert in quantitative analysis, Dr. Sanja Badanjak. This was transformative of the nature, ambition, scale and professionalism of the project. Sanja brought her own vision of what the database could be, came with a strong understanding of conflict data—and its constraints—and introduced me to terms such as 'data interoperability'. She created a system for relating country codes that link the data to nearly all the relevant conflict data (and wider), by using ISO country codes and the Gleditsch-Ward List of Independent States, that can account for things that ISO, being an official account of countries cannot (e.g., countries that no longer exist). This development meant that we could examine not just what was in peace agreements, but their implementation as measured by the effect on deaths in conflict, triangulated across three datasets UCDP, ACLED, and Correlates of War (which deals with civil wars and interstate wars). As noted earlier, these all have different thresholds of deaths, and have different methodology, which again need to be understood before using them.

Sanja's work meant that we could connect deaths in conflict to our data, and develop ways of standardise encoding data, and align with these datasets. She also brought a much more robust methodology to coding agreements and elaborating a code book.

We also continued to learn from other projects. For example, Constitute, the constitutions database had developed strong methodologies for ascribing text to topic. These included, an automated 'question-and-answer' function for enumerators of topic content to inquire about 'borderline' or unclear cases. A central decision-maker would respond with the decision recorded into an ongoing repository to inform consistent enumeration over time. We incorporated this design-feature into our database backend.

An amazing team of researchers also came on board, who engaged and co-developed how we defined and documented topics. The staff team developed topic definitions collaboratively, all suggesting modifications that would evolve a form of 'good practice'. At each point we would often need to modify our 'back end' and 'front end' interfaces for coding and enabling searching of data. Out of this process evolved quantitative innovations such as 'weighting' provisions quantitatively depending on whether they were purely rhetorical or made a clear commitment to change.

As our work has developed we have had to add skills and components: employing data engineers; and Visualizers. We have had to think how to architect and engineer our data into a more sustainable computing environment—for us using the Edinburgh Parallel Computing Centre (EPCC) supported by a new Edinburgh International Data Facility both with 'big data' capacity (EIDF). We have also tried to think about how we make what we have learned and done open source and reusable, by creating a curated data hub.

This has all involved also constant 're-training' and mutual learning, as we grapple with 'large-scale computing', CKAN platforms for curating data, data pipelines, data marts that coordinate different types of data in one database, and different ways in which databases can be created and maintained. As well as ethics, data protection, and security.

11.10 End-Users of Peace Analytics

We have always designed our peace process data with four main communities of end-users in mind, and all are active users of PA-X. We work in collaboration with these end-users in multiple ways, and many of the ideas of how to develop the data come from their articulation of needs and concerns.

Armed actors in conflict. These include both state security forces and non-state armed combatants, who seek to move to peace and want to know what a process looks like. They can often come from a position of little to no expert advice on peace process design because they are considering ending it for the first time. Providing a resource that armed actors can use is controversial. But if conflicts are not to continue forever, then they need to be brought to an end.

International organizations and mediators who are involved in negotiating conflicts. The idea of PA-X was that it would provide 'Peace Agreement Access' for mediators, to be able to draw on topic-based resources that they were encountering in negotiations, and also be able to look easily at regional or comparative examples.

Organizations focused on 'inclusion' in peace processes, in particular the inclusion of women. These can often be international non-governmental organizations—human rights groups, or peacebuilding organizations, who seek to try to ensure that people additional to those doing the fighting, get a chance to shape the peace agreement and the country's future.

Civil society actors in-country. These actors often seek to understand how they might shape the peace agreement, or work to secure its effective implementation.

Researchers. PA-X now supports most of the quantitative research on peace processes, as it provides a transparent and reliable basis of counting and quantifying peace agreement commitments over the duration of a peace process. This means that the research it supports now goes well beyond our own team. PA-X has enabled a new research capacity.

11.11 What Does 'Peace Analytics' Help Us to Do?

What use is this type of data—what type of support to peace processes does it enable?

Evidence-based innovation in peace process design and drafting. Our database is used frequently by mediators—of all different types—to understand how different issues in peace agreements are drafted, what is possible at what stage in a process, and what is at stake in the drafting. We have a set of 'Peace Agreements and…' publications that in part originated as response to mediator requests to understand how particular issues were dealt with in other contexts. Local peace mediators, and representatives of some of the protagonists of the conflict, also use the database, and call us up from the field. The database is not a set of drafts for cut-and-paste; it is more as being a 'tool for political imagination' illustrating how persistent issues in conflicts are resolved, in techniques that can be creatively repurposed and reused to work in a different context.

Development and monitoring of new norms addressing peace process inclusion. Since around 2000 the UN Security Council and international courts have increasingly produced new norms or 'laws' as to how peace agreements should deal with certain things. For example, UN Security Council Resolution 1325 of 2000, provided that women should be included in peace negotiations, and that peace agreements should reflect gender concerns. Early data helped provide the evidence base that issues relating to women were seldom included in peace agreements, and since that time the data has been used by the UN Secretary General to monitor implementation in annual reports.

What does PA-X tell us? Has anything changed? Yes! Sort of. Women and gendered issues such as sexual violence, are more likely to be included in comprehensive peace agreements since that norm was passed, particularly where the UN has been involved in the process (Bell & McNicholls, 2019). However, women are rarely present in pre-negotiation and ceasefire talks, or at the implementation negotiations, where pathways are set, or comprehensive peace agreements renegotiated. In Colombia, for example, significant gender elements were watered down in negotiations that took place after the peace agreement with the Revolutionary Armed Forces of Colombia (FARC) of 2016 failed to be passed in a referendum. This included negotiations directly between the FARC and Church leaders, as well as with the Colombian Government, that pushed back on gender rights, including some of the world's only peace agreement provisions addressing LGBTQ communities.

The UN Secretary General, who reviews the women, peace and security developments each year, responded to our data and analysis by recommending that new efforts take place to include women at *all stages* of a peace process (UN, 2015), and subsequent UN Security Council Resolutions have recommended that efforts for inclusion at early and late stages of peace processes take place (see eg., UN SC Resolutions 2242 (2015), and 2493 (2018)).

Supporting mediators, civil society, donors and international organizations, to understand that peace processes are dynamic and interactive and need long-term mediation support, rather than a once-off intervention burst at one moment. Our messy peace process visualization, and the data that underlies it has helped create a broader vista amongst international mediators, donor states and international organizations, of what a peace process is. It has shown the multiple iterations of peace that develop in multiple agreements over time. The peace agreement data provides important knowledge of context for people who often arrive in-field on short notice. But it also in a sense illustrates that a comprehensive agreement has had a 'before', and will have to have an 'after'—even if international actors are no longer present. Seeing things from a longer time perspective changes the ways in which people approach negotiation in the moment.

Understanding new dynamics and trends in conflict and peace, and supporting those involved in peace processes to adapt. More recently, our work has provided an evidence-base for understanding changes in patterns peace processes, and who mediate, that has helped paint a picture of what I have called the double disruption of peace processes that has come from shifting conflict patterns. This is now of central concern to a range of actors, and is underpinned by the clear evidentiary basis of our data and analysis, and resonates with those in the field. The data illustrates quantitatively, things that I described in Chap. 4, such as:

- comprehensive agreements are on the wane, and the UN is less involved in mediation over time
- interim transitional arrangements which contemplate social processes of reform are a prevailing modality for ending conflict, but go wrong all over the place for similar sorts of reasons
- we are now in an era of geopolitical competition over 'who mediates' in peace processes, which is part of a struggle to shape global order as codified in international legal norms
- many countries experience 'iterative transitions' against a background of fragmented conflict that is simply not amendable to a 'big elite deal, to establish a political settlement' that once characterized peace processes

This information has impacted on how mediators and international organization view contemporary conflict resolution challenges, and respond to them. It has also radically re-shaped our research agenda.

It is worth pointing out that all of the peace analytics efforts, have made similar tyes of contribution in different ways, related to their design. One of the most interesting is perhaps that of the Peace Accord Matrix (PAM). While developed across conflicts, the PAM team had members who were very trusted in the Colombian process. PAM was written into the Colombian peace agreement as a methodology that could be employed to monitor and support the peace agreement's implementation. The monitoring of whether agreement promises were kept, has been vital to the implementation process (see Colombia Barometer Initiative).

11.12 Where Next?

As we began to see in Chap. 10 on CEWS, there is an increasingly long list of data that can be understood as useful (or part of) to 'peace analytics'. As Richard Caplan points out, peace has no settled content, so we cannot easily measure whether it has been achieved (2021). Instead, he suggests, we have to consider what we might be a 'peace impact' and see if there is a way to measure that.

There are, however, data gaps. Relevant data does not always exist for conflict countries, or is not always reliable across case studies, or does not cover a long enough time period to capture a peace agreement implementation period. Data-matching is needed, and remains difficult. Nevertheless an expanding array of data for measuring peace impacts exists (see box below).

Composite data sets relevant to peace (that crunch many of the datasets below). For example, Global Peace Index.
'Institutional peace-related event' datasets. For example, NELDA Elections dataset, and COLPUS
Political indicators. For example, V-DEM Varieties of Democracy Data base.
Conflict and Security Indicators. For example ACLED, UCDP and Correlates of War, and SIPRI on issues like military expenditure.
Economic Indicators. For example, The Government Revenue Dataset, and Global Food Prices

The new disruption of peacebuilding efforts, and the unravelling of the global order that supported them, has re-shaped where peace analytics is beginning to go, and might go—including for ourselves.

11.13 Peace Analytics and Double Disruption

Concern to address changing conflict and peace dynamics has led us to work to develop a Peace and Transition Process Tracker—PA-X Tracker, to support innovation in how peace processes are designed, constructed, and implemented in a changed conflict context.

PA-X Tracker attempts to build a better picture of the types of new assembling and disassembling of actors for peace and for war unfolds, in ways that could support adaptive peacebuilding and the ongoing construction of 'multi-level' peace processes that appear needed for multi-level conflict systems. We want to do this in ways that are sustainable over time.

There is a tube station in the London Underground where when the train pulls in there is a dangerous gap between the train floor and the platform and famously a recorded voice warns 'Please mind the gap'. Covid dashboards illustrated the usefulness of minding gaps between areas with Covid infections, and where hospital beds, quantities of PVC masks and gloves, etc., were located.

Our project similarly aims to use Peace Analytics to suggest where to 'mind the gap' between peace agreement commitment and implementation. This could be the gap between promises made and actions unfolding, or between national and local perceptions of peace. We are therefore focusing on how to point to where processes are going well, and where gaps are opening up, that perhaps peacebuilding projects, including new forms of mediation, could bridge.

However, there are considerable issues that have had to be wrangled to take peace analytics in this direction, they include:

- Agreeing and defining what peace or 'peace impacts' are
- Finding appropriate data that is reliable and consistent in conflict settings, that might measure them
- Finding ways to bring different types of data together intelligently
- Localising data through new localised data collection, or finding ways to disaggregate it by area
- Connecting data findings to analysis

Our enterprise in a sense acknowledges that there is no settled meaning of peace—it is something that is constructed (remember Ken Bush and his knife). We therefore have created a Tracker with 'different ways of seeing' progress, across very different types of knowing and data. The interface has the following components, in this initial iteration at least.

A country timeline of formal institutional change. The timeline builds on earlier the 'process-oriented' data interoperability we set up to bring together automated timelines of peace agreements across all stages of the process, constitutions, elections, amnesties, and coups. We have capacity to add other events to customise timelines more contextually, but the event data provides for automated update. The timeline enables a more comprehensive political process tracking over time.

Peace agreement topic analysis linked to quantitative implementation data. A dashboard links agreements to a range of 'peace impact' indicators. We think the need in the field is not 'more' data, but 'less' with knowledge of interoperability and data limitations built into what is chosen. So we include only customised bundles of data that have time-periods and geographies that cover conflicts, and that we, and others in the field, trust and already use, such as those listed above, including deaths in conflict data across datasets. In countries where we have local researcher field teams, we add localised perception data.

Peace agreement qualitative implementation data. We have developed a natural language processing (NLP) methodology based on semantic similarity (see Gardner, 2023), to connect agreement text to where implementation of its key commitment are monitored in reports, to produce 'extracted' implementation data of a narrative type. For this, we need accurate implementation reports, which for some countries exist and for others do not, and we will have to source good quality consistent narrative information. The NLP tool is reusable for other tasks such as comparing how topics are treated in different drafts of agreements, topic modelling consultation responses in an automated way, and comparing peace agreement and constitutional content.

Actor Networks. Showing who has signed agreements, what third parties were involved, connecting this data to group dynamics within country. The work has involved using named actor entity recognition techniques to create dictionaries of armed groups (Henry, 2023). We are working to extend this type of visualization to 'mapping peace dialogues' and examining 'islands of agreement', and trace the connections between them.

We aim not for a 'measurement' of peace, but to paint a picture of—what is going well, what is going badly, and where indicators sit together 'oddly'. The intention is to support deliberation by actors in the field as to: is this real or an artefact of data collection efforts; why might the picture be mixed; what does it mean, and how should it be addressed?

11.14 Conclusion

Like Monet's Cathedral At Rouen series of paintings, or more obviously the wonderful Atlas of Economic Complexity that has served as inspiration, the Peace and Transition Process Tracker is designed to show things from multiple perspectives, all of which give a slightly different view. It aims to support peace process design and implementation in an era of peacebuilding disruption, by providing different ways of understanding and evaluating 'progress' in outcomes and processes that relate to peace. It is designed to encourage questioning and deliberation rather than to offer a straightforward statistical assessment of progress.

Questions

1. What types of data do you think are useful to peacebuilders?
2. What would make it more usable to a range of people?
3. What more data of what type could be helpful?

References[1]

Bell, C. (2000). *Peace agreements and human rights.* Oxford University Press.

Bell, C. (2006). Peace agreements: Their nature and legal status. *The American Journal of International Law, 100*(2), 373–412. http://www.jstor.org/stable/3651152

Bell, C., Bach, B., & Kauer, T. (2022). Ways of seeing: Peace process data-viz as a research practice. *Convergence, 28*(1), 150–169. https://doi.org/10.1177/13548565211050748

Bell, C., & Badanjak, S. (2019). Introducing PA-X: A new peace agreement database and dataset. *Journal of Peace Research, 56*(3), 452–466. https://doi.org/10.1177/0022343318819123

Bell, C., & McNicholl, K. (2019). Principled pragmatism and the 'InclusionProject': Implementing a gender perspective in peace agreements. *Feminists @ Law, 9*(1). https://journals.kent.ac.uk/index.php/feministsatlaw/issue/view/38

Caplan, R. (2021). *Measuring peace: Principals, practices, politics.* Oxford University Press. https://global.oup.com/academic/product/measuring-peace-9780198867708?cc=gb&lang=en&

Davies, S., Pettersson, T., & Öberg, M. (2022). Organized violence 1989–2021 and drone warfare. *Journal of Peace Research, 59*(4), 593–610. https://doi.org/10.1177/00223433221108428

Gardner, R. (2023). *Report on semantic analysis.* PeaceRep: The Peace and Conflict Resolution Evidence Platform, University of Edinburgh. (Forthcoming).

Henry, N. (2023). *Named actor recognition.* The Peace and Conflict Resolution Evidence Platform. (Forthcoming).

Paffenholz, T. (2021). Perpetual peacebuilding: A new paradigm to move beyond the linearity of liberal peacebuilding. *Journal of Intervention and Statebuilding, 15*(3), 367–385. https://www.tandfonline.com/doi/full/10.1080/17502977.2021.1925423

UN. (2015, September 16). *Report of the Secretary-General on women and peace and security.* S/2015/716. https://reliefweb.int/report/world/report-secretary-general-women-and-peace-and-security-s2015716

[1] All last accessed 1 May 2023.

PART III

PeaceTech Challenges

CHAPTER 12

Doing PeaceTech

Abstract PeaceTech reports seldom describe the practical trials of mounting a project. Yet those who reflect on the field suggest that the transformative or disruptive potential of PeaceTech lies less in the attempt to use technology and more in the curious and unpredictable ways that PeaceTech 'doing' modifies peacebuilding as a political practice. The chapter therefore offers lessons from doing.

Keywords failure • innovation • end-users • software choices • digital capacity

12.1 Learning Through Doing

When we began our work in the PeaceTech field, it was with a sense that everything was doable. It was a matter of bringing the right capacities to bear on the right problems.

Then, as I have described, we discovered lots of challenges. Getting things done seemed really hard. It often took longer than we thought, and more commitment. We discovered lots of wonderful people and good practice. But also some frequent issues. Tech wizards offered us unlimited potential, then started to hum and ha, and did not deliver. Businesses who we assumed would cost, plan and deliver work to clear specifications better

C. Bell, *PeaceTech: Digital Transformation to End Wars*,
https://doi.org/10.1007/978-3-031-38894-1_12

than our informal in-University collaborations—did not. They often wanted money up front, made no commitment to joint planning, and came back with outputs that only half worked. We encountered both innovative new start-ups who could not deliver what they promised, and established businesses who somehow could not work in straightforward planning processes. (And of course we also discovered lots of wonderful people and good practice!)

To be honest, it sometimes felt as if perhaps we were not 'doing things right'. Our work risked all turning into experimentation without clear result. We seemed to have entered a business world of smoke, mirrors, and potentially unpredictable and therefore unmanageable costs.

Over time, we have reflected and talked to others in the digital transformation and PeaceTech field, commissioned papers to inform our PeaceTech work, taken digital transformation courses, swapped notes with the most similar data projects, and watched some massive digital transformation failures in our own wider University environment (sighs). It seems the problems we encountered are in fact common.

Many of these PeaceTech problems have been touched on in other chapters. However, it seems useful to draw together lessons and choices.

12.2 Why Digital Transformations Fail

There are masses of business blogs, reports and academic articles dedicated to 'why digital transformations fail'. The lists that emerge are very similar, and interestingly, few reasons relate to the technology. Broadly, they include the following:

- **Transforming on the hoof.** Not having a clear vision of what you want to achieve in terms of sustainable business outcomes.
- **Not being able to take the range of stakeholders on the journey.** Whether those who pay for things in the business, those who must engage with the technology in your own organisation, or your end-users of the business or 'customers', leaving any behind spells failure.
- **Difficulty in appropriately staffing projects.** Often teams must change, to add the right tech skills, held by people you can talk to and understand, who stay with the project long-enough to give to continuity of delivery. Or with the right researchers, project managers and peacebuilders, to bridge between tech language and capacities, and what 'peacebuilders want to do'.

- **Getting long-term funding and commitment to the digital transformation efforts.** Production will involve 'invisible work' that is costly in time and money, particularly at the beginning. Longer-term you need to be able to sustain work, when the 'shiny' first iteration that the funder has already taken credit for is no longer good enough.
- **Not thinking tactically about technological tools** and capacities across the organization you work for, and of the end-users you work with.

In our particular 'peace and conflict field', we encountered challenges similar to these, in ways that were specific to the peace and conflict field. These often intersected with ethical and moral challenges, which will be dealt with next chapter.

You may encounter others problems, but what follows is an account of 'what I wish I had known'.

12.3 When to Do Something

Let's start with the positive: it is good to commit to innovation where things are not working.

The key commitment that drives PeaceTech is a commitment to innovation. Innovation works best when it responds to a problem. Understanding that there might be a technological solution, however, also requires being someone that is a bit interested in exploring innovative ways to solve problems and making some time commitment to understand technological advances and what they offer.

I became committed to digital innovation that led to the PA-X Tracker for the following quite simple reasons.

First, I have always been frustrated with how much we (researchers) replicate data efforts, in particular in the peace and conflict field, without considering what we might get from creating better ways to combine data. As some of my stories illustrated, data initiatives sometimes move forward in overlapping ways in different organisations. Forms of replication can be useful, even if it looks a bit chaotic. However, I was and remain convinced that as researchers and practitioners we could do much better in bringing data together in intelligent ways, to better support practice.

Digital developments such as APIs, i-framing visualizations into multiple websites, and using tools for collaboration, now offer forms of collaboration that make it easier to cooperate and connect data across institutions, without people having to give up institutional ownership of data and products. This is important because most data projects need ongoing institutional homes and support, meaning that ownership matters. Most big digital developments in the wider words, such as 3G to 4G to 5G mobile networks have come about not just due to better cabling, but about because protocols for sharing networks and collaboration and connectivity were created.

Second, conflict and capacities to mediate ends to it are indeed changing—for the worse. Given that diverse data now exists in good quality and can support what I have called 'Peace Analytics', it seemed useful to try to bring that data to bear on the types of agile and adaptive decision-making that those seeking to end conflict must make to address multilevel conflicts that operate as a complex system.

Third, as our own data collection efforts grew and our PA-X Peace Agreement data was more widely used, we garnered a range of quite different 'customers' or end-users for our data. This drove further innovation because it seemed useful to develop a range of ways for different types of people to enter the data and use it. This also built the reach of the large-scale work we had already invested in.

Our current drive to produce Peace and Transition Process Trackers, is tied up with these same impulses. But the larger point is—that the innovations all grew from a perceived need.

12.4 Shiny—Beware!

If you are a person who is attracted to digital innovation—and, strangely for someone so technically challenged, I am (!)—there is a tremendous seduction about the digital world. There can seem to be a million racy projects and a boat that is leaving without you on it. Also the potential seems really limitless. Everything can always go bigger and better, more comprehensive, multi-multi-functional.

I often thought that we could bring data together, or create visualizations or new technological ways of working, and then 'see what we could do' with it. Could we see new things? Get new insights? Have a whole new way of working that revealed incredible new research findings?

But that does not work. It doesn't work because in any digital or data innovation project you make a lot of decisions that could be made lots of different ways. It is impossible to make these decisions in any sort of consistent or coherent way, if you do not know why you are doing what you are doing.

This point may seem obvious. But there is something about the scale of potential of tech solutions and just how shiny they appear, that draws people into experimentation without purpose.

There may be reasons to experiment—if you are doing tech just to learn how to do tech, that is fine if you are honest about it, but even then you will have learning outcomes to drive your decisions. I am also all for exploration as creative enterprise, and in fact we have used 'visualization as exploration' as a research methodology in our work (See Bell, Bach and Kauer, 2022). But we still had a sense of 'why', that drove how we went about things.

If the why is clearly specified, it is worth also being somewhat agnostic as to whether tech is the answer. Rather than saying 'I want to create an App to support peace agreement implementation', it can be useful to be agnostic about the tool. 'I want to support peace agreement implementation.' This then involves a series of prior inquiries. What do we think amounts to peace agreement implementation? Where is it going wrong? What can be done about it?

At that point you can consider where technological solutions might solve particular problems such as: wouldn't it be great if instead of people in field missions all going individually to the same sources to manually put together very similar reports on 'how things are going', there could be a website that had this data in easy to 'visualise and grab' ways. Technology will only ever be a piece of the solution.

12.5 Scope Versus Usability

We also discovered a trade-off between the scope of a PeaceTech application and its usability. The story of 'doing one thing' in the Ceasefires tracker and PeaceFem App, reflects the advantages of limiting scope to one clear purpose. In Chap. 7, what I called PeaceTech Hacks—innovations that help with one task, were illustrated as a key way that PeaceTech has worked well.

This is a 'washing machine' lesson. New washing machines have 50 or more different wash-programmes, when one only really ever uses a maximum of four. These machines can take reading a 60-page manual for several hours to figure out how to use those four. If they just had four programmes it would be easier for most users.

It can be quite tempting at a design stage, to have your data or tech tool do all the things it could possibly do, in customisable ways. But this often takes it beyond what most users will want to do simply, and means it is only usable by the 'especially dedicated end-user'. And the timescales of production extend and extend. We often found levels of debate and constructive tension with our visualizers because we wanted to limit interactivity to a few features, rather than enable people to explore 'everything' from one interface.

Scope/usability trade-offs also exist with regards to data. In our Peace and Transition Process Tracker, which attempts to respond to double disruption, we think the challenge is not to create the 'ultimate tracker' with all possible data and complex algorithms, such as CEWS attempt. We think the problem is not 'more data', but 'less'. The PA-X Tracker aims to provide better access and connectedness to the data people already use and trust, in ways that better connect to the questions peacebuilders are asking in a process.

Doing one thing well, however, is not the same as 'once-off' PeaceTech design. The PA-X Tracker comes from a wider data collection effort that has a long hinterland and integrity. It repurposed data-interface design from the Amnesty database, and in turn has been repurposed for parts of our new Peace and Transition Process Tracker.

12.6 Know and Collaborate With 'End-Users'

'Know and collaborate with end-users, is the peace and conflict specific exhortation to 'know your customer and bring them on the journey'. Peacebuilders and researchers often do not think of end-users as customers because we try not to have products to 'sell' and the culture of 'partnership' predominates, rhetorically at least. But, like a business we want what we work on to be useful and used, and for this to happen PeaceTech innovations have to add value to the peacebuilding world. Our funders also expect this, and they—by the way—are second level 'customers' who look at download figures, and monitor and evaluate how well a PeaceTech innovation works and what value it has added (as compared to the money it cost). So, even not-for-profit PeaceTech experiments must respond to questions of 'value' and 'usability'.

We have already mentioned being specific about who you think the end-users are, and what they want to do. Different peacebuilders will have different needs and capacities to use technology. For example, international peacebuilders and local peacebuilders often have quite different agendas for change and ways of working and different levels of digital inclusion. The same tool might not work for both. Others will have different capacities due to things such as the bandwidth available to them, access to a computer, etc. The PeaceFem App, for example, is targeted on a very specific audience of women peacemakers and mediators, and in particular those in the Middle East, and designed to be low bandwidth.

At the design moment, it can be useful to try to describe the end-user and task the application is intended to help very specifically, for example, End-user: 'the person who arrives in a country field-team without much warning and has better knowledge than the lay person, but does not have the detail of the past peace process at their fingertips'. And Task: 'This person wants to be able to quickly access past peace agreements and get a sense of the main issues they covered, with capacity to open the whole document easily if they want.'

12.7 Making Good Tech Choices

The exhortation to 'make good tech choices' looks like a different version of 'shiny—beware'. But it is less an exhortation not to jump to tech solutions, than to make sure that the choice of tech is appropriate to the context and need. Remember PayPal advice: use technologies your customers already use. I would add: and remember if you are actually walking into a shop, cash can often be faster and easier (although PayPal I am sure might disagree). Making good choices requires asking, and even researching, what Tech people already use? Does it raise security issues that they may need to think about more? What band-width do they operate in? Who has capacities to use what?

'If you have a hammer, everything looks like a nail.' This phrase captures the idea that often our use of digital tools is 'supply driven' rather than 'demand driven', in ways that lead us to perhaps do silly and even unhelpful things (like hit something inappropriate on the head). Given that peacebuilding itself is criticised for being too 'supply-driven', replicating this problem in PeaceTech is to be avoided.

Critical Choices. We often faced choices relating to the tech tools we used. Sometimes the range of possible tools was overwhelming. Sometimes none of it seemed quite right and we faced whether to work with existing software and tools, or design our own. Low-code, or existing software can often make something quickly doable, sufficient to get 'up and running'. It can be used by a range of staff without technical expertise, and has often had a lot of time and thought go into making the output look good. It can be good value (or already on your computer), and efficient because you are using a tool rather than inventing one. But sometimes it is just not the right thing, and all the workarounds will become cumbersome.

For what it is worth, we have found that starting with low-code experiments, with software that you have skills to use is a really good way to consider what you are trying to do and what is possible. Over time, you may need to customise or invent. As described with our ceasefire tracker, we used Knight Lab's timeline tool initially in a no-code form. But when we wanted to design a bilingual timeline in both Arabic and English for Yemen, and those languages were read from right to left for the former, and left to right for the latter, we found it useful to design our own timeline (Yemen Timeline).

We have become less afraid to try to build our own customization when low-code tools start being restrictive. Sometimes this can mean jumping into the 'coding' version of a tool to modify it, and sometimes it has meant creating our own visualization completely. Creating our own visualization, also has the advantage that we can leave behind the code for what we did in open source way that is hopefully more useful to others in the peacebuilding field, than what is already out there—if we have found that to be limited for some peacebuilding purposes—such as bilingualism. We hope that this way we can contribute to creating a new research capacity, as well as new research. But we started 'low' or even 'no' code.

12.8 Building Digital Team Capacity

The right team capacities are needed at three levels. First, 'domain expert' capacity in our case that know the peacebuilding field, and then the right 'technical expert' capacities to deliver what you think will respond.

There is additionally a really important middle bit: you need 'creative translators' to think about how to connect problem and any proposed tech solution, who can bridge the 'domain expert / technical expert divide (see Fig. 12.1). Often 'bridgers' will have to be people that are domain experts, but have some digital leadership dimension. We have been really lucky on our team to have such people, and we have also worked to expand existing staff skills and think about the skills we need as we work. For smaller organisations, what I have called 'PeaceTech Enablers', such as Build Up, may be really vital partners to act as this connective tissue, while transferring skills.

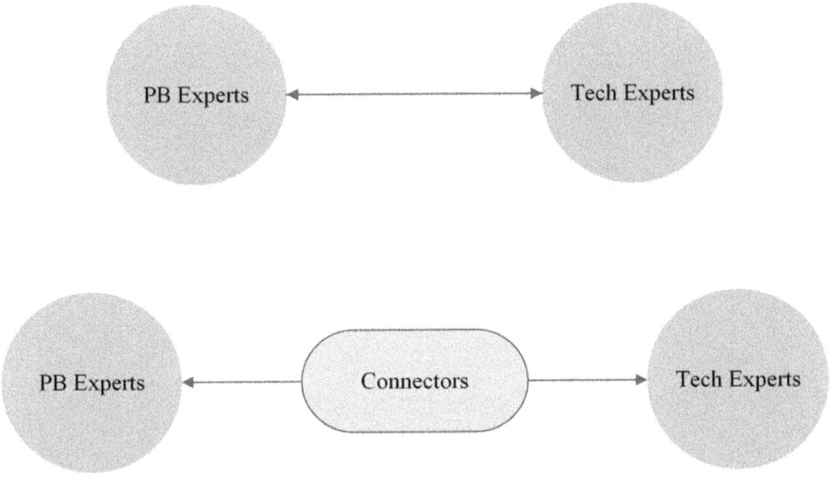

Fig. 12.1 Connecting Experts

Specific skills are needed for the bridgers who connect. In particular, having people who can write a technical specification that addresses the peacebuilding need is very important. So also is capacity to test prototypes and translate modifications into further clear specifications for improvement.

In the peacebuilding field, however, you are likely to need to connect groups who have different types of expertise at each end. You are likely to need a range of expertese and skills: peacebuilder practitioner skills, peace and conflict researcher skills, conflict and peace data knowledge and skills. Over time you may also need a larger range of technical skills: people who can install your data on a large scale computer, access to that large-scale computer or data storage facility, data engineers, database designers and visualizers, security advisors capable of evaluating whether the cybersecurity offered is sufficient in your conflict context and risks (see Fig. 12.2). How do you access this expertise?

Critical Choices. There is a choice here between whether **to stay in-house, or go 'out'.** That is, do you recruit someone onto your team with skills or build up the skills of a team member, or 'contract out' support to a partner, consultant or company? The choice will be shaped by budget,

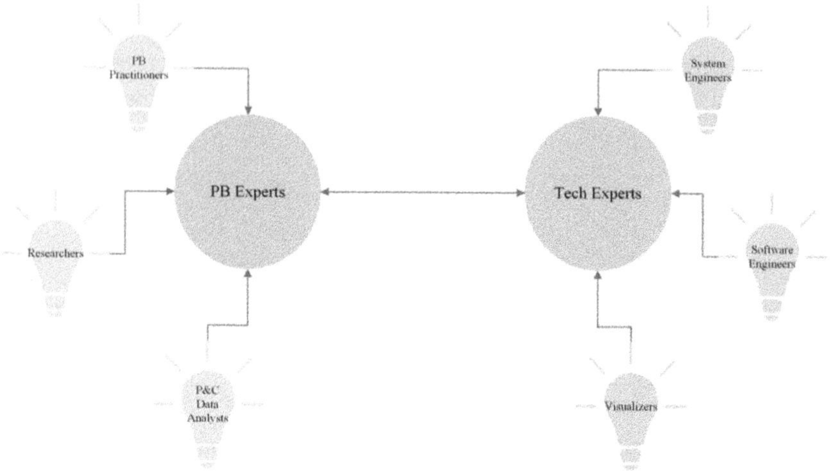

Fig. 12.2 Expert Clusters

and human resource and contracting matters. However, beyond those constraints, for us it often felt quite difficult to know which choice was 'best'.

We worked flexibly doing what seemed best sometimes in the moment, but looking also a little down the road. Both types of arrangement worked. What seemed important, however, was to create working relationships whether inhouse or outhouse, through forms partnership, business relationship, or other, to enable 'iterative design' and an ongoing processes of collaboration. This approach partly reflects that we find we are never just 'commissioning' a piece of technical work, but rather we need to engage in co-creation across tech and subject-matter experts. So we need a commitment from technical experts to that process. We can get this from relationships with business providers, but it does not work for us to fit within traditional business models of either 'buying a job', or 'Servitization'. More on that later.

In all peacebuilding expert to tech expert relationships, the most important ingredient to the relationship working is capacity to communicate across very different languages and forms of expertise. It may sound obvious, but again sometimes digital innovation seems as if you should have to take things on trust, as to technical to be able to be simply explained. I now tend to assume that if the technical experts cannot explain to me what they are doing using language and concepts I can understand or learn, and cannot commit to design as process, or I do not commit in the same way, then the project is not going to work.

12.9 Sustainability in All Decisions

So many PeaceTech initiatives have not been sustainable, although interesting pockets of innovation may have been usefully incubated on the journey. But if you value your project it is really important to think about sustainability in a number of ways.

Think in advance about what is logical to sustain. Some tasks we are engaged in have logical end-points from their start: e.g., the 'Ceasefires in a time of Covid-19' App, or our 'local agreements' data because we know that an ongoing census will be impossible. In others, we have had to consider: is our data collection effort undermined by thinking of this project as finite because funding will be finite?

Sometimes the answer is 'no'. The PeaceFem App, decision to focus on 'significant' examples, rather than all examples, was in part a sustainability choice, because it means the App remains useful and valid, even if every new gender provision is not added.

Work within frameworks that are not disproportionately costly. If you have created something that you want to sustain you need to think how it will be paid for into the future. Ambitions of scale need to be tempered. Or sometimes, you can work out digital ways to automate tasks at lower cost in sustainable ways, and work on those as part of the initiative. Questions of cost also involve thinking about the tech relationships you get into before commit to them in ways that are difficult to switch from.

Engage with 'Servitization'. I am not sure what the answer is, but servitization is a problem for sustainability. For Tech providers it is often their business model. Where you want to purchase a piece of work, providers will want to create a service relationship. However, if you end up with multiple service relationships you will have multiple rolling costs, that can suddenly add up to amounts that stop the project from being sustainable.

It can also be really difficult to be sure exactly what the 'service' servitization provides. We talked to related databases about whether they did their database design and storage in-house or not. Unlike us their database designers were external providers. The business charged for ongoing storage and all that goes with that. However, the company often announced they an update had created a new security risk in their system and then produced additional bills for fixing them. Our colleagues complained—'it sometimes feels like they break a window and then charge us to fix it.' I know the feeling.

Entering a servitization model makes co-creation and iterative design very difficult. So you may need to talk all that through and negotiate a different way of working, or build relationships with tech providers that somehow work around these models. As regards emergent PeaceTech providers, funders often want to see a plan for sustainability for 'self-payment' based on the PeaceTech innovation charging on a 'servitization' model. This can stand in tension with their desire also to have the tech produced 'for public good'. Pushing servitization can perpetuate a business model that stalls rather than enables iterative development. It can also mean innovative PeaceTech entrepreneurs are pushed to provide a static 'do a thing' business model, rather continue on creative journeys that are more open-ended. Yet, ongoing sustainability needs to be paid for.

12.10 Design to Future-Proof

There are three main aspects to future-proofing.

Thinking ahead. Sustainability can also be addressed by thinking ahead about the things you will need to change and commissioning the work to not just deliver the end product, but to also deliver easy ways for the product to be customised or extended in the future, as we did with the languages on PeaceFem.

Design for re-use. Often we have designed data interfaces not just for the immediate use in mind, but have also commissioned ways to modify the back-end design so we can 're-purpose and reuse' what has been developed to completely new uses. An example was the repurposing of the Amnesty interface, for the Covid 19 ceasefires.

Document as you go along. We always documented what we were doing, but now I would document even more. If you document your experiences you create capacity for new staff to come in and do the work, but also for the learning to be shared and used more widely than your own efforts.

Documentation to ensure your PeaceTech efforts and capacities do not disappear should really cover the nuts and bolts of how the system works, what servers it is on, and what relationships are needed to sustain use, the code used, the passwords, the decisions made, etc. Documentation should be 'internal' for new staff to pick up and know what is going on. Documentation should also have an external form—sharing learning and processes and even code with others. We are now working hard on this. This book, to be honest, is an element of our documentation and lesson-sharing efforts.

12.11 Returning Data and Feedback Loops

There are issues with where data comes from, and where it goes to, that we will discuss more next chapter. However, worth noting for now: it is important to have people 'participate' in, use and learn from their own data, and is their feedback itself data that tells us something interesting.

The whole of PA-X was in ways an attempt to pull a peace agreement repository together and return it to the people in-country who had helped create peace processes, and to make it available to others engaging in future peace processes. However, now we also collect perception information on peace processes as part of our new project. This data is collected in surveys from people in-country to compare data on 'how a peace process is going' with perceptions in-country, so we can identify where to 'mind the gap'. How, then, can this be used by the same communities?

Is returning data to those it was drawn from a business need, or an ethical commitment? If you are serious about peacebuilding support, both I would say.

12.12 Learn From the Local

Peacebuilding innovation is nearly always at its most innovative when responsive to conflict at the local level. This is no less true of PeaceTech. We have definitely struggled with this, but commissioning things in-country is nearly always possible.

12.13 Complicated Issues

Think about what you are doing 'really'? What does this even mean? Well.... I think it is useful to remain aware of the criticisms of PeaceTech and issues such as 'double disruption' and always question—what am I doing? Or perhaps—what practice of production am I engaged in? This reflexivity involves being aware of 'modularization', 'servitization', and conflict-peace nesting—all quite complicated things. Or in short: It requires you to think about the ways you are engaged in this world. Are you replicating problematic practices, are there consequences you should be worried about? I address this type of 'technomoral' reflexivity in next chapter.

Ethnics, harm, risk and safety. In addition to all these things, you have to think about the consequences of what you are doing in terms of well-established processes of managing ethics, data protection, and risk of harm to people and perhaps to the peace process itself. It is to these issues that we now turn.

Questions

1. How important to you think 'iterative design' is? Is it always important?
2. What challenges do these lessons raise for 'getting started', or doing PeaceTech as a small local group?
3. Is there something about digital innovation that causes us to think that normal ways of working are not to be applied? Which of the lessons apply to any project management, and what is distinctive to digital innovation in peacebuilding?
4. Do these lessons affect any PeaceTech ideas or plans you have?

References[1]

Bell, C., Bach, B., & Kauer, T. (2022). Ways of seeing: Peace process data-viz as a research practice. *Convergence, 28*(1), 150–169. https://doi.org/10.1177/13548565211050748

[1] All last accessed 1 May 2023.

CHAPTER 13

Ethics and Morals

Abstract PeaceTech raises distinctive ethical, data protection, risk and moral concerns, due to the particular risks that adhere to some digital technology uses, and the fact that peacebuilding interventions are used in contexts where conflict is conducted using forms of digital innovation, including cyberwarfare. PeaceTech innovation also raises questions of 'what constitutes good practice'? This chapter outlines these areas, to map the challenges, pointing to the gaps in existing ethical frameworks.

Keywords Ethics • Do no harm • Data protection • Corporate social responsibility • Techno-morality

13.1 PeaceTech WarTech Interfaces

In her book *First Platoon* (2021), prize-winning journalist Annie Jacobsen tells the following story from the conflict in Afghanistan. I summarise for my purposes, but she tells it better and it is worth reading in full.

Kevin is working for the US Army in Afghanistan as an expert in 'pattern-of-life' analytics, an experimental form of behavioural science. He monitors behaviour of suspected Taliban. He works in a unit that uses a 'Persistent Ground Surveillance System' involving an array of cameras attached to a giant tethered balloon, where he watches people from a remote bunker. He has spent time watching and analysing the daily habits

C. Bell, *PeaceTech: Digital Transformation to End Wars*,
https://doi.org/10.1007/978-3-031-38894-1_13

of a man wearing a purple hat, who is being tracked as part of an attempt to warn US platoons of impending attack, or track individuals associated with 'terrorism'. This man has been identified as a 'bomb emplacer' who buries improvised explosive devices (IEDs), for the Taliban. If he is identified as in the process of placing IEDs he can be targeted and killed legally according to army rules of engagement. All the information from Kevin, from the balloons and from other sources are fed into a Palantir knowledge foundry system (remember Chap. 9), where it is supposedly crunched with a range of other data. This system is used to identify people and make decisions about legitimate targeting of suspects, but permission to access it is above Kevin's paygrade so someone else reviews all the evidence and makes the decision.

Kevin is told one day, that the man with the purple hat has been located in the act of emplacement and is about to be killed. He looks at the image feed as the strike is being put in place. But what he sees does not match with the close personal study he has made of this man and his habits. While the computer algorithm has identified—'this is the man', Kevin doubts it, and calls-in his doubts, leading to the strike being called off.

Kevin was right, the target was a civilian farmer in a field.

13.2 Unpicking Ethical Concerns

In the story, Kevin's human analysis was more accurate than Palantir's machine-supported deductions. Jacobsen shows that there is really no transparency to enable understanding the Palantir algorithm and therefore why it 'went wrong'. Indeed, it is likely that those relying on the foundry did not understand how it worked, and—we may speculate—perhaps neither did Palantir entirely itself.

Jacobson's book is eye-opening in showing just how far WarTech has developed. She focuses on the use of personal and biometric data in Afghanistan, including iris scans, fingerprints, photographs, occupation, home addresses and names of relatives. Data was used to track Taliban as Jacobsen describes.

Personal biometric data was also used in Afghanistan as part of GovTech to try to address corruption—for example, the payment of 'ghost soldiers', that is people on the books as soldiers being paid salaries who did not exist. The existence of ghost soldiers has been blamed as one of the reasons why an army of 300,000 fell so quickly to the Taliban once the US pulled out, in August 2021—many of the 300,000 did not exist (see BBC, 2021).

In a further twist to the tale, when the US and UK and other NATO countries withdrew from Afghanistan, this biometric data was left behind without any security. It now appears it is being used by the Taliban to identify and kill former government workers who they perceive as enemy (Human Rights Watch, 2022). In other words, the systems used as GovTech to enable civicness, are now used by enemies of civicness to target and kill.

Afghanistan graphically illustrates how projects 'for good', become intertwined with war efforts in complex and unpredictable ways.

Also worth noting—the story opens a window into the fragmentation of conflict and peace that I have labelled one prong of 'double disruption'. Afghanistan was invaded in 2001, by an international coalition led by the US, to destroy Al Qaeda, post their involvement in the Twin Tower attacks in New York. This displaced also the Taliban who had supported them and were in government. What followed was a paradoxical international attempt to incubate a 'locally owned' transition focused on acheiving stable and democratic institutions. Over following 20 years, this transition became ever ongoing, and overlaid new transitional structures and processes on old ones. The transition negotiations and outcomes excluded the Taliban, until a parallel deal was signed in 2021, not between Afghans, but between the Taliban and the US, leading to US. This deal provided for US troop withdrawal the following summer. The Taliban used fragmentation to sweep to power in a show of unity, but now find themselves dealing with ongoing fragmentation, including in the range of armed groups they encounter. Afghanistan illustrates the flaws of internationally constructed transition, and the complex ways in which efforts connect to digital transformation of securitization and war. It also illustrates what our wider research indicates is a characteristic of the new conflict landscape: 'critical junctures' arise that have capacity to create sudden reversals from peace trajectories to war outcomes in a matter of days.

Against such a peacebuilding backdrop, how can we begin to think about the ethical challenges for PeaceTech, and what frameworks and regulations exist to govern them?

13.3 Ethical and Moral Concerns

Particular dynamics in the conduct of war, raise distinct ethical, data protection and harm issues than those of more peaceful contexts. Distinctive ethical challenges arise even more when new technologies are thrown into the mix. As the issues are legion and often very specific to the type of digital innovation in being deployed, I will point in a general way to the gaps in existing frameworks, and resources that are beginning to plug them.

There are three quite different sets of ethical questions, using the term broadly, that should be considered as part of PeaceTech design, that I use to structure this discussion.

Ethics and Impact concerns. The first set of concerns focus on the impact of PeaceTech interventions and ensuring that PeaceTech is not inadvertently supporting non-peaceful activities that can hurt people. That PeaceTech cannot be 'flipped' to WarTech. These concerns are common to all peacebuilding interventions, and have existing legal and policy frameworks, but digital innovation in conflict areas poses additional challenges that these frameworks often do not cover.

Good Practice and Process Concerns. The second set of concerns focus on questions of ethical design of PeaceTech. These concerns reflect a wish to design PeaceTech so as to protect against potential negative impacts on people and processes. Good practice ambitions are also driven by a wider set of ethical commitments to particular forms of practice that peacebuilders understand to go hand-in-hand with the type of peaceful outcomes that they are trying to achieve. These commitments include: equitable partnership between global north and south; fostering greater inclusion; mitigating climate impacts; and using practices that support rather than undermine social justice. There are emergent good process frameworks, but they are scattered and various in ways that undermine their systematic application.

Technomoral Concerns. A third set of concerns arise that we can label as 'technomoral' concerns that operate to try to deal with the 'what are we doing *really*' questions that I have asked at particular points in the book. Technomoral concerns focus on how digital innovation shapes our lives and world in ways that relate to human flourishing because they create or destroy a world we might want to live in (Vallor, 2016). We have very few systems at all for guiding technomoral approaches to PeaceTech into practice.

We will explore the challenges of conflict-contexts and the frameworks in each area as a form of mapping of gaps and emergent guidance.

13.4 Impact Concerns: Ethics, Harm and Data Protection

The first set of concerns attempt to ensure that PeaceTech does not harm people. These type of concerns are common to all research and peacebuilding enterprises, but PeaceTech poses five distinctive challenges for how we identify and manage risk of harm. All have been illustrated by stories throughout this book.

- Digital technologies often produce detailed geolocated population-specific data that can focus violence on groups. However, our ethical and data protection frameworks tend to evaluate the risk in terms of individuals. Geolocated population data, in a context of conflict, raises a need to evaluate PeaceTech plans in terms of whether and how it could be used to target vulnerable groups of people.
- Any digital innovation needs awareness of cybersecurity risk to be able to account fully for the risks to individual and populations. Using data responsibly is more than just a matter of individual consent and privacy issues. It involves being aware of what data is feeding analysis, understanding where it is stored, pre-identifying risk of issues like hacking, and putting in place mitigations strategies, that may themselves need digital fixes such as forms of online security (UN OCHA, 2016).
- Digital technologies such as satellite or other aerial technology, even when used for peace research and peacebuilding, produce forms of knowledge that have a value as 'intelligence'. They come close to the knowledge that intelligence agencies gather, with consequences for unpredictable spill-overs from PeaceTech to WarTech.
- Peace processes, and institutions and organizations providing public authority, are themselves a vital target of peacebuilding or civicness initiatives. Damaging them has consequences for the long-term levels of violence and trajectory of the conflict. Current ethical frameworks often do not require consideration of how a process or set of institutions might be affected.

In Universities, frameworks and processes exist to manage ethical concerns, through ethics approval systems, data protection frameworks, and risk management matrices. These types of frameworks also exist in business organizations, and non-governmental organizations that inhabit the PeaceTech ecosystem. However, how robust the framework is, whether it is a guide or is independently reviewed, and whether review has any context-specific expertise, will vary between different types of actor in the PeaceTech ecosystem, and often is also dependent on their size. On our PeaceTech collaborations, as we think these issues through, we have found that there are also tensions in how levels of risk are understood between Western institutions, and researchers in the field. While University processes are robust as processes of formal review, NGOs sometimes have better practical protocols for the actual practice of safety in the field.

Often countries experiencing conflict, legal and policy frameworks do not exist, although of course good practice can still be implemented and frameworks used. Afghanistan, for example, had and still has no data protection law. However, in the US, UK and EU, for example, data protection is backed up by legislation, and tends to apply to research projects 'abroad' because it focuses on where data is held and processed, which is 'at home'. Even where there may be technical legal gaps, organizations act to apply legal standards even beyond where they are strictly enforceable as institutional good practice.

Let us look at a few of the relevant frameworks in general terms, to understand how they deal, and do not deal, with the above challenges.

13.4.1 Ethical and Data Protection Frameworks

University researchers have to apply for ethical approval which consider issues of ethics and risk, and also need to file data protection plans. These will be governed by organizational policy and by law, and often also by the terms of any funding.

However, relevant ethical frameworks are modelled at heart on medical ethics frameworks and a model that works a bit like the questions that we might ask before we test a new drug. These frameworks ask whether the person has given free and prior informed consent to be a 'research subject', and been made adequately aware of risks that the researcher understands to exist, and has been given capacity to withdraw at any time. Typically, the forms also ask about potential risks to researchers from conducting the research. Some risks can be mitigated, and all risks have to be balanced against the value of the research. Some risks cannot be mitigated and are too high, and then the research cannot take place.

The ethical frameworks therefore focus on whether there is an anticipated harm to individual research subjects and whether it has been adequately dealt with.

Universities and some peacebuilding organizations will have in place similar rules and procedures for data protection. These are also individual-focused. They are driven by the idea of an individual having privacy rights with respect to their own data, and consent is the basis its for use by others. Data protection requirements rise the more that 'personal data' such as name, address, race, gender, that could specifically identify is recorded and used. They also tie the use of scope of permission to use data to evaluation of what information is strictly needed for the research.

As regards PeaceTech innovation in conflict contexts, these frameworks and procedures leave clear gaps, as outlined above. Most critical is what the UN Office for the Coordination of Humanitarian Affairs (OCHA), calls data relating to the 'time and place-specific activities of affected populations' that is, 'spatiotemporal metadata' (UN OCHA, 2016, p. 3). Ethical and data protection policies, forms and processes, do not prompt researchers to consider whether, even when there are no individual 'research subjects', whether population-specific risks can be created by PeaceTech methods and data.

Group-based data in conflicts is highly political. In Bosnia, at one point during the conflict in the 1990s, there was graffiti saying 'every Yugoslav war started with a referendum'. Referendums used to ascertain sovereign wishes, could also be used as geolocated targeting maps for those who wanted to create ethnically 'pure' areas that would enable borders to be re-drawn and future referenda to be won. Time and place population data regarding activities, identity, or political views, has a WarTech value. In practice, most peacebuilders are acutely aware of the controversy of group-based spatial data in the contexts they work in. However, there is no protection framework for these concerns within many of the key institutions supporting PeaceTech, unless those undertaking the work create them.

Second, there is no specific framework for considering whether and how cyber-risks have been evaluated, and whether sufficient research has taken place to understand what they might be in a conflict zone characterised by cyberwarfare.

Third, ethical and data protection processes often have little context-specific expertise to offer the question of how data might be misused in the conflict in question. If those involved do not alert to the right risks, those reviewing, certainly in Universities, are unlikely to have country or conflict expertise at all.

Consider, for example, satellite data as described in Chap. 12. It will often not focus on individuals, will not therefore need their consent according to standard ethics review practice, but is now sufficiently low cost or open access to be used on occasion by researchers and non-governmental organizations. Yet, researchers and organizations may have little contextual knowledge or capacity to anticipate how the data might be used by local actors (remember Nick from Chap. 1). They may also be insufficiently technological expert in the type of data to understand its possible flaws and misrepresentations (remember the Palantir system from the story at the start of this chapter). The ethical forms involved are unlikely to uncover these issues or deal with them.

The Harvard Humanitarian Initiative (HHI) in 2010 has usefully shared its experience. HHI joined the Sentinel Project to use satellite imagery to monitor the border region of Sudan and South Sudan to detect threats to the civilian population. They reported on troops massing or moving, and what looked like possible attacks on civilian housing, and possible mass graves. While the satellite imagery provided access to areas that otherwise could not have been monitored internationally, and while precautions were taken on how images were released (for example editing out landmarks and coordinates), the HHI concluded over time that:

> the impact of the collection of imagery and the release of reports on many different types of actors, on the ground and at the international level, became increasingly consequential yet unpredictable. Thus HHI could no longer assess the potential risk the project was exacerbating, not could it causally determine when it either mitigated threats or magnified them. (UN OCHA, 2016, p. 12)

Whew!

Having assessed that it simply could not act responsibly on the project, HHI acted responsibly by leaving the partnership, and working to research what a good framework of common operational doctrines and ethical standards to address these issues might be. (UN OCHA, 2016, p. 12).

Beyond satellite data, other data such as social media t groups of people with place and time, depending on how it is used.

13.4.2 *Research or Intelligence?*

Where information such as the satellite images HHI used, the data can really be a form of 'intelligence', that governments may have better access to already, but may not. Again, we have no frameworks to enable us to draw a clear line as to what makes something a 'research methodology' and what makes it 'intelligence', or to prompt how to evaluate when and how that might matter. Technically all research that provides 'data' can be used for all sorts of purposes. But use of open source imagery has an immediacy that is illustrated by Nick's story, and just feels different. Heather Marquette suggests that some protection from toppling from research into intelligence gathering is given by simple application of rigorous research standards. These include: specifying a research purpose of using satellite imagery; justifying its use; adhering to research ethics principles such as anonymity; openness the use of the of the images and of the research; and educating people about how to interpret the images. But she also calls for honesty that even research rigor will not protect against intentional use of data as intelligence and points out that this will typically happen without the researcher's knowledge (XCEPT seminar).

13.4.3 *CyberWar Risks*

The application of ethical and data protection standards to digital innovation in conflict zones, is further complicated by the heightened cybersecurity risks of many conflicts. Cyber-insecurity in conflict zones is often of a different nature and scale and quality than in other places. It cannot be accounted for by quickly racking one's brains and asking 'are there any risks?' while filling in a form. Cyber-risk has to be researched in-context to understand the consequences of even non-personalised data collection.

In Yemen, for example, internet provision is itself a key 'front' in the conflict—so much so that any quick explanation of exactly how, is not possible (for more detail see Combs, 2020). Suffice it to say, the Houthis who are a key armed actor involved in the conflict, and the current fractured government of Yemen which is tied up with Saudi Arabia and United Arab Emirates who are also involved in the conflict, have two different internets. YemenNet is controlled by Houthis and AdenNet, was set up using another ISP by United Arab Emirates and Saudi Arabia to break Houthi control. These rival internets have different geographic coverages, and operate different forms of censorship. This type of cyber complexity means that something as simple as encouraging people to communicate thought computer, and which internet provider they use (something that is easily remotely discoverable), can give a sense of location and possible political affiliation. Plus, internet providers can monitor all individual online activity. Knowledge of the realities of internet provision, censorship and capacity to monitor, is clearly relevant to a range of PeaceTech methodologies. Without an audit of how the internet works, how is is controlled, key insecurities and risks will be missed.

In fact, a whole lot of things that we think of as fairly 'safe' or having non-physical consequences in Western societies, can be subject to a different level of consequence in conflict countries. WhatsApp groups that can easily be hacked and people targeted for views; use of Twitter/X can be monitored at scale; a 'self-learning environment' computer may fall into the control of local armed leaders.

13.4.4 Dual Use Restrictions

There are other forms of ethical framework in place which seem potentially able to 'get to' PeaceTech issues. Dual use frameworks in research ask researchers: 'does your research have a military application'? If one answers 'yes', the research cannot be undertaken under normal grant frameworks, for example be funded by the EU. Yet again, however, the framework does not seem to fit. The challenges of double disruption and 'modularization' means that almost any digital innovation that can be developed for PeaceTech to make peacebuilding more effective, can also be unscrewed and attached to war, to make war more effective. So nearly all use of normal digital devices to gather information is dual use in this broad sense.

The dual use tick-box does not seem to contemplate this. It creates a system where things are either 'in' or out'. For example, the ERC Frontiers grant requires a declaration to the following effect: 'We declare that the proposal has an exclusive focus on civil applications (activities intended to be used in military application or aiming to serve military purposes cannot be funded)' (see for example Horizon 2022 Small Grants). Whether, a software application, for example, is dual use therefore seems dependent on the intent the user brings, rather than the possibility of actual dual use.

To be fair, there are other dimensions to the policy, including guidance for researchers, and a link from this research policy, to a legal framework for export licences to help elaborate dual use. However, these merely help in ruling-in very particular types of military-related hardware as always requiring a licence because they are always potentially dual use, and ruling-in forms of public software as always ok, and not requiring licences. This approach may be appropriate for grant of export licences, but the policy as a whole is not designed to guide questions of how digital methodologies designed for non-military purposes and used in research, could still be considered to raise a risk of dual use in ways that need considered and mitigated. Working groups continue to try to work out a better framework (see for example, Bromley & Gerharz, 2019).

13.4.5 *Risk to Peace Processes: Too Much Knowing*

PeaceTech entrepreneurs working to support mediation processes to end wars, might also want to be concerned not just about harm to individuals, but harms to the peace processes they are aiming to support. Our current formalised standards within the research environment do not raise this question as relevant to ethical or data protection concerns. But should they?

What if even good data harms a perfectly good peace process, damaging the prospects for a good outcome. As I grew up in Northern Ireland, it was heartbreaking when secret peace talks were revealed before they had a chance to produce any real compromise and the parties who did not want to be seen to be compromising all jumped away from the process. Decades of conflict and death often followed.

Investigative journalism and public transparency is a good thing. But where a sensitive process is at play that holds the prospects of life or death, should that process be protected from things like 'publicity' or 'transparency' at particular moments? This might be particularly important where we have all sorts of innovative ways of digitally communicating so that any form of secrecy is difficult to achieve. Discussion with local political leaders in several contexts points to the dangers of 'too much knowing'—who has met with who, and discussed what, and why? Often political exploration of unthinkable moves, needs space.

If we seek to undertake PeaceTech to support wars ending, should we think in terms not just of a duty of care towards research subjects (that is people) and geolocated populations, but also a duty of care towards peace processes? Or is that too political? Do just we trust to our broader ethical standards as sufficient, and require people try to protect their peace processes in other ways—for example, building public buy in for the idea of political compromise as having a value? Or is there sometimes 'too much knowing'?

13.4.6 *'Do No Harm' Frameworks*

For issues such as harm to processes, humanitarian actors seem to have a slightly more appropriate framework than that of ethics or data protection. That is the 'do no harm' framework. This framework also has its roots in medicine and the Hippocratic Oath. In the humanitarian world it is understood as a framework to help apply the seven fundamental principles of humanitarianism: humanity, impartiality, neutrality, independence, voluntary service, unity and universality. 'Do no harm' evaluations, aim to support questions of what these values mean when applied to a particular proposed intervention. Do no harm, involves asking not just about risk to people, but of unintended harm to institutions and processes. Harm could include how emergency healthcare might affect a national healthcare system down the road, or how food aid might impact on the livelihoods of local farmers. Do no harm frameworks in essence critically question the range of short and long-term consequences that could flow from trying to 'do good' (see eg, ICRC Principles).

Yet, there are problems with adopting do no harm in practice. Steeped in debates regarding the philosopher John Stewart Mill, I have always found it less than helpful in deeply divided societies experiencing conflict. How do we know what harm might result? When should that stop immediate action—how would we calibrate the risks of doing something, versus the risks of doing nothing? It is always easier to do nothing, because that has no risk, right?

People living in conflict, seldom do nothing. They work around and through the conflict, they create 'normal lives' in the midst of abnormality. They take incredible risks to travel through war zones to possible safety, or to build peace, or fight for justice. They risk their political capital to call a ceasefire, and take a chance of something different. They experiment with how to make connections, or create new ways of doing things. They do all this because they do not have the luxury of doing nothing. Sometimes that carries the biggest risk of all. Yet, they own their own context, and can make these decisions as political decisions. External researchers must make them another way.

With all its faults, applying a 'do no harm' approach to PeaceTech design is useful in prompting consideration of issues of harm that go beyond immediate harm to people, to consider possible political consequences, and at least prompts useful deliberation that can inform how things move forward. Ethical review processes could usefully ask for a do no harm evaluation that is broader than harm to individuals.

13.5 Process Concerns: Ethical Design

Our second set of ethical questions relate to ethical design. That is, whether the ethics of the methods match the ethics of the outcome. The issues again, have been touched on throughout, and the main ones can just be outlined.

Inclusion. Peacebuilding at many levels is about inclusion, and inclusion has been a major challenge and concern regarding peace processes. Particular, norms exist on the inclusion of women in peace mediation, such as UN Security Council Resolution 1325. Legal challenges have been made to peace agreements and the constitutions that result, on the basis of the exclusion or non-dominant minorities by peace process power-sharing or devolution deals (see eg *Sejdić and Finci v. Bosnia and Herzegovina, Grand Chamber, European Court of Human Rights, 2009*). Digital innovation, as we have seen, is often justified as increasing inclusion. Yet, digital inclusion in fragile and conflict settings continues to be a major issue.

For example, women often have much lower use of mobile phones, and rural peripheral communities where minorities may reside can lack internet access or mobile connectivity at all. As we have seen in the Yemen example, divided societies and tactics of cyberwarfare and censorship often mean conflict-related biases in provision of digital connectivity. Further, we may simply not know what the conflict-relevant biases of technology and its use—such as 'who uses twitter'—are.

Other problems can be created by PeaceTech, such as uneven inclusion. Women in many conflict areas will face cultural and safety barriers and additional costs to travel, for example, where they have to be accompanied by a male family member. Digital access to peace talks, post-Covid has occasionally seen men participate in person and women facilitated remotely. Yet these are quite different forms of access.

All of these factors can mean the offer of PeaceTech inclusion, can come with more hidden exclusions. The biases of who has access to technology can damage the peacebuilding outcome, or peace process itself, particularly in a context already full of exclusions, distrust and disinformation. Use of PeaceTech therefore needs to involve a prior audit of digital inclusion, and steps to account for or remedy bias, often through supplementary analogue processes.

Environmental Protection. PeaceTech offers ways of cutting down environmental impact, such as where online meetings are used rather than in-person ones. Data, however, has energy needs that are sometimes quite significant—for example in the large data warehouses behind the cloud. Mobile phones use precious metals that are often mined in conflict zones, in ways that fuel war economies, such as in Democratic Republic of Congo. Thousands of small satellites create space debris. Plus, Planet Lab's five year partnership with Musk's SpaceX, supports a project that also aims to make space travel an ordinary and regular human adventure, an aim that is paralleled by other similar ambitions of other Tech billionaires. If achieved, mass space travel would have large-scale environmental consequences. The environmental impact of PeaceTech, and the connection to conflict itself, is now always easy to unearth and quantify against the alternatives.

Corporate Social Responsibility. Most large-scale businesses have adopted some form of corporate social responsibility standards that commit them to reviewing their own practice on issues such as inclusion and diversity and environmental impact. PeaceTech entrepreneurs can therefore choose partners carefully in this regard. However, it is more difficult to understand and assess the multiple relationships that digital providers are involved in as illustrated by the Planet Labs-SpaceX partnership. Additional issues can arise due to the secrecy surrounding some proprietary technology of PeaceTech providers, that can preclude understanding what firewalls are in place between different customer uses. In 2019, for example, Palantir, the company in the Afghanistan story at the start of this chapter was engaged by the UN's World Food Programme (a Nobel Peace Prize winner in 2020), at a cost of $45 billion, with potential to improve alleviation of hunger, but raising serious concerns about data protection of millions of the world's most vulnerable people (Parker, 2019).

Good practice for the use and design of digital technologies in peace processes, requires that frameworks for assessing, avoiding or mitigating these process concerns are developed and applied.

13.6 Techno-Moral Principles

Even deeper ethical questions arise related to 'what are we doing *really*'? The idea of techno-morality for the digital revolution, tries to understand how digital technology changes our life invisibly by structuring our relationships, our aspirations, our activities, and our use of time. Remember the social media algorithms promoting disagreement, based on turning all our interactions into a chance to advertise? Shannon Vallor suggests

(2016), we should ask, are we using digital technology in ways that will lead to humans flourishing because it creates a world worth living in?

Technomorality switches the question asked by ethical frameworks of—'what are we doing with the technology, and are we doing it safely?', to consider, 'what is the technology doing to *us*, as humans, as a society'? Should PeaceTech providers think about this question, and how? Again, we have seen a number of persistent concerns that seem relevant.

North-South empowerment and equity. How should supply and demand relate to digital innovation, and where it occurs? Digital innovation clearly should not always come from the north to add 'hacks' to peacebuilding interventions undertaken in the South. PeaceTech efforts to develop digital innovation responsively, seek to avoid supply-driven PeaceTech. However, digital innovation does not happen 'in one place', so how should we consider equity and participation in the underlying structural capacity for PeaceTech arises: where data warehouses, fabrication and innovation have their infrastructure located? What does ethics require—would replication say of data warehouses in the global South be a good thing? Or is this about using existing capacity in better service of global South inclusion? There can be arguments either way.

Morality of relationships, knowability and distance. Multiple instances of PeaceTech are about engaging bigger populations, through remote engagement. Is this a good thing? Even if we could factor out disinformation and inequities of who it reaches? How does remote participation restructure relationships of trust if we focus on 'knowing' as exchange of information, rather than focusing on 'getting to know'?

What if remote access enables international actors to work ever-more remotely. There are gains of efficiency, capacity and even perhaps local ownership. Or is there an ethic of 'being present'? Seán, does not exist, and if he had was 'in-country', but similar people were at pains to tell me that most 'Seáns' are knowing and uncomfortable with the inadequacies of their 'presence'. As local expertise illustrates, a micro-knowledge is gained invisibly through every movement through a street, every interaction at a marketplace, and through the interpersonal relationships of friendship and co-working. It is even gained in every ride in a taxi taken between UN buildings, and observed even through darkened windows.

From CSR to Cultivating Technomoral Virtues? And should we be concerned, beyond CSR about how the providers of PeaceTech are creating the wider digital transformation world? Some of the personal views of key providers of PeaceTech technology, seem completely at odds with notions of 'civicness', with no commitment to inclusion, moderation of hate speech, or even democratic elections. Some of these personal views translate into their business models. How does this sit with the idea of 'technomorality'? Is there a need to ask, not just, 'is this company engaged in providing something I do not like?', but also, 'is this company creating a world I do not like'?

To be clear, technomorality is not a matter of judging the moral worth of Tech entrepreneurs, it is a matter of considering one's own moral stance with reference to the social reality being created. Asking—'is this a world I want to participate in building?' Our discussion of whether we view PeaceTech practices of retro-fitting, modularlization and hacktivism, in a sense engages with trying to understand what sort of world PeaceTech World is and what we are doing when we participate.

13.7 Emergent Responsive Standards

New ethical standards addressing all of the above types of concern are emerging both for particular new technologies, but also for PeaceTech in particular. One difficulty is that there are so many different ones, and they are emerging and being developed so constantly, it can be quite a task to try to synthesise them all and use them to guide action. We have found the following really useful, so I offer them as examples.

The UN advocates and aims to comply with the use of FAIR Principles for Scientific Data Management and Stewardship, regarding the generation and use of data, and these Principles capture many of the lessons I have shared. FAIR Principles elaborate a framework for ensuring that data is: accessible; interoperable; reusable. I also find OCHA guidance on data management very practical and useful in providing both standards and process advice, for data-driven projects in conflict contexts (UN OCHA, 2016).

Particular sets of standards have been developed for particular technologies. Use of earth observation technology, for example, has multiple guidance frameworks address issues such as how to understand error and interpret images properly. A quick appraisal of these standards provide a sharp warning as regards the scale of expertise needed to use these technologies responsibly. Perhaps the best advice is to partner with knowledgeable organizations and research the relevant frameworks, if delving into a new area.

Standards are also emerging from within the PeaceTech ecosystem to offer PeaceTech-specific guidance relevant to the above challenges.

Build Up for example, has established Principles for Digital Development, that are intended to guide good digital development, as part of an ongoing commitment to establish good practice frameworks. The Principles resonate strongly with our learned-experience of what constitutes good practice articulated earlier. The Principles focus on how to build processes that establish the right types of relationship, rather than evaluating just uses of data for harm. They are also working to address 'current ethical challenges' and plan further development of PeaceTech guidance.

ConnexUS, of which Build Up is a part, has set out frameworks which go much more to the underlying technomoral issues. A Peace Impact Framework (PIF) for example, tries to go beyond 'do no harm' to suggest the type of iterative cooperative practice that might be useful to doing good, based on three pillars—lived experience; aligned measures; and shared reflection. This PIF in essence aims to build civicness as a practice of PeaceTech, rather just concentrate on avoiding harm. ConnexUS is also piloting a 'grounded accountability' (GAM) model along with Everyday Peace Indicators, to create more community-driven ways of monitoring and evaluating peace outcomes. While not focused on digital innovation, the GAM offers ways of approaching data ownership, feedback loops, and equitable partnership.

Guides are also emerging on particular PeaceTech methodologies that focus on the mediation at the heart of peace processes. The UN Department of Mediation has set out Guidelines on Digital Mediation in the form of a Toolkit, mentioned earlier (UN DPPA, Centre for Humanitarian Dialogue, n.d., 2019). UN DPPA and Swiss Peace have also set out a practical framework for using social media in mediation (UN DPPA & Swiss Peace, 2021).

These efforts are weaving good practice standards around PeaceTech, in ways that are thoughtful about the particular peacebuilding challenges in peace processes, and tailored to helping navigate them.

Yet, they face a central difficulty of keeping pace with digital innovation. Sullivan, for example, argues we live in a world where we simply cannot regulate to keep up with digital transformation because 'how the tech works' constantly outpaces ethical frameworks (2022). His ideas suggest that the value of new frameworks may lie less in providing static 'regulation', and more in how they create assemblages of people who entangle in ethical deliberation across the PeaceTech ecosystem and its very different types of provider with very different ethical commitments. Sullivan argues that 'applying ethics' involves asking how knowledge and relationships, empowerment and disempowerment, are being defined and co-created.

This is a shift-shaping approach to ethical regulation, for a shift-shaping digital conflict world. It seems to respond to the reality of digital innovation, and to involve a form of 'technomoral' commitment. However, ethics as creating relationships, also seems difficult to translate into a clear-cut practice whose outcomes institutions can stand-over.

13.8 Conclusion

Thinking back to the idea of Peacebuilding ripples, and peacebuilding as the practice of building civicness, it becomes clear that impact ethics, process ethics and techno-morality are deeply connected. The means of peacebuilding such as creating trust, are often also its ends. Supporting civicness means embedding civicness as an ethic of production. Doing PeaceTech requires being part of a community that develops ethical strategies, as much as ethical frameworks. Those involved should work to develop a practice of behaving ethically, legally, inclusively, equitably, environmentally, and techno-morally.

Got that? Right.

Questions

1. How concerned are you about the peculiar ethical, data protection and technomoral challenges of PeaceTech?
2. How confident are you that we can design better ethical, data protection and technomoral frameworks to deal with them?
3. Is there a risk that overthinking leads to inaction, whose harm we seldom evaluate?

References[1]

BBC. (2021, November 10). *Afghanistan's ghost soldiers undermined fight against Taliban—Ex-official*. BBC online news article. https://www.bbc.co.uk/news/world-asia-59230564

Bromley, M., & Gerharz, P. (2019, October 7). *Revising the EU Dual-use regulation: Challenges and opportunities for the trilogue process*. Stockholm International Peace Research Institute (SIPRI), blog. https://www.sipri.org/commentary/

[1] All last accessed 1 May 2023.

topical-backgrounder/2019/revising-eu-dual-use-regulation-challenges-and-opportunities-trilogue-process

Combs, C. (2020, 10 March). *In Yemen the internet is a key frontline in the war.* https://www.codastory.com/authoritarian-tech/yemen-internet-conflict/

Human Rights Watch. (2022, March 30). *New evidence that biometric data systems imperil Afghans; Taliban now control systems with sensitive personal information.* Human Rights Watch Press Release. https://www.hrw.org/news/2022/03/30/new-evidence-biometric-data-systems-imperil-afghans

Jacobson, A. (2021). *First platoon: A story of modern war in an age of identity dominance.* Penguin.

Parker, B. (2019, February 5). *New UN deal with data mining firm Palantir raises protection concerns.* The New Humanitarian, Online news story. https://www.thenewhumanitarian.org/news/2019/02/05/un-palantir-deal-data-mining-protection-concerns-wfp

Sullivan, G. (2022). Law, technology, and data-driven security: *Infra*-legalities as method assemblage. *Journal of Law and Society, 49*(2), 31–50. https://doi.org/10.1111/jols.12352

UN DPPA, Centre for Humanitarian Dialogue. (n.d.). *Digital technologies and innovation toolkit 1.0.* UN Department of Political and Peacebuilding Affairs and Centre for Humanitarian Dialogue online digital toolkit. https://peacemaker.un.org/digitaltoolkit

UN DPPA, Global Pulse. (2019, January). *E-Analytics guide: using data and new technology for peacemaking, preventive diplomacy and peacebuilding.* Department of Political and Peacebuilding Affairs, UN Global Pulse United Nations University Institute on Computing and Society E-Analytics Guide. https://www.unglobalpulse.org/wp-content/uploads/2019/04/e-analyticsguide2019.pdf

UN DPPA, MSU and Swiss Peace. (2021). *Social media in peace mediation. A practical framework.* UNDPPA MSU and Swiss Peace.

UN OCHA. (2016, May 18). *Building data responsibility into humanitarian action.* OCHA Policy and Study Series. United Nations. https://www.unocha.org/sites/unocha/files/Building%20data%20responsibility%20into%20humanitarian%20action.pdf

Vallor, S. (2016). *Technology and the virtues: A philosophical guide to a future worth wanting.* Oxford University Press.

CHAPTER 14

PeaceTech Futures

Abstract This chapter assesses 'where PeaceTech' is, in terms of hype, disillusionment and a plateau of steady-state use. In conclusion a small manifesto for PeaceTech's future is offered.

Keywords Gartner hype cycle • Manifestos

14.1 A PeaceTech Hype-Cycle Audit

The Gartner Hype Cycle is a graphic representation of the maturity life-cycle of new technologies and innovations divided into five phases, which I adapt to PeaceTech (see box).

Gartner Hype Cycle

1. **Innovation Trigger.** Interest in a PeaceTech possibility is sparked by seeing an application of a new digital innovation.
2. **Peak of Inflated Expectations.** People's excitement and expectations for the innovation exceed the reality of its current capacity to deliver. This excitement can generate considerable financial speculative support.

(*continued*)

C. Bell, *PeaceTech: Digital Transformation to End Wars*,
https://doi.org/10.1007/978-3-031-38894-1_14

(continued)

3. **Trough of Disillusionment.** Peacebuilder and funder excitement dissipates and is offset by disillusionment, due to poor performance, length of time to deliver, or lack of sustainability in cost-outcome terms.
4. **Slope of Enlightenment.** Early PeaceTech adopters overcome the initial hurdles and begin to realise the innovation's benefits. Other organisations benefit from the experience and gain better knowledge regarding where and how the innovation will deliver significant value (and where it will not).
5. **Plateau of Productivity.** The PeaceTech innovation demonstrates real-world benefits, and more organizations feel comfortable with the greatly reduced level of risk. Others adopt the PeaceTech innovation until the innovation (modified or not) becomes mainstream.

Where would be plot the PeaceTech innovation to end wars on this cycle? I offer a speculative graph below (Fig. 14.1). What follows is my assessment of 'where PeaceTech is at'. I offer it for deliberation rather than as a final judgment.

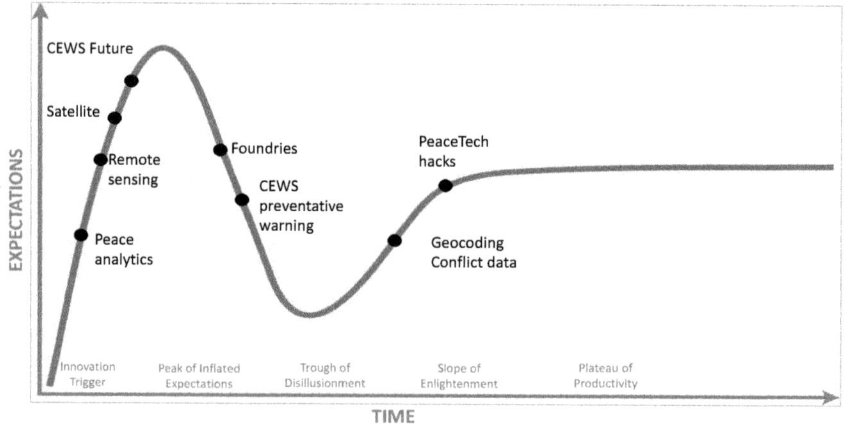

Fig. 14.1 'PeaceTech' Gartner Hype Cycle

PeaceTech as Hack. The innovation trigger for PeaceTech as a disaggregated set of ad hoc responses, and 'one good thing' approaches, means that the Gartner Hype Cycle is in a sense repeated in mini-ways, with different technologies. Many of the 'once-off's' have not been sustained, or have not fully delivered. I place it in the Plateau, however, because across the peacebuilding field there is a sustained turn to technology and methodological innovation. Even discrete initiatives have opened minds as to positive new applications of tech in the peacebuilding field, and generated a new ecosystem that enables new forms of collaboration across actor-type, and across skills.

Ad hoc digital peacebuilding is therefore 'mainstreamed', but characterised by ongoing experimentation, rather than attempt a wholesale digital transformation of practice, including the practice of peace processes and mediation. Once-off experimentation is in part due to the ad hoc nature of peacebuilding itself, which was always not very 'joined up', across interventions, actions and actors. Peace processes seldom, if never, are able to mobilise strong cross-organisation strategisation and coordination, but often see vast amounts of replication, competition and supply-led practice. PeaceTech as 'hack' at worst replicates this pattern, but at least retro-fits some new techniques onto it.

Yet organisations now know and use the 'easy-to-use' technology that is low-cost, and are open to responding to other innovations on a 'trial-and-error' basis. Over time, some PeaceTech providers have found ways to build business models based on 'reusability' across a range of peacebuilding needs, expanding the possible capacity for organisations to draw on—as Ushahidi illustrates. There are of course vast gaps in who does PeaceTech, and where it can be done, but these do not challenge the broad idea that digital methods are now in the frame as a new 'go to' in the peacebuilder toolkit.

Conflict Early Warning Systems. These remain a central focus of international attention, and governments, and are likely to remain so, not least because they are also big tech business. Today they are a normal part of security intelligence systems. As regard their use in peacebuilding and PeaceTech World, I divide them into the 'nowcasting' CEWS and the more Future-scanning EWS, and put these in slightly different places on the Hype Cycle graph.

Personally I am sceptical about prevention capacity to 'predict' the imminent onset of violent conflict through purely quantitative data-driven methods, and mobilise effective pre-emptive responses. I am reinforced in this by writing at time when the conflict in Khartoum is unfolding. No-one really predicted this specific armed conflict would erupt when it did on the basis of data, even though politically the peace process was widely known to be shaky and likely to fall apart somehow at any moment.

In my view, our understanding of conflict drivers and how they interact show a mix of structural cause and human agency, and the former are so difficult to predict, and the latter so inherently unpredictable, that the idea that probabilistic statistical modelling would somehow prove usefully predictive is misplaced. Even if I am wrong, I suspect this feeling is shared in peacebuilder circles, meaning that warnings will not generate sufficient confidence to provoke coherent political reaction that might prove useful. I suspect that good context-specific political analysis, based on simple observation of data, supported by digital innovation perhaps, will continue to be the main driver of response. But of course, I could be proved wrong, and may have leapt too early into the trough of despondency. However, because I am there myself, I place CEWS as data-driven automated warning in the trough of despondency.

However, when we turn to the peace process 'peace agreement implementation' area of work, in my view, CEWS have a value. Here the challenges often are in the platform design, and how not to introduce so much data that it remains unable to be deliberated on, or impose massive logistical data-collection jobs on staff who already risk spend more time filling in reports than peacebuilding in any meaningful sense.

CEWS, in my view, can usefully support 'future scenario planning'. That is, as a longer-term tool to support strategic analysis of the range of people involved in supporting peace processes, as to how best to do so. CEWS for future-scanning avoids some of the CEWS warning-response gap problems, because rather than give a predictive analysis of what will happen next, it suggests emergent risks and creates a conversation as to whether a mission or country-team or set of local actors should 'adapt' what they are doing to address that risk. CPAS attempts to do this, and our PA-X Tracker platform aims to support this type of deliberation. I can see this travelling round to the plateau of productivity if the right choices are made.

GIS and Remote Sensing Technologies. Technologies, such as satellite are offering a new capacity to peacebuilding in the form of access to technologies that were once beyond their capacities and budgets. They are also offering things like drones that we might think of as WarTech now reinvented as a module to be added to peace technology. This type of GIS PeaceTech has had the innovation trigger pulled and is hurtling up the curve of inflated expectations. As a PeaceTech tool in the making it seems to offer peacebuilders, and other peace process implementers such as peacekeeping forces, amazing new possibilities. UN Peacekeeping appears to have seized on the potential for new capacities for 'intelligence' to support peace implementation with gusto.

Whether GIS develops to support peace processes will depend on delivery of low cost provision of new satellite capacity, and peacebuilders having sufficient resources and expertise to use it. Connectors such as Earth Blox type projects that offer 'low- or no-code' ways of accessing and using images may play a part. However, my jury is out on how mainstream this type of work will become for peacebuilders. Some other forms of remote sensing such as sensors in the ground are remarkably cheap, but aside from warning of bombs, it is difficult to see the wider peace process function they would provide.

Perhaps the bigger PeaceTech limitation for aerial observation lies in the ethical civilian protection issues encountered by HHI, of 'switching modules' from war to peace. Can remote sensing technology be used as a module that can be unscrewed from war ends, and re-attached to peace ones? Peacebuilders may find it is simply impossible to build organisational firewalls to stop 'intelligence for peace' becoming 'intelligence for war'. Capacity to move beyond a trough of despondency to steady-state use will involve adequately addressing these challenges.

Geocoding. Beyond new remote sensing technologies, Geocode/ geocoding of conflict and peace data, has reached—in my opinion—a plateau of productivity due in no small part to the good practices of ACLED and UCDP and the wide usage of both data sources. Further standardisation of things like administrative sub-unit geocoding, and methodologies of plotting—boring as they may be—would be very useful for peace process monitoring, and could help visualize local peace perception surveys, such as we have been conducting (Deng et al., 2022), with other information such as local agreements or peacebuilding projects.

The remaining issues for geocoded data is the existence of data gaps, and whether and how people trust deaths in conflict data as providing a 'real' picture. Here, paradoxically, different datasets at least enable questions to be asked of 'whether this is real or an artefact of the data collection model'. Some interesting in-country projects, provide further more locally-collected data, to compare with the larger global datasets. There is a lesson for funders here- sometimes more is more, and replication has a value.

The other key gap, is a methodological and data gap in understanding how to measure peace, usefully contributed to by Caplan (2021) who points to the need to measure 'peace impacts', and then the difficulty of matching peace impacts onto data that is often 'slow data', and has country and quality gaps, as well as gaps in disaggregation of data. In the peace process context, there is a need to better think through what types of change are relevant to measure, and what should be the expected timescales of change, before jumpin into monitoring.

14.2 Peace Analytics

There is, in my view, a clear capacity and need to bring together the very considerable data collection efforts relating to conflict and peace into better articulation in peace analytics. Peace analytics will not change the world, but at present, as the stories right at the start indicated, multiple organisations repeat the same tasks to write similar reports, using the same data, in ways that they cannot share, to try to support peace processes. They face the same silly obstacles. How can I disaggregate the data by the local administrative districts we have projects in? How can I easily visualise information in a way that supports strategic decision-making, and adaptive management? How can I communicate levels of confidence about what it tells us and what it does not? How can I connect the quantitative data to our own organisational assessments? These are all issues that if solved could support peace process implementation tasks, and create massive efficiencies across organisations in-country (see e.g., Brusset et al., 2022, for an excellent report, that bears similarity to Paul's story). If done in an open source way, as we are trying to do, the enterprise might also enable collaborative conversations between people whose own platforms cannot be shared for diplomatic reasons.

I am biased, of course, as this is what we are doing. I also would not like to try to shoot us up the 'inflated expectations' curve, but rather jump over it and the associated trough of despondency, to land in a place of productivity. So I would want to emphasise that our peace analytics 'is what it is'—an attempt (still ambitious we feel), to create new ways of seeing, new ways of sharing information and analysis, and new ways of making comparative process information available. Whatever its ambition, it is what happens next in the real world that will change that world or not.

However, I believe these types of platform, and the methodologies we are working with, have potential to increase the opportunity for local actors and priorities to be more easily incorporated into peace process development, and seen and heard. Projects like Everyday Peace Indicators are good examples that giving voice to local definitions of peace can have power even in high places like the World Bank. Giving voice to local priorities is perhaps even more important in a context of double disruption where international actors no longer know 'what to do' and are floundering, and often displaced overnight from the country altogether, as Sudan and Afghanistan illustrate.

14.3 PeaceTech Manifesto

This book has given a short and—I hope—somewhat enticing introduction to PeaceTech efforts focused on ending wars. There is clearly much more that could have been said.

However, as part of encouraging that discussion, I leave with a short 'PeaceTech Manifesto'. The word 'manifesto' is deliberate. To quote Wikipedia (let's not be academically snobby in a PeaceTech book—it is a wonderful crowd-sourced tool, and we all use it):

> A manifesto is a published declaration of the intentions, motives, or views of the issuer.... [It] usually accepts a previously published proposition or public consensus or promotes a new idea accompanied by prescriptions the author believes should be made. It often is political, social or artistic in nature, sometimes revolutionary, but may present an individual's life stance.

Yes to all of that. Here goes.

1. Digital transformation in all aspects of life is here to stay, it has a lot to offer peace processes, but also raise new ethical, technomoral and practical challenges that we must rise to meet. As a rule of thumb, if a PeaceTech innovation feels creative and collaborative, and responds to a problem in the field, it is worth exploring. Inaction also has risks.
2. Conflict patterns are changing and a range of intersecting threats mean that the last decade has become much more dangerous to the point of our extinction. New models on how to mediate ends to conflict and reinvent responsive peace processes, need to be fashioned, and combined with innovative thinking about technology for war and technology for peace.

3. Ending conflict through practices of mediation and compromise is worth saving. We have few safe alternatives. Compromise between armed actors has moral costs, but these are nearly always less than the moral costs of continuing conflicts, particularly ones that it is clear neither side can 'win'. All conflicts have legitimate and illegitimate interests on all sides, even where there appear to be clear transgressors on one side and warriors for social justice on the other. Good practice matters as to whether an honourable and sustainable compromise is reached or not, and useful digital support to that end, is a good thing.
4. Peace and transition processes, while not transformative of all social relations, have made important contributions to reducing deaths in conflict, without which other transformation is not possible. The practice is in decline, and the world is more dangerous. Criticism of how good they have been should not lead to throwing the baby out with the bathwater. The iterative nature of peace and transition processes shown by PA-X, indicates that we should be more open to understanding peace processes as the complex ongoing business of politics and innovate to support.
5. To this end, digital capacities can help us to understand and map, and provide comparative information as to how people in conflict assemble and disassemble for peace and for war, with a view to supporting pockets of civicness where they emerge.
6. Beyond that, digital innovation has a vital role to play in addressing past peace process critiques by:

    (a) Enabling creative communities committed to peace to come together across different skill sets
    (b) Helping local priorities to be more visible, heard, and accepted by international peace process supporters.
    (c) Support monitoring and implementation of peace promises by armed actors.

7. To be effective PeaceTech will have to continue to develop two things:

    (a) Better composite agreed frameworks to assess ethics, data protection and harm to people and processes
    (b) Technomoral virtues for the field that connect understanding of PeaceTech innovation, to understanding of the wider impacts of digital transformation on our world (for this reason I have focused on drawing the connections).

8. People seldom shift positions and begin to trust each other by simply getting better information about 'the other'. They do so, through relationships and encountering the other. Supporting face-to-face encounter remains important.
9. PeaceTech promises inclusion, but risks exclusion. The rush to innovate should not bypass considering digital exclusion in design.
10. PeaceTech promises better collaboration but risks the same patterns that have emerged in the peacebuilding field itself. Funding models often reflect funder needs to show value, and so both project and funder in need to claim ownership of shiny new things. These incentives run counter to a field needing better sharing, reusability and interoperable data, which might require demonstrating an effort to build on what came before, rather than touting small modifications of existing data as 'new datasets'. More consideration of how the PeaceTech field as a coherent field should be built into innovative funding models that incentivise cooperation, open acces, and where appropriate, mutual ownership, and things like 'reusability'.
11. No-one wants to pay for ongoing data development. Everyone wants to fund 'shiny' new data even when it is unproved and overlaps with the old, but without any capacity for data continuity. Funders need to flip to support data sustainability and reuse better. Servitization is not the answer. Plus someone needs to support projects that have capacity to develop good models of 'standardisation' and 'interoperability'. Not sexy, hard to claim the result as a major thing leading to the outbreak of peace, but none of the sexy stuff happens without it. Good data is a major thing.
12. Finally, finally. There is a real opportunity to think through much better how PeaceTech could be systematically part of peace process design, rather than left to moments of experimental incubation. Not all things would need done in all circumstances, but having some form of open-source blueprint, to provide a systematic starting point would be useful. We have been involved in projects to design in-country digital peace processes. In my view, further considering what the 'digital peace process' might look like could usefully come together to support thinking about what peace processes should be in the age of double disruption. Perhaps a new way forward could be found for a peacebuilding field that has in a sense been always characterised by fragmentation and lack of strategy across varied organisations and actors. Whoops, there, I've said it!

Thank you for reading.
The End.

Questions

1. How would you place PeaceTech developments on the PeaceTech Hype Cycle graph?
2. What is your manifest, are there bits of mine you particularly agree or disagree with?

References[1]

Brusset, E., Milante, G., Riquier, M., & Delgado, C. (2022). *Measuring peace impact: Challenges and solutions.* Stockholm International Peace Research Institute. https://www.sipri.org/publications/2022/other-publications/measuring-peace-impact-challenges-and-solutions

Caplan, R. (2021). *Measuring peace: Principals, practices, politics.* Oxford University Press. https://global.oup.com/academic/product/measuring-peace-9780198867708?cc=gb&lang=en&

Deng, D., Dawkins, S., Oringa, C., & Pospisil, J. (2022). *Perceptions of peace in South Sudan* (Detcro and PeaceRep Policy Brief). PeaceRep: The Peace and Conflict Resolution Evidence Platform, University of Edinburgh. https://peacerep.org/publications-database/

[1] All last accessed 1 May 2023.

Authorities (Legal and Related)

Cases

Application of the Convention on the Prevention and Punishment of the Crime of Genocide (Bosnia and Herzegovina v. Serbia and Montenegro), International Court of Justice, 11 July 2006. https://www.icj-cij.org/case/91/judgments

Sejdić and Finci v. Bosnia and Herzegovina, (Applications nos. 27996/06 and 34836/06), Grand Chamber, European Court of Human Rights, 22 December 2009. https://hudoc.echr.coe.int/fre#{%22itemid%22:[%22001-96491%22]

Constitutions

Ethiopia Constitution of 1994, see the constitution here https://www.constituteproject.org/constitution/Ethiopia_1994.pdf

Peace and Transition Agreements

Joint Declaration between the Federal Democratic Republic of Ethiopia and The Ogaden National Liberation Front, 2018, https://www.peaceagreements.org/viewmasterdocument/2231

Minsk I Agreements, Protocol on the results of consultations of the Trilateral Contact Group with respect to the joint steps aimed at the

C. Bell, *PeaceTech: Digital Transformation to End Wars*,
https://doi.org/10.1007/978-3-031-38894-1

implementation of the Peace Plan of the President of Ukraine, P. Poroshenko,and the initiatives of the President of Russia, V. Putin (Minsk Protocol, or Minsk I Agreement), https://www.peaceagreements.org/view/1363

Transitional Period Charter of Ethiopia, 1991, https://www.peaceagreements.org/viewmasterdocument/1300

UN Resolutions

UN GA Resolution 70/262, 27 April 2016, A/RES/70/262, https://www.un.org/en/development/desa/population/migration/generalassembly/docs/globalcompact/A_RES_70_262.pdf

UN SC Resolution 1325 of 2000, 31 October 2000, S/RES/1325 (2000), https://peacemaker.un.org/sites/peacemaker.un.org/files/SC_ResolutionWomenPeaceSecurity_SRES1325%282000%29%28english_0.pdf

UN SC Resolution 2242, 13 October 2015, S/RES/2242 (2015), https://www.un.org/sc/ctc/news/document/sres2242-2015-women-and-peace-and-security-adopted-on-13-october-2015/

UN SC Resolution 2282, 27 April 2016, S/RES/2282 (2016), https://digitallibrary.un.org/record/827390?ln=en

UN SC Resolution 2493, 9 October 2018, S/RES/2493 (2019) http://unscr.com/en/resolutions/2493

Websites Referred To[1]

Amazon Data Centers, https://aws.amazon.com/compliance/data-center/data-centers/

Amnesties, Conflict and Peace Database (ACPA), https://www.peaceagreements.org/amnesties/

Armed Conflict Location and Event Data (ACLED), https://acleddata.com/, see also, Volatility and Risk Predictability Index (VRI), https://acleddata.com/early-warning-research-hub/volatility-and-risk-predictability-index/

Atlas of economic Complexity, https://atlas.cid.harvard.edu/

Atrocity Forecasting Project (AFP), Australian National University, https://politicsir.cass.anu.edu.au/research/projects/atrocity-forecasting; https://politicsir.cass.anu.edu.au/research/projects/atrocity-forecasting

Bosch, on AI in fitness watches, https://www.bosch-sensortec.com/news-and-stories/stories/ai-revolutioniztes-fitness-tracking.html

Britannica, Arabia Felix, https://www.britannica.com/place/Arabia-Felix see also, Borgia and Italian Wars and Imola, at https://www.britannica.com/place/Forli-Italy

[1] All last accessed 28/4/23.

C. Bell, *PeaceTech: Digital Transformation to End Wars*,
https://doi.org/10.1007/978-3-031-38894-1

Build Up, https://howtobuildup.org/, see also Build Up Principles for Digital Development, https://digitalprincip.wpengine.com/principles/ and Current ethical challenges, https://howtobuildup.org/rise/key-ethical-challenges_current/

Busara, https://work.busaracenter.org/

Butterfly Works, https://www.butterflyworks.org/. Arabia Felix, https://www.butterflyworks.org/storage/app/media/One%20pagers/BW_ArabiaFelix.pdf. Facebook page, https://www.facebook.com/thesecretofarabiafelix/

Carter Center, Support for Peace in Syria, https://www.cartercenter.org/peace/conflict_resolution/syria-conflict-resolution.html

Ceasefires in a Time of Covid-19 Tracker, https://pax.peaceagreements.org/static/covid19ceasefires/

Centre for Humanitarian Dialogue, https://hdcentre.org/

Centre for International Governance Innovation, Rohozinski bio, https://www.cigionline.org/people/rafal-rohozinski/

Christine Bell, University of Edinburgh, https://www.research.ed.ac.uk/en/persons/christine-bell

Cisco, https://www.cisco.com/site/uk/en/index.html, Cisco-Mercy Corps partnership, https://www.mercycorps.org/blog/technology-for-change-cisco-partnership#

CKAN, https://ckan.org/

Conflict forecast (CF), https://conflictforecast.org/about

Colombia- Sole Self-organised Learning Environment, Colombia, https://startsole.org/blog/primer-SOLE-remoto)

Colpus Dataset, https://www.johnjchin.com/colpus

ConnexUS, Digital Peacebuilder's Guide, https://cnxus.org/digital-peacebuilders-guide/. see also, Peace Impact Framework, https://cnxus.org/peace-impact-framework/, and 'grounded accountability model (GAM)', https://cnxus.org/gam/

Constitute, https://www.constituteproject.org/

Correlates of War, https://correlatesofwar.org/

Comprehensive Planning and Performance Assessment System (CPAS), https://peacekeeping.un.org/en/cpas

Covid Collective, https://www.covid-collective.net/

Crisis Group, Crisis Watch, https://www.crisisgroup.org/crisiswatch

Database in Constitution-Building Processes in Conflict-Affected States, http://pccbp.constitutionnet.org/

Deep Root Consulting, https://www.deeproot.consulting/

Dove Satellites, PlanetSpace, https://www.planet.com/pulse/we-call-them-doves/ see also, Planet Lab News, https://investors.planet.com/news/news-details/2023/Planet-Reports-Financial-Results-for-Fourth-Quarter-and-Full-Fiscal-Year-2023/default.aspx

Earth Blox, https://www.earthblox.io/

Edinburgh International Data Facility, https://www.ed.ac.uk/edinburgh-international-data-facility

Edinburgh Law School, https://www.law.ed.ac.uk/

Edinburgh Parallel Computing Centre, EPCC, https://www.epcc.ed.ac.uk/

ETH Zurich, ETH/PRIO Civil Conflict CeaseFire (CF), https://css.ethz.ch/en/research/datasets/civil-conflict-ceasefire.html

Enhancing Women's Leadership for Sustainable Peace in Fragile Contexts in the Middle East and North Africa (MENA) Region, https://www.unwomen.org/sites/default/files/Headquarters/Attachments/Sections/What%20We%20Do/Peace-security/WPS-Brief-Womens-meaningful-participation-in-peace-and-political-processes-in-fragile-contexts-en.pdf

European University Institute (EUI), Global PeaceTech Hub, https://www.globalpeacetech.org/ see also, PeaceTech digital mapping, https://www.globalpeacetech.org/gptmap/

EUI School of Transnational Governance, https://www.eui.eu/en/academic-units/school-of-transnational-governance

Everyday Peace Indicators, https://www.everydaypeaceindicators.org/

eyeWitness to Atrocities, https://www.lexisnexisrolfoundation.org/projects/eyewitness.aspx?p=projects

FAIR principles for data: https://www.go-fair.org/fair-principles/

Foreign Commonwealth and Development Office, UK, https://www.gov.uk/government/organisations/foreign-commonwealth-development-office

Futuring Peace, https://futuringpeace.org/about.html#about

Gartner Hype Cycle, https://www.gartner.co.uk/en/methodologies/gartner-hype-cycle

Gleditsch and Ward list of independent states, https://www.andybeger.com/states/reference/gwstates.html

Global Food Prices Database, https://data.humdata.org/dataset/wfp-food-prices/resource/12d7c8e3-eff9-4db0-93b7-726825c4fe9a

Global Partnership for Responsible Artificial Intelligence (AI), https://www.gpai.ai/
Global Peace Index, https://www.visionofhumanity.org/
Global Urban Analytics for Resilient Defence (GUARD), Turing Institute, https://www.turing.ac.uk/about-us/impact/predicting-conflict-year-advance
Google Maps, https://www.google.com/streetview/how-it-works/
Harvard Humanitarian Initiative, https://hhi.harvard.edu/
Humanitarian Data Exchange, https://data.humdata.org/
Imola Plan, Da Vinci, Royal Collection Trust, https://www.rct.uk/collection/themes/exhibitions/leonardo-da-vinci-a-life-in-drawing/the-queens-gallery-buckingham/mapmaker-and-engineer
INCORE, CAIN, Memorials, https://cain.ulster.ac.uk/victims/memorials/search.html
Inclusive Peace, https://www.inclusivepeace.org/
Independent Diplomat, https://independentdiplomat.org/
Instability Monitoring and Analysis Platform, US Department of State, https://www.state.gov/about-us-bureau-of-conflict-and-stabilization-operations/instability-monitoring-and-analysis-platform/
International Committee of the Red Cross (ICRC), Digital Innovation (RCView), https://www.redcross.org/about-us/who-we-are/innovation.html see also, Principles, ICRC Principles
International Catalan Institute for Peace, https://www.icip.cat/en/
ISO Country Codes, https://www.iso.org/iso-3166-country-codes.html
Israel Ministry of Foreign Affairs, Peace Process Agreements, https://www.gov.il/en/departments/general/israel-palestinian-negotiations
John Hopkins University, Corona Virus Resource Center, https://coronavirus.jhu.edu/map.html
Kluz Ventures, https://www.kluzventures.com/, https://www.kluzventures.com/about/
KoboToolBox, https://www.kobotoolbox.org/
Kroc Institute for International Peace Studies, University of Notre Dame, https://kroc.nd.edu/about-us/what-is-peace-studies/what-is-strategic-peacebuilding/#
Legacy Series, BBC, (https://accounts.ulster.ac.uk/repo24/collections/show/111)
Marconi PLC (history), https://www.referenceforbusiness.com/history2/4/Marconi-plc.html
Mercy Corps, https://www.mercycorps.org/

Nelda, National Elections Across Democracy and Autocracy, https://nelda.co/

New York University, Center for International Cooperation (NYU-CIC). https://cic.nyu.edu/ see also, ecosystem map, https://cic.nyu.edu/data/data-for-peacebuilding-and-prevention/

NorthEastern University, Knight Lab, US, https://knightlab.northwestern.edu/projects/

Open AI 'GPT-4', https://openai.com/research/gpt-4

Oracle, India, https://www.oracle.com/in/internet-of-things/what-is-iot

Organization for Economic Cooperation and Development, Principles for AI, https://oecd.ai/en/ai-principles

Oxford English Dictionary, https://www.oed.com/

Palantir, World Food Programme Partnership, https://www.palantir.com/impact/world-food-programme/

PAM, Peace Accords Matrix, https://peaceaccords.nd.edu/, see also, COmobia Barometer Initiative, https://peaceaccords.nd.edu/barometer

PA-X Peace Agreement Database, https://www.peaceagreements.org/ see also, Visualizing Peace: Time and Space, https://www.peaceagreements.org/visualizing-peace?visualisation=time-and-space see also, Visualizing Peace: Messy Timeline, https://www.peaceagreements.org/visualizing-peace?visualisation=messy, and Yemen Timeline, https://www.peaceagreements.org/yemen-timeline

PA-X Gender, (PA-X Women, Girls, and Gender Database), https://www.peaceagreements.org/wsearch

PA-X Tracker, Ukraine, forthcoming https://www.peaceagreements.org

Palantir, https://www.palantir.com/uk/, see also, Palantir, Edge AI, https://www.palantir.com/offerings/edge-ai/

Peace and Conflict Resolution Platform, PeaceRep, https://peacerep.org/

See also, Ceasefire key findings and policy recommendations,

Peace and Security Data Hub (https://psdata.un.org)

Peace Innovation Lab, University of Stanford, https://www.peaceinnovation.stanford.edu/

Peace Innovation Institute (in the Hague), https://www.peaceinnovation.com/

PeaceFem App, https://peacerep.org/digital-resources/peacefem/, See also, PeaceFem google player, https://play.google.com/store/apps/details?id=app.trigyn.PeaceFem&pli=1, apple store for iphone, https://apps.apple.com/gb/app/peacefem/id1520152849

PeaceTech Lab, https://www.peacetechlab.org/what-is-peacetech, see also, Hate Speech Lexicons, at https://www.peacetechlab.org/hate-speech-lexicons

PeaceTech Lab, Netherlands, https://peacetechlabnl.org/

PeaceRep research team, https://peacerep.org/about/people/

Principles for Digital Development, https://digitalprinciples.org/about/

Principles for Peace Initiative https://principlesforpeace.org/

Pulse Lab Jakarta, https://pulselabjakarta.org/

Pulse Lab Kampala, https://www.unglobalpulse.org/lab/kampala/#:~:text=Pulse%20Lab%20Kampala%20works%20with,sharing%20data%20sets%20for%20analysis

Royal Society of Edinburgh, https://rse.org.uk/; and Mary Sommerville Medal aware for PeaceRep, https://rse.org.uk/outstanding-achievement-recognised-by-2023-rse-medals/

SalamaTech Syria, https://en.salamatech.org/

Search for Common Ground, https://www.sfcg.org/

SecDev Foundation, https://secdev-foundation.org/

SecDev Group, https://digital.secdev.com/

SIPRI Databases, https://www.sipri.org/databases

Strata, https://unepstrata.org/

Strava, https://www.strava.com/, and on fitness score calculation, https://support.strava.com/hc/en-us/articles/216918477-Fitness-Freshness

Sudan, Conflict Sensitivity Resource Facility (CSRF) https://www.csrf-southsudan.org/#top

Towards Inclusive Peace, Mapping Gender Provisions in Peace Agreements, Monash University, http://mappingpeace.monashgps.org/

The GDELT Project, https://www.gdeltproject.org/

TheGovLab, https://thegovlab.org/

The UNU-CS Digital Peace Lab, United Nations University, Institute in Macau, https://cs.unu.edu/research/labs/digital-peace

The Government Revenue Database, https://www.ictd.ac/dataset/grd/

The World Bank Govtech, https://www.worldbank.org/en/programs/govtech

Ukraine, Donbas-Dialogues Programme, https://www.donbassdialog.org.ua/

Ukraine, Interactive Map, https://liveuamap.com/

United Nations, Digital Innovation Cell (DPPA), https://dppa.un.org/en/innovation

United Nations, Global Issues, Peace and Security, https://www.un.org/en/global-issues/peace-and-security
United Nations, Global Pulse, https://www.unglobalpulse.org/
United Nations, Innovation at the UN Quickguide, https://research.un.org/en/innovation
United Nations, Innovation Network (UNIN), https://www.uninnovation.network/
United Nations, Mediation Support Unit (DPPA), https://peacemaker.un.org/mediation-support
UN Office for the Coordination of Humanitarian Affairs, (OCHA), https://www.unocha.org/
United Nations Peacebuilding Commission, https://www.un.org/peacebuilding/commission
United Nations, UN Secretary General's Covid19 Global Ceasefire Call, https://www.un.org/en/globalceasefire
UNHCR, Innovation Service, https://www.unhcr.org/innovation/, and Digital Inclusion programme, https://www.unhcr.org/innovation/digital-inclusion/
UNICEF, Digital Transformation Mission, https://www.unicef.org/globalinsight/digital-technology, see also Office of Innovation, https://www.unicef.org/innovation/drones
UN OHCHR, Hub for Human Rights and Digital Technology, https://www.digitalhub.ohchr.org/about
UN Peacemaker, https://peacemaker.un.org/
UN Women, https://www.unwomen.org/en see also, Digital Innovation Strategy, https://www.unwomen.org/en/digital-library/publications/2017/7/making-innovation-and-technology-work-for-women
United States Geological Survey, remote sensing definition
https://www.usgs.gov/faqs/what-remote-sensing-and-what-it-used#/, see also geographic information system, https://www.usgs.gov/faqs/what-geographic-information-system-gis
United States Institute of Peace, https://www.usip.org/ see also, Peace Agreements Digital Collection, https://www.usip.org/publications/2008/02/peace-agreements-israel-palestine
University of Lucerne, Institute of Social Ethics, https://www.unilu.ch/en/faculties/faculty-of-theology/institutes-and-research-units/institute-of-social-ethics-ise

Uppsala Conflict Data Programme (UCDP), https://ucdp.uu.se/ see also Violence Early-Warning System (ViEWS), https://www.pcr.uu.se/research/views/ and Peace Agreements, https://ucdp.uu.se/downloads/index.html#peaceagreement

Ushahidi, https://www.ushahidi.com/

V-Dem, Varieties of Democracy, https://www.v-dem.net/

XCEPT, https://www.xcept-research.org/, see also, Vigil Monitor research and research seminar, https://www.xcept-research.org/how-can-researchers-better-navigate-the-profits-and-perils-of-satellite-and-open-source-investigations-2/

Zero-Point Security, https://www.zeropointsecurity.co.uk/

References[1]

Allison, J., Badanjak, S., Bach, B., Bell, C., Bhattacharya, D., Knaussel, F., & Wise, L. (2020). An interactive tracker for ceasefires in the time of Covid-19. *The Lancet Infectious Diseases, 21*(6), 764–765. https://doi.org/10.1016/S1473-3099(20)30932-4

Anderson, B. (1983). *Imagined communities: Reflections on the origin and spread of nationalism*. Verso.

Arana-Catania, M., van Lier, F., & Procter, R. (2022). Supporting peace negotiations in the Yemen war through machine learning. *Data and Policy, 4*(e28). https://doi.org/10.1017/dap.2022.19

Ascendix. (2023, March 20). *What is proptech and how it changed the real estate industry*. Ascendix blog. https://ascendixtech.com/proptech-real-estate-definition/

Barrett, P. M. (2022, September). *Spreading the Big Lie: How social media sites have amplified false claims of U.S. election fraud*. Stern Center for Business and Human Rights report, New York University. https://bhr.stern.nyu.edu/tech-big-lie

Barrett, P. M., & Hendrix. J. (2022, June). *A Platform 'Weaponised': How youtube spreads harmful contents—And what can be done about it*. Stern Center for Business and Human Rights, New York University. https://static1.squarespace.com/static/5b6df958f8370af3217d4178/t/62a38fc022745a7274601da0/1654886337000/NYU+CBHR+YouTube_Final_June10.pdf

[1] All last accessed 1 May 2023.

C. Bell, *PeaceTech: Digital Transformation to End Wars*,
https://doi.org/10.1007/978-3-031-38894-1

BBC. (2021, November 10). *Afghanistan's ghost soldiers undermined fight against Taliban—Ex-official*. BBC online news article. https://www.bbc.co.uk/news/world-asia-59230564

Bell, C. (2000). *Peace agreements and human rights*. Oxford University Press.

Bell, C. (2006). Peace agreements: Their nature and legal status. *The American Journal of International Law, 100*(2), 373–412. http://www.jstor.org/stable/3651152

Bell, C. (2008). *On the law of peace agreements: The new lex Pacificatoria*. Oxford University Press.

Bell, C. (2017). Peace settlements and human rights: A post-cold war circular history. *Journal of Human Rights Practice, 9*(3), 358–378. https://doi.org/10.1093/jhuman/hux025

Bell, C. (2020, March 24). *COVID-19 and Violent Conflict: Responding to predictable unpredictability*. Just Security blog. https://www.justsecurity.org/69340/covid-19-and-violent-conflict-responding-to-predictable-unpredictability/

Bell, C., Bach, B., & Kauer, T. (2022). Ways of seeing: Peace process data-viz as a research practice. *Convergence, 28*(1), 150–169. https://doi.org/10.1177/13548565211050748

Bell, C., & Badanjak, S. (2019). Introducing PA-X: A new peace agreement database and dataset. *Journal of Peace Research, 56*(3), 452–466. https://doi.org/10.1177/0022343318819123

Bell, C., & McNicholl, K. (2019). Principled pragmatism and the 'Inclusion Project': Implementing a gender perspective in peace agreements. *Feminists @ Law, 9*(1). https://journals.kent.ac.uk/index.php/feministsatlaw/issue/view/38

Bell, C., & Wise, L. (2022). The spaces of local agreements: Towards a new imaginary of the peace process. *Journal of Intervention and Statebuilding, 16*(5), 563–583. https://doi.org/10.1080/17502977.2022.2156111

Bell, C., Wise, L., Beaujouan, J., Epple, T., Forster, R., and Wilson, R. (2021). *A globalised practice of local peace agreements*. In C. Bell, J. Pospisil & L. Wise (Eds.), Local Peace Processes (pp. 7–14). The British Academy, London.

Berns, J. (Ed.). (2015, March). *#Peacetech everything you need to know, from social media in Afghanistan to humanitarian drones in Syria* (Vol. 5). Building Peace, Alliance for Peacebuilding. https://creativeconomy.britishcouncil.org/media/uploads/files/Alliance_for_Peacebuilding_-_PeaceTech_Doc.pdf

Bhattacharya, D., Badanjak, S., Bell, C., Knäussel, F., Wise, L., Allison, J., & Bach, B. (2021). Designing an interactive real-time web-mapped dashboard to visualise conflict ceasefires data over COVID-19 infection rates: Facilities and the way ahead. In *IEEE global humanitarian technology conference article* (pp. 200–207). https://doi.org/10.1109/GHTC53159.2021.9612457.

Björkdahl, A., & Buckley-Zistel, S. (2022). Space for peace: A research agenda. *Journal of Intervention and Statebuilding, 16*(5), 659–676. https://doi.org/10.1080/17502977.2022.2131194

Bradshaw, T. (2020, June 9). Planet Labs to expand earth imaging as rocket-launch costs fall. *The Financial Times*, Online news article. https://www.ft.com/content/1070bb0e-4899-48b9-9321-c4571f74c8ac

Bressan, S. (2021, June 29). *Crisis early warning: Berlin's path from foresight to prevention.* PeaceLab Blog. https://peacelab.blog/2021/06/crisis-early-warning-berlins-path-from-foresight-to-prevention

British Council, Build Up. (n.d.). *Innovative Peacebuilding in Syria: A scoping study of the strategic use of technology to Build Peace in the Syrian context.* British Council and Build Up Report. https://creativeconomy.britishcouncil.org/media/uploads/files/Peacetech_Report_Web_En.pdf

Bromley, M., & Gerharz, P. (2019, October 7). *Revising the EU Dual-use regulation: Challenges and opportunities for the trilogue process.* Stockholm International Peace Research Institute (SIPRI), blog. https://www.sipri.org/commentary/topical-backgrounder/2019/revising-eu-dual-use-regulation-challenges-and-opportunities-trilogue-process

Brusset, E., Milante, G., Riquier, M., & Delgado, C. (2022). *Measuring peace impact: Challenges and solutions.* Stockholm International Peace Research Institute. https://www.sipri.org/publications/2022/other-publications/measuring-peace-impact-challenges-and-solutions

Burke, J. (2023, April 30). *A War for our age: how the battle for Sudan is being fuelled by forces far beyond its borders.* Guardian online news article. https://www.theguardian.com/world/2023/apr/30/a-war-for-our-age-how-the-battle-for-sudan-is-being-fuelled-by-forces-far-beyond-its-borders

Butcher, C., Goldsmith, B. E., Nanlohy, S., Sowmya, A., & Muchlinski, D. (2020). Introducing the Targeted Mass Killing Data Set for the Study and Forecasting of Mass Atrocities. *Journal of Conflict Resolution, 64*(7–8), 1524–1547. https://doi.org/10.1177/0022002719896405

Caplan, R. (2021). *Measuring peace: Principals, practices, politics.* Oxford University Press. https://global.oup.com/academic/product/measuring-peace-9780198867708?cc=gb&lang=en&

Capoot, A. (2023, February 13). *Shares of Palantir pop as it reports first profitable quarter.* CNBC Online news article. https://www.cnbc.com/2023/02/13/palantir-q4-earnings-2022.html

Card, B. L., Raymond, N. A., & Baker, I. L. (2015). Conflict-related displaced population camps commonly visible in high-resolution satellite imagery.

Carl, A. (2023). Understanding PeaceTech [Peace Analytics Series]. PeaceRep: The Peace and Conflict Resolution Evidence Platform, University of Edinburgh. https://peacerep.org/publication/understanding-peacetech

Carothers, T., & Samet-Marram, O. (2015). *The global market-place of political change.* Carnegie Endowment for International Peace report. https://carnegieendowment.org/files/global_marketplace.pdf

Cassidy, A. (2023, April 24). *The wedding tech now at the heart of couples' nuptials.* BBC online news article. https://www.bbc.co.uk/news/business-65322101

Cerf, V., & Himelfarb, S. (2018, September 29). *Can the peacetech industry save the internet?.* CNN Opinion. https://edition.cnn.com/2018/09/29/opinions/technology-harm-better-application-help-world/index.html

Chandler, D. (2017). Securing the Anthropocene? International policy experiments in digital hacktivism: A case study of Jakarta. *Security Dialogue, 48*(2), 113–130. https://doi.org/10.1177/0967010616677714

CMI. (2020, September 17). *Digital technologies and peace mediation—Can Finland drive peacetech development?.* Martti Ahtisaari Peace foundation blog. https://cmi.fi/2020/09/17/digital-technologies-and-peace-mediation-can-finland-drive-peacetech-development/

Combs, C. (2020, 10 March). *In Yemen the internet is a key frontline in the war.* https://www.codastory.com/authoritarian-tech/yemen-internet-conflict/

Davies, S., Pettersson, T., & Öberg, M. (2022). Organized violence 1989–2021 and drone warfare. *Journal of Peace Research, 59*(4), 593–610. https://doi.org/10.1177/00223433221108428

De Coning, C. (2018). Adaptive peacebuilding. *International Affairs, 94*(2), 301–317. https://doi.org/10.1093/ia/iix251

De Coning, C., & Brusset, E. (2018). *Towards a comprehensive results-based reporting and performance assessment framework for UN peacekeeping operations.* Norwegian Institute of International Affairs research report. https://nupi.brage.unit.no/nupi-xmlui/handle/11250/2496840?locale-attribute=en

De Meyer, C., Franco, C., & Otto F. (2019). *Warning about war: Conflict, persuasion and foreign policy.* Cambridge University Press. https://www.cambridge.org/core/books/warning-about-war/2B8E3B55370AF392411BBDDD33DDD0B9

Defontaine, K. (2019, February 15). *Setting up early warning and response systems to prevent violent conflicts and save lives.* World Bank Blog. https://blogs.worldbank.org/dev4peace/setting-early-warning-and-response-systems-prevent-violent-conflicts-and-save-lives

Demombynes, G., Gubbins, P., & Romeo, A. (2013). *Challenges and opportunities of mobile phone-based data collection: Evidence from South Sudan*". The World Bank Africa Region Poverty Reduction and Economic Management Unit Policy Research Working Paper. https://papers.ssrn.com/sol3/papers.cfm?abstract_id=2202683

Deng, D., Dawkins, S., Oringa, C., & Pospisil, J. (2022). *Perceptions of peace in South Sudan* (Detcro and PeaceRep Policy Brief). PeaceRep: The Peace and Conflict Resolution Evidence Platform, University of Edinburgh. https://peacerep.org/publications-database/

Desai, D., & Lang, A. (2022). From mock-up to module: Development practice between planning and prototype. *Law and Critique, 33*, 299–318. https://doi.org/10.1007/s10978-022-09326-1

Dorith Kool, L., Pospisil, J., & van Voorst, R. (2021). Managing the humanitarian micro-space: The practices of relief access in Syria. *Third World Quarterly, 42*(7), 1489–1506. https://doi.org/10.1080/01436597.2021.1896359

Dorn, A. W. (2011). *Keeping watch: Monitoring, technology and innovation in UN peace operations.* United Nations University Press. https://digitallibrary.un.org/record/708466?ln=en

Douglas, S. (2022, December 4). *These are the World's fastest marathon runners.* Runner's world blog. https://www.runnersworld.com/races-places/a20823734/these-are-the-worlds-fastest-marathoners-and-marathon-courses/

Druet, D. (2021). *Enhancing the use of digital technology for integrated situational awareness and peacekeeping-intelligence.* Thematic Paper for the DPO Peacekeeping Technology Strategy. Not published. https://peacekeeping.un.org/sites/default/files/20210430_-_sa-pki_technologies_research_brief_final_clean.pdf

Falisse, J. B., & McAteer, B. (2022). Visualising policy responses during health emergencies. Learning from the COVID-19 policy trackers. *Convergence, 28*(1), 35–51. https://doi.org/10.1177/13548565211048972

Farquhar, A. (2023). *A primer on geocoding for peace and conflict studies.* [The Peace Analytics Series]. The Peace and Conflict Resolution Evidence Platform. https://peacerep.org/publication/geocoding-primer

Fintech Weekly. (2023, March 12). *Fintech definition.* Fintech weekly blog. https://www.fintechweekly.com/fintech-definition

Firchow, P., & Mac Ginty, R. (2020). Including hard-to-access populations using mobile phone surveys and participatory indicators. *Sociological Methods and Research, 49*(1), 133–160. https://doi.org/10.1177/0049124117729702

Firchow, P., Martin-Shields, C., Omer, A., & Mac Ginty, R. (2017). Peacetech: The liminal spaces of digital technology in Peacebuilding. *International Studies Perspectives, 18*, 4–42. https://cpb-us-e1.wpmucdn.com/blogs.gwu.edu/dist/8/846/files/2017/11/ekw007-1y3cfw7.pdf

Foley, C. (2023). *The protection paradox: How the UN can get better at saving civilian lives.* Palgrave Macmillan.

Fournier, J. (2021, November 10). *How algorithms are amplifying misinformation and driving a wedge between people.* Changing America, The Hill blog. https://thehill.com/changing-america/opinion/581002-how-algorithms-are-amplifying-misinformation-and-driving-a-wedge/

Fritsch, S. (2014). Conceptualizing the ambivalent role of technology in international relations: Between systemic change and continuity. In M. Mayer, M. Carpes, & R. Knoblich (Eds.), *The global politics of science and technology—Vol. 1. Global power shift* (pp. 115–138). Springer.

Galov, N. (2023, March 30). *17+ Impressive PayPal statistics to pay attention to in 2023.* Webtribunal blog. https://webtribunal.net/blog/paypal-statistics/#gref

Gardner, R. (2023). *Semantic Analysis to Support Peace Analytics.* [Peace Analytics Series]. PeaceRep: The Peace and Conflict Resolution Evidence Platform, University of Edinburgh. https://peacerep.org/publication/semantic-analysis

Gardner, R., & Bell, C. (2022). *Global realignments: Understanding peace process interventions through news.* (PeaceRep Report: Global Transitions Series). PeaceRep: The Peace and Conflict Resolution Evidence Platform, University of Edinburgh, Edinburgh. https://peacerep.org/publication/global-realignments-peace-process-interventions-through-news/

Greenall, R. (2023, April 17). *EU rejects Ukraine grain bans by Poland and Hungary.* BBC. Online News. https://www.bbc.co.uk/news/world-europe-65292698

Guadagno, R. E., Nelson, M., & Lee, L. L. (2018). Peace data standard: A practical and theoretical framework for using technology to examine intergroup interactions. *Frontiers in Psychology, 9*(734). https://doi.org/10.3389/fpsyg.2018.00734

Guo, W., Gleditsch K., & Wilson, A. (2018). Retool AI to forecast and limit wars. *Nature*, Comment. https://www.nature.com/articles/d41586-018-07026-4

Haider, H. (2022, April 14). *Humanitarian access issues linked to peace processes: Advantages, disadvantages and examples.* Institute of Development Studies, K4D Helpdesk report 1123. https://opendocs.ids.ac.uk/opendocs/handle/20.500.12413/17397

Hegre, H. (2022). Early-warning Systems for Political Violence: How Should We Define our Prediction Targets?, in *Taking Stock of Early Warning for Atrocity Prevention. Report from the 2021 Sudikoff Interdisciplinary Seminar on Genocide Prevention.* Washington, DC, United States Holocaust Memorial Museum (10–12).

Hegre, H., Allansson, M., Basedau, M., Colaresi, M., Croicu, M., Fjelde, H., Hoyles, F., Hultman, L., Högbladh, S., Jansen, R., Mouhleb, N., Muhammad, S. A., Nilsson, D., Nygård, H. M., Olafsdottir, G., Petrova, K., Randahl, D., Rød, E. G., Schneider, G., Von-Uexkull, N., & Vestby, J. (2019). ViEWS: A political violence early-warning system. *Journal of Peace Research, 56*(2), 155–174. https://doi.org/10.1177/0022343319823860

Heidebrecht, P. (2022, September 16). *Peacetech commentary.* IEEE Technology and Society Magazine: 101–2. https://ieeexplore.ieee.org/stamp/stamp.jsp?tp=andarnumber=9893514; https://technologyandsociety.org/peacetech

Heinzelman, J., Brown, R., & Meier, P. (2011). Mobile technology, crowdsourcing and peace mapping: New theory and applications for conflict management. In M. Poblet (Ed.), *Mobile Technologies for Conflict Management. Law, governance and technology series* (Vol. 2, pp. 39–53). Springer.

Henry, N. (2023). *Extracting Named Actors from Text: Using Named Entity Recognition in Peace and Conflict Studies.* [Peace Analytics Series]. The Peace and Conflict Resolution Evidence Platform. https://peacerep.org/publication/extracting-named-actors-from-text

Hirblinger, A. T. (2020, September). *Digital inclusion in mediated peace processes: How technology can enhance participation.* United States Institute of Peace report, 168. https://www.usip.org/publications/2020/09/digital-inclusion-mediated-peace-processes-how-technology-can-enhance

Hirblinger, A. T. (2023). Building a peace we don't know? The power of subjunctive technologies in digital peacebuilding. *Peacebuilding, 11*(2), 113–135. https://doi.org/10.1080/21647259.2022.2154957

Hirblinger, A. T., Hansen, J. M., Hoelscher, K., Kolås, Å., Lidén, K., & Martins, B. O. (2022). Digital peacebuilding: A framework for critical–reflexive engagement. *International Studies Perspectives, 24*(3), 265–284. https://doi.org/10.1093/isp/ekac015

Human Rights Watch. (2022, March 30). *New evidence that biometric data systems imperil Afghans; Taliban now control systems with sensitive personal information.* Human Rights Watch Press Release. https://www.hrw.org/news/2022/03/30/new-evidence-biometric-data-systems-imperil-afghans

ICRC, Privacy International. (2018, October). *The humanitarian metadata problem: "Doing no harm" in the digital era.* International Committee of the Red Cross and Privacy International report. https://reliefweb.int/report/world/humanitarian-metadata-problem-doing-no-harm-digital-era-october-2018

ICVA. (n.d.). *Learning stream: Navigating the nexus, topic 1: The "nexus" explained".* International Council of Voluntary Agencies, humanitarian learning briefing paper. https://www.icvanetwork.org/uploads/2021/08/Topic-One-Briefing-Paper-The-nexus-explained.pdf

Idler, A., Belén Garrido, M., & Mouly, C. (2015). Peace territories in Colombia: Comparing civil resistance in two war-torn communities. *Journal of Peacebuilding & Development, 10*(3), 1–15. https://doi.org/10.1080/15423166.2015.1082437

International Catalan Institute of Peace. (2020, October). *Co-existence and polarization in Catalonia.* ICIP Survey. https://www.icip.cat/wp-content/uploads/2021/01/Enquesta_ICIP2020_Eng.pdf

Jacobson, A. (2021). *First platoon: A story of modern war in an age of identity dominance.* Penguin.

Kaldor, M., & Radice, H. (2022). Introduction: Civicness in conflict. *Journal of Civil Society, 18*(2), 125–141. https://www.tandfonline.com/doi/full/10.1080/17448689.2022.2121295

Krause, J. (2019). How do wars end? A strategic perspective. *Journal of Strategic Studies, 42*(7), 920–945. https://doi.org/10.1080/01402390.2019.1615460

Krause, J., Krause W., & Bränfors P. (2018). Women's Participation in Peace Negotiations and the Durability of Peace. *International Interactions, 44*(6), 985–1016, https://doi.org/10.1080/03050629.2018.1492386

Lanier, J. (2018). *Ten arguments for deleting your social media accounts right now*. Vintage Penguin Random House.

Lanz, D. (2021). Envoy envy? Competition in African mediation processes and ways to overcome it. *International Negotiation, 26*(3), 499–526. https://doi.org/10.1163/15718069-bja10039

Lanz, D., & Eleiba, A. (2018, December). *The good, the bad and the ugly: Social media and peace mediation*. Swiss Peace policy brief. https://www.swisspeace.ch/assets/publications/downloads/Policy-Briefs/aa3fc8830f/Social-Media-and-Peace-Mediation-Policy-Brief-12-2018.pdf

Mac Ginty, R. (2022). Conflict disruption: Reassessing the peace and conflict system. *Journal of Intervention and Statebuilding, 16*(1), 40–58. https://www.tandfonline.com/doi/full/10.1080/17502977.2021.1889167

Manning, N. (2018). *Keeping The Peace - The UN Department Of Field Service's And Peacekeeping Operations Use Of Ushahidi*. https://www.ushahidi.com/about/blog/keeping-the-peace-the-un-department-of-field-services-and-peacekeeping-operations-use-of-ushahidi/

Martin-shields, C. (2013). Inter-ethnic cooperation revisited: Why mobile phones can help prevent discrete events of violence, using the Kenyan case study. *Stability: International Journal of Security and Development, 2*(3), Art. 58. https://stabilityjournal.org/articles/10.5334/sta.cu

McGinnis, D. (2023, February 2). *What is the fourth industrial revolution?*. Salesforce, The 360 blog. https://www.salesforce.com/blog/what-is-the-fourth-industrial-revolution-4ir/

Mouly, C., Idler, A., & Garrido, B. (2015). Zone's of Peace in Colombia's borderlands. *International journal of Peace Studies, 20*(1), 51–63. https://www3.gmu.edu/programs/icar/ijps/Vol20_1/Mouly_Idler_Garrido.pdf

Mueller, H., & Rauh, C. (2018). Reading between the lines: Prediction of political violence using newspaper text. *American Political Science Review, 112*(2), 358–375. https://doi.org/10.1017/S0003055417000570

Mueller, H., & Rauh, C. (2022a). The hard problem of prediction for conflict prevention. *Journal of the European Economic Association, 20*(6), 2440–2467. https://doi.org/10.1093/jeea/jvac025

Mueller, H., & Rauh, C. (2022b). Using past violence and current news to predict changes in violence. *International Interactions, 48*(4), 579–596. https://doi.org/10.1080/03050629.2022.2063853

Muggah, R., & Whitlock, M. (2022). Reflections on the evolution of conflict early warning. *Stability: International Journal of Security and Development, 10*(1), 1–16. https://doi.org/10.5334/sta.857

Nathany, M. (2021, September 1). *Fintech, Medtech, Edtech, Regtech and all the other terms ending in 'tech'*. UCL Finance and Technology Review (FTR) blog. https://www.uclftr.com/post/fintech-medtech-edtech-regtech-and-all-the-other-terms-ending-in-tech

Nicolaïdis, K., & Giovanardi, M. (2022). *Global Peacetech: Unlocking the better angels of our techne*". European University Institute, Global Governance Programme working paper. https://hdl.handle.net/1814/74985

NYU Center on International Cooperation, Netherlands Ministry of Foreign Affairs, & UN Peacebuilding Support Office. (2019, July). *Data for peace and security: Report of the practitioners workshop on harvesting best practices and building a community of practice.* Center on International Cooperation, New York University. https://cic.nyu.edu/resources/data-for-peace-and-security-report-of-the-practitioners-workshop-on-harvesting-best-practices-and-building-a-community-of-practice/

Ondaatje, M. (1979). *There's a trick with a knife I'm learning to do: Poems 1962–1978.* W. W. Norton and Co Inc.

Paffenholz, T. (2021). Perpetual peacebuilding: A new paradigm to move beyond the linearity of liberal peacebuilding. *Journal of Intervention and Statebuilding, 15*(3), 367–385. https://www.tandfonline.com/doi/full/10.1080/17502977.2021.1925423

Panic, B. (2020, October). *Data for peacebuilding and prevention ecosystem mapping: The state of play and the path to creating a community of practice.* Center on International Cooperation Report, New York University. https://s42831.pcdn.co/wp-content/uploads/1662/65/data_for_peacebuilding_and_prevention_-_ecosystem_mapping_-_october_2020.pdf

Parker, B. (2019, February 5). *New UN deal with data mining firm Palantir raises protection concerns.* The New Humanitarian, Online news story. https://www.thenewhumanitarian.org/news/2019/02/05/un-palantir-deal-data-mining-protection-concerns-wfp

Peter, M., & Rice, H. (2022). *Non-Western approaches to peacemaking and peacebuilding: State-of-the-art and an agenda for research.* (PeaceRep Report: Global Transitions Series). The Peace and Conflict Resolution Evidence Platform. https://peacerep.org/publication/non-western-approaches-to-peacemaking-and-peacebuilding-state-of-the-art-and-an-agenda-for-research/

Pospisil, J. (2022). Dissolving conflict. Local peace agreements and armed conflict transitions. *Peacebuilding, 10*(2), 122–137. https://doi.org/10.1080/21647259.2022.2032945

Raleigh, C., Kishi, R., & Linke, A. (2023). Political instability patterns are obscured by conflict dataset scope conditions, sources, and coding choices. *Humanities and Social Science Communications, 10*(74), 1–17. https://doi.org/10.1057/s41599-023-01559-4

Reichert, E. (2020, October 8). *What is climatetech?*. Greentown labs blog. https://greentownlabs.com/what-is-climatetech/

Restrepo, E. M. (2018). Online technology as a pathway for citizen deliberation and depolarization. *Perspectives on Global Development and Technology, 17*(3), 239–263. https://doi.org/10.1163/15691497-12341477

Russell, I., Wise, L., & Badanjak, S. (2021). *Breathing space: Vaccination ceasefires in armed conflict* (PSRP Research Report). Global Justice Academy, University ofEdinburgh. https://peacerep.org/publication/breathing-space-vaccination-ceasefires-in-armed-conflict/

Sabbach, D. (2023, February 9). *Fury in Ukraine as Elon Musk's SpaceX limits Starlink use for drones.* Guardian online news article. https://www.theguardian.com/world/2023/feb/09/zelenskiy-aide-takes-aim-at-curbs-on-ukraine-use-of-starlink-to-pilot-drones-elon-musk

Schwab, K. (2015). *The fourth industrial revolution*. Penguin books.

Smith, A. (2022, October 5). *SpaceX was paid by US government to send some Starlink terminals to Ukraine despite claiming it wasn't.* Independent online news article. https://www.independent.co.uk/tech/spacex-ukraine-elon-musk-starlink-government-b2055491.html

Suhrke, A., & Samset, A. (2007). What's in a figure? Estimating recurrence of civil war. *International Peacekeeping, 14*(2), 195–203. https://doi.org/10.1080/13533310601150776

Sullivan, G. (2022). Law, technology, and data-driven security: *Infra*-legalities as method assemblage. *Journal of Law and Society, 49*(2), 31–50. https://doi.org/10.1111/jols.12352

Sweijs, T., & Teer, J. (2022, February 21). *Practices, principles and promises of Conflict early warning systems.* The Hague Centre for Strategic Studies Report. https://hcss.nl/report/practices-principles-and-promises-of-conflict-early-warning-systems/

Thrift, N. (2003). Space: The fundamental stuff of geography. In S. L. Holloway, S. P. Rice, & G. Valentine (Eds.), *Key concepts in geography* (pp. 95–107). Sage.

UN. (2014). *Performance peacekeeping.* UN expert panel on technology and innovation in UN peacekeeping final report. United Nations. https://peacekeeping.un.org/en/final-report-of-expert-panel-technology-and-innovation-un-peacekeeping

UN. (2015, September 16). *Report of the Secretary-General on women and peace and security.* S/2015/716. https://reliefweb.int/report/world/report-secretary-general-women-and-peace-and-security-s2015716

UN. (2018). *UN Secretary General's Strategy on New Technologies.* New York, United Nations. https://www.un.org/en/newtechnologies/images/pdf/SGs-Strategy-on-New-Technologies.pdf

UN. (2019). *The age of digital interdependence.* UN Secretary-General high-level panel on digital cooperation report. https://www.un.org/en/pdfs/HLP%20on%20Digital%20Cooperation%20Report%20Executive%20Summary%20-%20ENG.pdf

UN. (2021). *Strategy on digital transformation of UN peacekeeping.* UN peacekeeping online strategy article. https://peacekeeping.un.org/en/strategy-digital-transformation-of-un-peacekeeping

UN, Centre for Humanitarian Dialogue. (2019, March). *Digital technologies and mediation in armed conflict.* United Nations Peacemaker and Centre for Humanitarian Dialogue Report. https://peacemaker.un.org/sites/peacemaker.un.org/files/DigitalToolkitReport.pdf

UN DPPA. (2021, July 12). *Virtual reality bites: using technology to bring post-conflict situations to life.* United Nations Department of Political and Peacebuilding Affairs online blog. https://dppa.medium.com/virtual-reality-bites-using-technology-to-bring-post-conflict-situations-to-life-bd5cb98ce3f6

UN DPPA, & Centre for Humanitarian Dialogue. (n.d.). *Digital technologies and innovation toolkit 1.0.* UN Department of Political and Peacebuilding Affairs and Centre for Humanitarian Dialogue online digital toolkit. https://peacemaker.un.org/digitaltoolkit

UN DPPA, Global Pulse. (2019, January). *E-Analytics guide: using data and new technology for peacemaking, preventive diplomacy and peacebuilding.* Department of Political and Peacebuilding Affairs, UN Global Pulse United Nations University Institute on Computing and Society E-Analytics Guide. https://www.unglobalpulse.org/wp-content/uploads/2019/04/e-analyticsguide2019.pdf

UN DPPA, Mediation Support Unit & Swiss Peace. (2021). *Social media in peace mediation. A practical framework.* UNDPPA MSU and Swiss Peace.

UN OCHA. (2016, May 18). *Building data responsibility into humanitarian action.* OCHA Policy and Study Series. United Nations. https://www.unocha.org/sites/unocha/files/Building%20data%20responsibility%20into%20humanitarian%20action.pdf

UNDP. (2015). *Predicting peace: The social cohesion and reconciliation index as a tool for conflict transformation.* United Nations Development Programme. https://reliefweb.int/report/world/predicting-peace-social-cohesion-and-reconciliation-index-tool-conflict-transformation

UNICEF. (2017, June 29). *Africa's first humanitarian drone testing corridor launched in Malawi by Government and UNICEF.* Press Release. https://www.unicef.org/press-releases/africas-first-humanitarian-drone-testing-corridor-launched-malawi-government

Vallor, S. (2016). *Technology and the virtues: A philosophical guide to a future worth wanting*. Oxford University Press.

Waidyanatha, N. (2010). Towards a typology of integrated functional early warning systems. *International Journal of Critical Infrastructures, 6*(1), 31–51. https://doi.org/10.1504/IJCIS.2010.029575

Walker, N. (2023). *Europe's constitutional retrofit*. Global Constitutionalism, forthcoming.

Wang, B. Y., Raymond, N., Gould, G., & Baker, I. (2013). Problems from hell, solution in the heavens?: Identifying obstacles and opportunities for employing geospatial technologies to document and mitigate mass atrocities. *Stability: International Journal of Security and Development, 53*(2(3)), 1–18. https://doi.org/10.5334/sta.cn

Wise, L. (2023). *From protests to paper: Using PeaceFem to analyse women's inclusion in peace processes*. [Peace Analytics Series]. The Peace and Conflict Resolution Evidence Platform. https://peacerep.org/publication/from-protests-to-paper

Wise, L., Badanjak, S., Bell, C., & Knäussel, F. (2021, March 22). *Pandemic pauses: Understanding ceasefires in a time of covid-19*. Political Settlements Research Programme research report. Global Justice Academy, University of Edinburgh.https://peacerep.org/publication/pandemic-pauses-understanding-ceasefires-in-a-time-of-covid-19/

Wittke, C. (2023). *Creating islands of agreement and civility' through humanitarian negotiations: A conflict management and disaster-mitigation strategy in Russia's war against Ukraine* (PeaceRep Report). Conflict and Civicness Research Group, London School of Economics. https://peacerep.org/publication/islands-of-agreement-conflict-management-russia-ukraine/

World Bank. (2018). *Pathways for peace: Inclusive approaches to preventing violent conflict*. World Bank and UN Report. http://hdl.handle.net/10986/28337.

Index

C. Bell, *PeaceTech: Digital Transformation to End Wars*,
https://doi.org/10.1007/978-3-031-38894-1

Negotiation, 40, 45, 46, 48, 55, 74, 101, 139, 145, 146, 152–154, 181

Milton Keynes UK
Ingram Content Group UK Ltd.
UKHW021141080724
445247UK00010B/350

9 783031 388965